I0786103

TIAGO LAMEIRAS

HYPATIA

EMPRESS
OF ALEXANDRIA

HISTORICAL FICTION

HYPATIA

EMPRESS OF ALEXANDRIA

Authored & Edited by
Tiago Lameiras

In honor of all the women who, throughout History, have been fighting for gender equality.

Hypatia: Empress of Alexandria – Edited by Tiago Lameiras. Includes an index, images, and footnotes.

Cover: *The Consummation of Empire* (1836), part of a series titled *The Course of Empire* (1833-36), by Thomas Cole (1801-1848) – detail;
Frontispiece: *Portrait of Hypatia* (1908), by Jules Maurice Gaspard (1862-1919).

Printed and bound by CreateSpace Independent Publishing Platform.

ISBN–10: 1723388408
ISBN–13: 978-1723388408

Typeset in Sabon Roman
by Linotype

Charleston, SC, United States

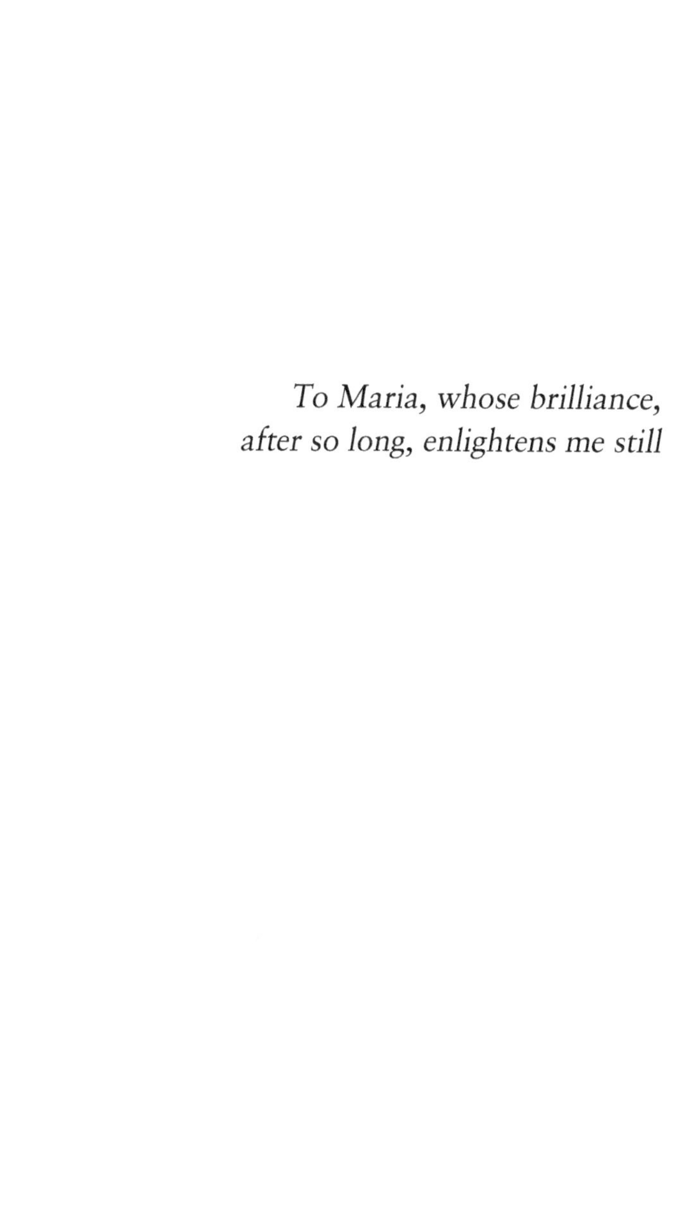

*To Maria, whose brilliance,
after so long, enlightens me still*

"Was not Hypatia the greatest philosopher
of Alexandria, and a true martyr
to the old values of learning?
(…)
[The Christians] could not argue
with her, so they murdered her".

— Iain Pears

Index

NOTICE

Hypatia of Alexandria (born circa 350-370 CE – died 415 CE), daughter of Theon of Alexandria (b. c. 335 CE – d. c. 405 CE), the last Director of the University of Alexandria in Antiquity, is a historical figure whose existence has been proven in fact, though much of her life remains a mystery to this day, given that none of her works have survived. Sadly enough, there are many more accounts concerning her martyrdom-like death, despite their duality regarding scholarly reliability and consequent academic satisfaction.

This is a work of fiction and, therefore, the following story is both novelized and romanticized, for which reason historical accuracy may not always be favored as the plot unfolds.

— The Author

The Roman Empire in 395 AD[*]

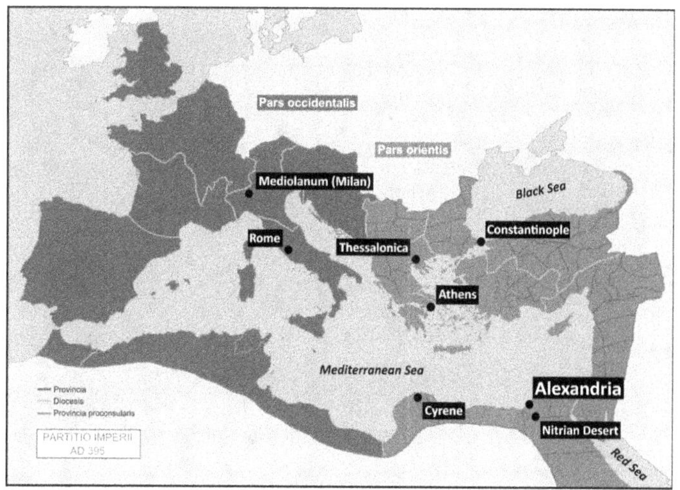

* Following the death of Theodosius the Great, the last Augustus to rule both portions alone (beginning in 392 AD). The cities and locations highlighted on the map are both the most often mentioned and the most important in the plot.

Alexandria During Hypatia's Lifetime**

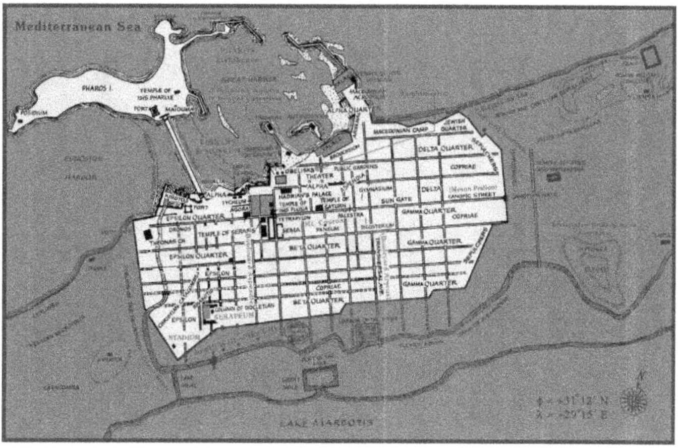

** This rendering of 4th-century Alexandria is based on architectural evidence retrieved from the remnants of a few of the structures mentioned in the map, though some speculation is obviously involved, as it is impossible to fully pinpoint their exact location because of the massive destruction the city endured over the centuries (mostly due to fires [both natural and provoked] and earthquakes [one of them having originated in Crete, followed by a tsunami, in 365]), though complete chaos settled in under Roman rule, namely throughout the transition from Paganism to Nicene Christianity.

Chapter I
Pharos, a Beacon in the Sandstorm

In the year of Our Lord three hundred and seventy, the Roman Empire no longer set its cornerstones in Greek culture and tradition, despite the Christian coexistence with Paganism. This newly-forged trend was owed to the great conqueror of the City of Byzantium, Constantine, who renamed the imperial-friendly urban center Constantinople, a brand-new capital where the Eastern portion of a nearly four-hundred-year-old conquest was to be governed from in straight connection with Rome herself.

Naturally (Alexander the Great lived almost long enough to see it happen, had he not been murdered because of his insatiable ambition), the larger the domain, the likelier it is for the entire body to break into small pieces, one at a time, like the bread resting on the table, the same loaf we all feed from, until no more than crumbs play the role of pointing out there once was something substantial that lay in that exact place – hence the reason why not even The Roman Senate and People, the most respectable authority the Western world has been ruled by, was bound to hold its seams together, as much as it tried to continuously mend them.

In three hundred thirteen, Licinius, the man in charge of the Balkans, met with the Augustus in Mediolanum, in the Northern Italic Peninsula, where a few changes as far as policy toward Christianity was concerned were turned into law via the Edictum Mediolanense. A faith whose lifespan was just a little over three centuries old and had been vehemently repressed by long dead Caesars across their reigns had managed to stay alive after all, mostly in secrecy, thus avoiding an oppression usually seeking the Circus as an example to all the newly-converted, which is to say being fed to the lions in the arena; either that, or dying as martyrs nailed to the cross, hoping to ascend to the company of the Messiah in Heaven once the torturing was over. Because the power of this faith was much stronger than that of the Pagan gods, Rome began to gradually embrace it through Augustus himself

– Galerius, who had decided (two years prior to Constantine and Licinius' laws) to at least tolerate the presence of Christians among Roman Pagans, therefore halting the persecution and conviction to death of the first for not abiding by the Pantheon. Instead, it was asked of them that they pray to their one true god for the protection of the State and the people, given his followers would never turn their back on him, even if it meant their being purged from this world. In fact, Maximinus Daia, emperor of the Eastern provinces, did not hesitate to restore the capture and killing of Christians once Galerius died, as he considered the followers of Jesus Christ to intentionally disrespect the predominance of the gods led by Jupiter. The Tetrarchy was eventually bound to fall as Maximinus, a committed Pagan, was taken down by Licinius in what turned out to be a civil war for total control of the Roman nation. The victor took his place in the East, always in direct competition with Constantine. Despite their differences, their agreement on Christianity stood its ground, and the pursuit for the fishermen was brought to an end. Not only that, the Edict of Mediolanum made sure all property taken away from Christians would be returned to them, including their churches, and the current owners paid a compensation. Constantine the Great, sole ruler of the Empire from three hundred twenty-four onward after beating a treacherous Licinius, intended to achieve peace across the State as soon as possible, therefore enabling freedom of religion, so as to create a balance between the Christian god (whom he feared and deemed the strongest) and the Greco-Roman deities. There was no better way to become a prosperous Caesar than to protect every Roman citizen, no matter their origin or creed, instead of choosing a side and oppressing the other, from which no sympathy would obviously be shown. Governors of any kind only remain so for as long as the people allow it; once their authority has gone too far, even if it takes decades for the counter-strike to happen, the divine right to rule is immediately revoked, punishable with either exile or death, just to make sure no followers are gathered for an attempted overthrow.

Unfortunately, the concept of Democracy is just that – an ideal. It bears no concrete consequences in the day-to-day life of a people. That is how extremism finds its way into daylight. It is impossible to create balance within Humanity. One belief alone must prevail above all others, whose fate is none other than extinction – by any means necessary.

Over the years, the following emperors became all the more receptive of Christianity, in line with the successors of Saint Peter, the Popes. Simeon himself, as he was also known, made Prince of the Apostles by Jesus, had been killed by Pagan Rome under Nero's reign, under the form of crucifixion, though he asked of his executioners to be placed upside-down on Vatican Hill, deeming himself unworthy of perishing the same way the Lord had about thirty years prior. There, the headquarters of the New Church would be erected, becoming the most powerful institution of the known world.

Through Pontius Pilate, Prefect of Judaea, Rome pleased the Pharisees by murdering Jesus, looking to avoid a rebellion. Even though he washed his hands concerning the matter, the Empire realized what it had done, and began avenging the Savior by cursing the Jewish people for eternity, regardless of having escaped Egyptian tyranny under Moses. Put bluntly, the Covenant had been broken. Once the Son of God was tried for blasphemy and capital punishment was demanded from Pilate, the Children of Israel sentenced themselves to perpetual persecution.

Constantius II, for instance, Rome's only Augustus for eleven years, beginning in three hundred fifty, made sure the Hebrews would pay for their ultimate sin, releasing numerous edicts forbidding procreation between Jews and Christian women, the possession of Christian slaves and even the attempt to physically mark them via circumcision, which was punishable by death. Anyone willing to convert to Judaism, and not the other way around, would see their properties confiscated by the State.

As for the remaining Pagans, there would be no more sacrifices or worshipping in temples. Any sign of witchcraft was to be purged. The Christians, on the other hand, kept collecting exemptions that were progressively extendable not only to the clergy, but also their families. Should a prostitute prove herself acceptant of the one faith, only another believer would be allowed to purchase her.

But for a brief moment, Julian took over – a scant two years. During that short a period, a great deal of changes took place, viewed by many as a grave regression, especially because of the opposition made against Christianity. Although Julian had sought to provide freedom of religion across the Empire, Paganism was clearly his view, which was both a faith and a form of tradition. It was his undermining of the power the clergy had been gaining mostly since Constantine that eventually led the people to show nothing but disdain for him. Being a Neoplatonist (and the last Pagan Augustus), Julian believed men and women had been divinely created, but not through Adam and Eve. On the contrary, Jupiter's blood falling from the skies was the true origin of humanity.

Pragmatically speaking, polytheistic literature penned by masters such as Homer himself was not to be used in Christian schooling, which had the youth believe the Homeric poems were indeed the result of divine inspiration, though inflated by the one god, as opposed to the muse. Pretending to be merciful, despite costing Christian pedagogues students and property in general, so as to reopen Pagan temples, Julian allowed the return of exiled bishops, but only to provoke sectarianism within the Church, forcing the clergy to fight among themselves and, therefore, weakening the concept of a hierarchy intended to top the Emperor, who was to be the ultimate ruler and provider for his people. However, Constantine had been a bigger source of funding for Christians, thus halting the Pagan festivities organized to bring people together, instead of breaking them apart, now opposing two different beliefs. The truth was, no matter how decisive Julian's stomping of Christianity, and though a consensus could not be found within the clergy, segregated into Catholics, Arians, and Nicene Christians, the Church's political power was much too underway to be prevented. As Julian was about to be killed in the Persian campaign he would soon launch, there still was time to appease the Hebrews and attempt to rebuild their temple in Jerusalem. Sabotaged by the followers of Jesus, the intention was dismissed, but not without branding the Emperor a friend to the Jews, the murderers of Christ.

Before the fourth century was over, the Roman Empire would never again be the same, regardless of having yet another Augustus to rule both ends of the known world. The damage had already been done, and there was no turning back from the fragmentation, with only one city left where prosperity was seamless. That city, of course, was Alexandria, in the Egyptian province, overlooking the Mediterranean, founded by the homonymous Macedonian king circa the year three hundred thirty-two, prior to the first coming of Jesus. From that moment onward, the culture of millennia-old Egypt was absorbed into the Hellenistic world, becoming one of its most important epicenters of trade and knowledge, once Ptolemy I Soter took over this part of Alexander's vast empire, founding a kingdom of his own, which would only see its end three centuries later, with both Cleopatra VII and Mark Antony's (being the latter once a triumvir) suicide after Rome's conquest of the Nile lands under Octavian, the first ever Augustus, three decades prior to the immaculate conception and birth of Christ.

Alexandria defined the border between the Western and Eastern halves of the Roman Empire, remaining for some time inhabitable by people of every faith, whether it be Greco-Roman Paganism (coupled with its Egyptian counterpart), Coptic Christianism, or even Judaism. It is not that there was not any tension between the several factions, but each of them had their own space, thus contributing to some sort of neutrality, depending on the religious proclivity of the Co-Emperor ruling from the Hellespont's Northern bank, in Constantinople.

People from all over the Empire came to Alexandria to pursue an education under the finest and most brilliant tutors of the day, where once had stood a remarkable academic complex – the Musaeum and its renowned Great Library, created by the first of the Ptolemies and boosted by his son and successor, the second to bear that name. The Latin designation loosely translates to the Home of the Muses, the nine daughters of Jupiter, which was not only built in their honor, but also as a shrine falling under their protection, mainly housing Music and Poetry in the field of the Arts, but also encouraging the development of research and science. Alexandria wasn't merely the administrative capital of Egypt, but also a remarkable competitor of its Pergamum counterpart, from which Antony (according to Plutarch) had taken a vast collection of two hundred thousand scrolls to both appease Cleopatra VII with a wedding gift and plenish the Great Library's storage rooms. It is rumored there may have been as many as four hundred thousand papyrus scrolls, as that is how books are compiled and edited at this time, utterly depending on the scribes in charge of copying all the originals that came into the city. It had been so ever since Ptolemy I Soter's time, he who asked Athens for the original manuscripts of the golden trio of classic tragic playwrights – Aeschylus, Sophocles, and Euripides, paying the city-state a total amount of fifteen talents as collateral. The successor of Alexander, naturally, kept them for the Library and returned to the Athenians their respective copies, the same fate other texts went through, not only to increase Alexandria's trade core, but also to concentrate all of the world's knowledge in one monumental institution where scholars could discuss scientific progress and even comment on theories of the past, offering them new and improved explanations, thus contributing to the early stages of textual criticism. The combination of both the Musaeum and the Library had resulted in the cornerstone of what an academic facility really is, providing scholars with unlimited resources throughout their lives, of which Archimedes, Claudius Ptolemy, Euclid, and Hipparchus are but a few examples. Researchers were able to dine together, lecture their disciples in halls specifically built for that purpose, take a walk under the peripatos while teaching or debating, and experience a wondrous oasis to behold in the gardens. Several subjects were dealt with at the Musaeum, including Astronomy, Geography, Mathematics, Physics, Physiology, Zoology, and many others. The Ptolemaic dynasty, being the most generous patrons of the institution, benefitted its staff and scholars with complimentary slaves, meals, residential areas, and tax exemptions. Over a thousand people may have lived in the Musaeum at its height.

Through the years, the Musaeum suffered severe modifications to its structure, both by human and natural action, thus igniting several fires that eventually consumed a great deal of the Pinakes, which is believed to be the first catalog of the papyri-filled rooms. There are two notorious occasions during which the Great Library endured a great deal of destruction: first, in the year forty-eight before the current era, when Julius Caesar, sided by Cleopatra VII, burned his own fleet, moored at the port of Alexandria, in order to stop the advances of Ptolemy XIII and Queen Arsinoe IV, an episode of the Great Roman Civil War, marking the transition from the Roman Republic to the Empire, as Gaius Octavius is appointed the heir of Caesar, Perpetual Dictator until his assassination on the Ides of March, in the year forty-four prior to the Christian era; the second occurrence took place between the years of Our Lord two hundred seventy and two hundred seventy-five, as Aurelian suppressed a rebellion from Queen Zenobia of Palmyra, damaging the territory in which the institution was located even further.

In the year of Our Lord three hundred seventy, only two structures from the Musaeum and its Ancient Library remained: the Serapeum and the Neoplatonic School; by then, most of the collected knowledge both the Ptolemies and scholars had worked so hard to preserve (if not all of it) had disappeared, thus crippling and subjecting an entire millennium of human progress to writings no one was bound to defy – the Holy Scriptures.

The Serapeum, a subsidiary temple of the former Great Library, was named after the Pagan god it was dedicated to, Serapis, a deity whose main purpose was to bring Hellenes and Egyptians closer, minimizing any differences between the two peoples. Considering the Greeks had ruled the once independently prosperous Nile-reliant nation for nearly three hundred years, it became imperative for Ptolemy I Soter to promote the cult of a merged Pantheon that would appease both parties. Serapis was neither Grecian nor Egyptian to begin with, which is sounding proof mythologies contaminate each other by the hand of Man, in order to unite different human factions under one faith. Whether there is enough humility to distribute the several powers of Nature across numerous deities who complete each other, or full-blown supremacy attributed to a singular god, that is a different topic entirely.

Serapis is first mentioned by the time of Alexander the Great's death, shortly before the tetrapartite distribution of the Macedonian king's empire and consequent founding of the Ptolemaic dynasty at the Egyptian capital. There was a temple which had been erected in honor of the deity in Babylon, where Aristotle's former disciple was slowly fading away from this world, but not without sending out directives for the god to be consulted on his behalf. The divinity became so influential in Greek culture that Ptolemy I Soter was sure he had chosen the best idol to worship in exchange for the protection of his family, their ruling, and the very city he had seen rise as one of the generals of Phillip II of Macedonia's son's army, campaigning through the desert to Persia. Having made that choice, Ptolemy I Soter needed to materialize Serapis for everyone to see and believe in his might, the time when Greco-Roman biographer Plutarch speaks of a dream the general had, induced by the god himself, telling him to go to the Hellenic settlement in Sinope, Asia Minor, in the South bank of the Black Sea, and take to Alexandria a statue that he, the future Pharaoh, believed to represent the embodiment of the deity. The statue's authenticity was sponsored by religious experts who, favored by both Greeks and Egyptians, had perhaps been illuminated in their spirituality to accept it as the true identity of Serapis. The god was generally accepted by both sides and even became popular after the Roman conquest of the province, remaining so despite the severe imbalance caused by the escalating number of newly converted Christians. In time, Serapis came to be respected as much as and identified with Osiris, god of the Duat, the Egyptian underworld (and the first Pharaoh, succeeded by his earthly representatives), his face and beard looking like that of Pluto, while wearing on top of his head a modius, associated by the Greeks to Tartarus. Even though Osiris wasn't represented with the head of an animal, many other deities pertaining to the North African culture were depicted as such, to the repulse of the Hellenes. Anubis, however, both the Egyptian guide of the deceased in the afterlife and guardian of the Duat's gates, was allowed to keep the head of a canine – in fact, he was given another pair of heads and the full body of a canid from the necks down, thus incarnating Cerberus, who, in turn, was the guardian of the gates to Tartarus. This mythological crossing between the Egyptian god and the Greek creature only a handful of people had seen without being dead became the companion of Serapis, dressed in garments matching those of Egypt's original traditions. The scepter in his hand was demonstrating of his power, along with the uraeus, a symbol of rulership in the shape of a cobra. Together with Isis, sister of Osiris and queen (much like Juno), and their son, Horus, readapted into a new god called Harpocrates, Alexandria's principal cult survived over seven hundred years, long after the disappearance of the Ptolemies and their legacy with the death of Cleopatra VII.

Hypatia: Empress of Alexandria

As for the Neoplatonic School, it was officially called Mouseion, in honor of the Musaeum that had included the original Great Library before its successive episodes of destruction, headed by Theon of Alexandria, astronomer, mathematician, and philosopher. As Professor and Director, the «Man from the Mouseion», as he was known, his work consisted mostly of lecturing his disciples with the compiled knowledge obtained by Claudius Ptolemy, especially as far as Astronomy was concerned, recurring to the 'Almagest' as a reference, which he eventually commented, looking to simplify the description of the second century astronomer's cosmos. With respect to Mathematics, Euclid's 'Elements' were essential to establish a treatise of propositions combining logic with digits, either expanding the author's argument whenever too short to serve as proof, or summarizing it if too long and redundant, also standardizing the writing style of the mathematician in order to make the textbook easy to understand during lectures or when in the hands of autonomous students. Of course, with every edition comes a given number of errors that Theon would end up overlooking. Nevertheless, before reaching the age of thirty, the multitalented Neoplatonic master had been able to successfully pinpoint eclipses on their exact day of occurrence, showing a remarkable comprehension of both Hipparchus and Ptolemy's cosmological notions, as described in the sixth book of the 'Almagest'.

In the year of Our Lord three hundred seventy, at age thirty-five, Theon of Alexandria would soon gain knowledge about an aspect of life no philosophical doctrine, mathematical calculation or astronomic unit of measurement could teach, for one only becomes aware of what it is like once Nature has decided it is time for one to know.

As the Director sat with his disciples in the lecture hall of the Serapeum, discussing the Neoplatonic principles of Plotinus, as opposed to those of Iamblichus, which he firmly rejected, one of his servants came in running, drawing everyone's attention as he struggled to regain his breath, approaching at last his master with household news to deliver.

Though the slave whispered his every word unto Theon's ear, it seemed impossible to prevent a bit of echoing across the lecture hall.

The moment he stopped talking, the slave stood upright and met the sight of his master, waiting for instructions from a man who had never been this bedazzled in his entire life. Theon quickly swept his curious audience with his gleaming eyes, rose from his seat and said, frantically:

'We're done for the day, gentlemen. A matter of the utmost importance has just come up and I'm afraid our debate must be kept on hold. I must go.

Collect my papyri', he told the slave, who soon obeyed the command. One of the students showed his concern and did not hesitate to ask:

'Sir? Is everything all right?'.

'Oh!, yes, yes, it's quite all right. It's just that my water broke. I mean – my wife is having our child. Never mind the books, just prepare the chariot', Theon ordered the servant, dropping the notes back on the desk where they initially lay without an apparent pattern of organization and running back out.

This was the day Theon of Alexandria would be inducted into fatherhood, not knowing whether a son or a daughter was on their way, but, whichever the gender, all he wanted was to get home straight away, as the Sun traversed the sky and the beacon of the Lighthouse of Alexandria on the isle of Pharos was lit for the night, and feast his eyes on the body of a newborn soul emanating from the Good, the ultimate immaterial cause of all existing things.

Chapter II
Beyond Reason

Quickly following his master, the slave helped Theon onto the chariot, which another servant had been watching over as his equal entered the Serapeum. They both took the horse's reins at the same time, once Theon gave the order. The arid streets of Alexandria were progressively becoming upmarket, as the merchants closed their stalls and the passersby headed to their rightful home, cooled off by the Mediterranean's breeze after yet another scorching day in the desert.

One by one, the oil lamps of the homes facing the agora were lit by slaves, whether it be men or women, depending on each homeowner's wealth, the subject's abilities and, consequently, the kind of housework they had been purchased to perform, in the first place. It is no surprise that the men dealt with duties requiring a physical strength their female counterparts did not biologically possess, whereas the latter handled the cooking, the sewing, and the domestic hygiene, granted this last task was often shared with the males. Although Rome had created useful infrastructures such as public latrines and sewage systems outflowing to nearby streams or the sea, thus preventing the existence of still waters and parasites, not all homes were necessarily connected to said systems because there was a general fear rats might show as both an unexpected and unpleasant surprise, which is why excrements were left in buckets for the servants to throw out the window. As far as urine is concerned, it would simply be collected in a pot and saved as detergent to wash the clothing. Public toiletry would usually be located out in the open, making it a place for fraternization, including the tersoria – sponges retrieved from the Mediterranean on the tip of a stick, communally used for wiping and left inside vinegar or salt water, unless running water was available to help clean them up; such were the sanitation standards.

Theon had the privilege of inhabiting a home with a view to the lighthouse. The moment the slaves stopped the chariot at the front door, their master did not wait for help getting off and quickly entered the vestibulum, where he left his hooded cloak on the floor for someone to pick up later. The chariot was taken to the stable and the horse was fed.

As Theon showed in the atrium, several female servants paced between the culina and the main cubiculum, where the mistress was in labor, right in front of the peristylium. A couple of slaves noticed the presence of the master while he was on his way to see his wife, for which reason they abruptly halted their running and bowed. They were both carrying wet pieces of cloth, leaving a dripping trail behind.

'How is the Mistress?', Theon asked the pair.

Without looking him in the eye or raising her head back up, one of the women said:

'The Mistress isn't faring well, Master. Her blood's been boiling ever since the water broke and has not yet refrained from rising. The midwife is doing her best to keep the Mistress awake, but the delirium is beyond disproportional'.

Clearly, the slave in question knew how to read, considering how enriched her vocabulary was. The other one did not feel that much comfortable around words, but what she had to add was enough to make her point, maintaining exactly the same posture as her equal:

'The child is still to come'.

'All right, move along. Do what you can to stop her temperature rising', Theon ordered the servants, who, in turn, immediately obeyed.

From the cubiculum came a concoction of mumbling and moaning, every now and then interrupted by sharp intakes of breath and screaming due to excruciating pain, the kind not even a sky-rocketing fever was strong enough to numb. The intermittent commotion, made louder at each step taken forward, somehow held Theon back. He had already walked to the first column of the gardens, past the tablinum, where he spent a great deal of his time, bringing his work home. Being Head of the Neoplatonic School was not an easy feat, especially because of the escalating tension between religious groups, though it was policy to welcome everyone to his academy regardless of faith. That office was his personal shrine, and for some reason only he was aware of, that is where he took refuge, shutting the door behind him.

There is not much we can hint that could explain the Director's behavior apart from sheer speculation, but if such is the only road available, so be it. Our guess is, though Theon was a sociable man (for one cannot teach without being properly instructed in the arts of Oratory, Public Speech, and Rhetoric), the philosopher within sought constant interest for knowledge, but not necessarily any new theories in particular, no – making what was already known of the cosmos a great deal more understandable to anyone pursuing an education was, indeed, the essence of it all. Unfortunately, a paradox takes shelter in this noble cause, and that is the lack of pathos, as opposed to a more noticeable presence of the other two artistic proofs, according to Aristotle: ethos and logos. Theon's pupils take his credibility for granted, along with the scientists of whom he speaks in his lectures, and his passionate appeal to reason is one of the main factors drawing the students' interest into learning more each day; however, Philosophy is the only link providing this pedagogue with a purpose to communicate with others. Any other subject discussed without a philosophical approach is pointless, anything that cannot be explained through logic is not worthy of starring in a conversation. Common sense must mandatorily be rationalized. In short, what is there to learn from loving another? It was the thought of it that scared Theon away from an intimate reality and into books, with which he felt far more comfortable than people he shared no pedagogical relation with, especially his dying wife, about to give birth to the one person capable of reminding him he had once forgotten what it was to think, the product of pure emotion – his descendant.

Ptolemy's geocentric model had taken over Theon, sitting in the center of the universe with his visage hidden in the palm of his hands, as the Sun in his personal life progressively turned into a red giant, feverishly exploding in the void, sparing neither the Five Wanderers, nor the Earth, the steady ground, which was also within its blast radius. If the Sun was to disappear, circling around the fixed globe of dirt, Theon would only be able to count on another light source to illuminate his path and keep him from stirring in the shadow – the Moon, pearlescent in the night sky. Whether sound can travel through emptiness is a mystery; the truth is he was able to heed the calling, the mistress wanted him in the cubiculum, having the walls work as muffled emissaries.

On a dry throat, Theon gulped and looked away into the distance, unspoiled by the physical barrier the door presented itself to be. He kept hearing his name being called upon, but his ears seemed shut for the moment. Inside his mind, the master of the house was running past every memory stored, brought up as if he were the one about to perish. In thirty-five years of carnal existence, from the very first reminiscences to that particular moment, intimacy was the least present. He was certain he had fallen in love with his wife, regardless of how such an event can be put into words, and he knew he had made the right choice as to marrying her, but it was precisely the rational contemplation of something as natural as love that left him adrift. There really was nothing to think about, no conclusion to extrapolate. That was the way it was, end of story.

It was not until a slave opened the tablinum door and called out for his master that Theon woke up from his stroll down recollection lane. Once muffled, the screaming was now much more audible, which gave the Director a much-needed click, realizing how foolish he had been all that time he could have paid more attention to his life companion, choosing isolation instead. The moment he got up from behind his desk and ordered the servant to step out of his way was the same he had decided he could still make it up to his devoted spouse, before death did them part, as the Christians would put it.

As he rushed, holding his tunic to prevent a nasty fall, the sound of pain came to an end and was replaced by another one – the crying of a new-born infant. Predicting what had just taken place, Theon leaned against the wall on his free hand, his sight drifting into the void once more, though his mind was well aware of what was going on. From the corner of the supporting structure and into the master cubiculum, the Director came face-to-face with irreparable damage; every servant assisting their mistress had their chins pasted to their chests, not as a sign of subservience, but rather pain and sorrow for a caring woman who had never taken upon the habit of either mistreating or punishing the slaves of her household. They were all standing in a semicircle around the bedstead, as if shielding her; some could not even hold their tears back, and not just the women, for crying does not pertain to a gender alone, the one some would think to be the weakest for their delicateness or lack of muscle.

In the center, at a ninety-degree angle, the midwife held in her arms the ultimate parental sacrifice – quid pro quo, one life for another, and the mother's last breath became the first of her only successor. Theon walked in at last, unable to avert his sight from his wife's lifeless body turned horrifyingly clearer at each step he took forward. The slaves, in turn, stepped back and allowed the master to come closer. The cubiculum was silent; the infant had had their share of crying for the time being, having already made sure they were breathing properly, and nothing was wrong concerning their health. Once positioned at the deceased mother's bedside, Theon noticed both her arms were extended, her hands still clenched to the sheets after putting her every bit of strength she had left into safely delivering their child before departing to the elemental world. The man who was known for his – perhaps – excessive rationality was now cascading a tear stream from his eyes, gutted and overwrought. Trembling in shock, his legs gave in and had him abruptly sit on the bed, by the mistress's rigid fist. His breathing had become heavy, as if an anvil had been dropped on his chest and he were struggling for air.

As gently as he could, Theon took the hand of his wife without forcing it open and gave it shelter within both his palms, still feeling the remnants of a high fever. The poor woman's eyes were trans-fixed as light went through the irises but was not absorbed; they somehow resembled a candle that had just been put out – a small flame using up all the air that was left before becoming extinguished, leaving nothing but a trace of darkness and smoke behind. The young widower kept staring at that gaze until her hand met his lips, which was when he closed his eyes in fervor. The sodium of his tears mixed with that of the sweat dripping still from the tip of her fingers… it was his plead for forgiveness in the form of a bittersweet kiss, one that seemed to perdure through the desert sand, the same that had suddenly stopped running from the upper to the lower end of an hourglass no one could see. Theon and his wife were sharing with each other a moment of their own, undisturbed by the sur-rounding environment; though she could not reply, he spoke to her in an undecipherable whisper, for his lips had not interrupted their contact with her hand. At some point, the widower halted his mur-muring and reopened his eyes. The lack of blood flow was drawing the color away from his wife's, for which reason he drove his free hand to her lids and pulled them down with the tip of his index and ring fingers, as the middle one slid on her nose; those three fingers then rested upon her heated lips. Absolutely no one dared move the slightest, grieving in silence as much as humanly possible.

The only living being in the room who was obviously unaware of this scene of desolation was the infant, simultaneously stretching and yawning, two correlated events that drove everyone's attention to them. Without turning back, Theon spoke to the midwife in the tone of a request, not a command:

'Would you please… bring the child to me?'.

The woman walked toward her master and stood in front of him, waiting for his eye contact.

'Which is it?', he asked, finally glancing at his offspring, wrapped inside a bundle of cloth.

'It is a beautiful baby girl, Master', the midwife responded, leaning over in order to put the infant in her father's arms, as she instructed him to mind the little girl's head and support it.

Theon took hold of her just like the woman told him, and the sadness he felt for the passing of his wife, who had born such a wondrous creature to behold, right there, alive and twitching, began to slowly fade away, yielding its place to the joys of fatherhood. The Director was proud of his life companion for the gift she had left him, so sweet, so beautiful. As he lay the child's entire body on the length of his hand and forearm, he held the mother's rigid hand once more, still warm, and placed it on the girl's stomach together with his atop, saying:

'Look, my Love, see how wonderful our daughter is… I've never felt this replenished in my entire life, and only just now I felt like I had aged twenty years… I promise you this – our baby won't be like any other, condemned to perpetual silence and a mind placed under arrest. I shall raise her to become the honorable woman her mother was, hopefully surpassing the wits of her father'.

Theon left one last kiss on his wife's forehead, handed his daughter over to the midwife again and told the latter to take excellent care of the girl, a request she happily obliged. As the woman took her leave, the newly minted father rose and spun on his axis, feasting his eyes on his little spawn while intertwining the fingers of both hands, plac-ing them against his abdomen. As far as the other servants in the cubiculum were concerned, the mas-ter asked of them to mourn with him in a moment of silence, as he prepared to lay the body of his spouse to its rest in the phenomenal world, granted her soul was now in the company of the One once more.

Chapter III
Trick of the Trade

By default, women in the fourth century of the current era, to the likes of their ancestors, were not raised to interfere with a world laid out for men; indeed, they were no better than an accessory of a true male citizen's life, which, not so surprisingly, was a sacrament people of all faiths seemed to agree upon without presenting any sort of significant resistance – women accepted their fate and dared not question it. The only men they were able to control were slaves; their respective husbands, on the other hand, did not fit the profile.

It is rather intriguing to think whether the daughter of Theon of Alexandria would have grown to become just another woman, had her mother survived labor. However, and granted the Director of the Neoplatonic School was sure to keep the promise made to his wife on her deathbed, Hypatia – so he decided to name her – was bound to acquire the kind of weaponry capable of defeating a full army, unsettling, even, the very pillars of an apparently steadfast empire, and that arsenal was made of Philosophy and knowledge, no less, reshaping the establishment of an absolute truth yet to be thoroughly refuted.

Throughout the infancy stage of her life, Theon hardly intervened regarding the correct approach to Hypatia's upbringing, for he could not tell the difference between right and wrong in this specific matter. While it is true the Director gave his best to bond with the child by deliberately acting silly with the purpose of making her laugh and, perhaps, present himself as the father figure he biologically was, thus having her progressively place her trust in him, some of the women slaves often pointed out to their master it took time for infants to begin recognizing familiar faces, whereas others mentioned the connection began right from the start, inside the mother's womb, meaning that, even though they had no logical method of expressing themselves like bigger children, who repeat and mime everything adults say or do, therefore developing their cognitive process, babies were capable of acknowledging the genitor's presence, especially whenever breastfeeding occurred, transmitting the same source of information that had traveled through the umbilical cord before. Of course, nothing concerning this matter was philosophical in any way; it was merely an assumption these women believed in, despite not having a family of their own. The circumstances concerning this particular case, however, were everything but common – the mother was gone and the only possible solution to suppress Hypatia's hunger was recurring to a wet nurse, who is, quite bluntly put, a woman paid to lactate and feed the children of others. It had never gone through Theon's mind hiring such a service would ever be necessary; he was naturally aware of the practice, but it was something a lot more regular among royalty.

There were also times when crying did not always mean feeling starved. The manifestation seemed annoyingly dull to the father, as he could not tell the difference between wanting to eat, sleep, or having intestinal cramps; nevertheless, the fact the slaves knew exactly what the infant wanted nearly just about every time seemed to not cease to amaze him, further convincing him it was perfectly possible for everyone to exchange sageness of all sorts, even when apparently they could not be explained in ways he was a lot more used to.

Over the next few years, when the puerile stage came to an end and Hypatia formally became a child, Theon put in place his own agenda for his daughter's development, taking up his fatherly role to an entirely different level, the kind usually restricted to girls – a proper academic education, and just like a mother would be responsible for the raising of a daughter, so was Theon responsible for the blossoming of an extraordinary personality in Hypatia, without detriment to her femininity, which, in a patriarchy, was permanently a weakness, but not as far as the little girl was concerned.

The fact there were biological differences between her and boys her age was not a synonym of having a different attitude regarding the innate need she felt to question things other girls were simply taught to hold their peace about.

Luckily for Hypatia, having the Director of the Neoplatonic School for a father meant free access to the remaining documentation that had once pertained to the original Musaeum complex. Staying at home under the care of slaves was something Theon firmly discouraged, thus prizing himself for being able to keep the promise made to his late wife and, somehow, making Hypatia his successor, the flesh and bone continuity of all he would have for a legacy, once he departed the phenomenal world, just like other fathers would teach their firstborn sons the basic principles of whichever activity they practiced to live a full, happy life.

Catching up on the mother idiom of a Hellene,

which was also the de facto idiom spoken in the Eastern portion of the Empire, together with Latin as the official language, Hypatia quickly became an avid reader, learning from Theon both at home and at the Serapeum, not only consuming every spare bit of papyrus she could lay her hands on, but also sitting in on lectures presented by her father and other professors. Needless to say, even though it shall be mentioned, not every pedagogue accepted this kind of rule-breaking lightly, but denying the Director would only have them risk an unnecessary conflict which could end up stripping them from both their intellectual authority and other advantages of being an academic.

Whenever she did not follow Theon, she took the time to continuously pursue the understanding of the most assorted matters, inclusively sparing some time to teach any willing slave to read and write, which was rather uncommon. Though she was still a child and innocence was a part of the growing up process, something told Hypatia information was power, indeed, but considering she had her father as a reference, such treasure was not one to be concealed; regardless of slavery being perfectly normal, that didn't mean they didn't have the right to at least learn to better interpret the tasks they had been purchased for, raising their chance of improvement and, consequently, achieving the best possible correlation between productivity and efficiency.

At night, after the Sun moved West of the lighthouse and the sky became clear of its predominant clarity, the little girl would often pretend to be asleep and wait for everyone to actually do the same, hoping to silently leave her cubiculum, despite the evident lack of tidiness concerning copies made of manuscripts found in the Serapeum, together with a Ptolemaic System still under construction from small pieces of wood scattered across the desk and a dissected Apollonian Cone, revealing the four geometric shapes applied, for instance, in architecture and engineering – the circle, the ellipse, the parabola, and the hyperbola. Her purpose was to go up to the balcony overlooking the peristylium and identify the Wanderers (Mercury, Venus, Mars, Jupiter, and Saturn), the only five a naked eye was able to differentiate in a firmament of one thousand and twenty-two stars, which, put together, gave birth not only to the twelve constellations of the Zodiac signs, but also to a system of coordinates listed in Ptolemy's star catalog with both latitude (unchangeable) and longitude.

Theon was not a heavy sleeper by nature, which is why there was this once he heard his daughter, who had been slightly careless concerning the noise, on her way up to the roof. Drawn by curiosity, the master of the house rose from his bed and followed the somewhat reverbing sound of Hypatia's bare feet on the floor, as if she were walking through a pond, splashing water at each step, though she was actually doing her best to tip-toe. When the father, now in the early stage of his forties, reached the top of the stairwell, he was a wee bit breathless – he was an old man, after all. Life expectancy under the circumstances of the present time was far too short; surviving infant mortality by overcoming the age of ten meant the new average target was twenty-five years, which was subsequently doubled, and that was definitely calling it a longshot, pushing one's luck. According to basic Arithmetic, Theon most likely had less than ten years to live, hence his dedication concerning his daughter's preparation, aimed at having her know how to achieve and maintain greatness in a world from which he would soon be gone, unable to shield her anymore – the reason why it had been and still was crucial for Hypatia to learn how to handle herself practically since birth; her mother had already gone without even holding her own child... the father was the only family and inspiration left. Regardless of how unconsciously he could have made his decision, Theon was without a doubt defying the rules of a society he, as a man, had always been expected to thrive among. The same could not be said about Hypatia or any other female.

The wheezing eventually caught the child's attention, diverting her from the focus she had placed on the revolving dome above, from which it was possible to tell each time an equinox or a solstice began, considering the constellations drifted in their longitude, holding, however, the same latitude. She abruptly turned around, rotating on her own axis, supported by her heels.

'Father…! I'm truly sorry, I didn't mean to wake you', Hypatia said, worried she might be in trouble and reprimanded by her old man.

Leaning on his right hand against the stairwell banister and having recovered his breath, Theon started walking toward his daughter while speaking in a tone of reassurance:

'There's no need to upset yourself, child. I suppose that, much like you, I wasn't feeling too sleepy, so I thought I'd come and join you. Doing a bit of late-night reading, are we? From the heavens, I mean', he said, standing next to his offspring while pasting his eyes to the firmament. Hypatia rested her forearms on the balcony's marble balustrade, which she surpassed in height by a few inches only and, ostensibly hypnotized by the dots of light in the dark sky, she replied:

'Oh!, yes, definitely… each celestial body is like a chapter in a book, with a story of its own, though correlated to all others in the same magnum opus – the constellations, in this case. If only there were a way we could get somewhere close and observe them, study their composition, reformulate Ptolemy's findings with new evidence and, perhaps, add a few addenda to your own commentaries, Father', Hypatia enthusiastically suggested.

Theon smiled before the child's candor, though he quickly dragged his eyes from above, all the way down to the flora in the peristylium, simultaneously letting go of all the air he had contained in his lungs, though his daughter did not seem to notice this surreptitious exasperation. Placing his left hand on Hypatia's left shoulder, he took another deep breath and told her:

'Do you know something, my child? Your drive is my most meaningful source of inspiration. No matter how long one may study the great minds of the past, one cannot feel whole without a decent enough reason to make it all somehow personal. Hoarding knowledge for the mere sake of it leads us nowhere. In all my life, there isn't anyone or anything I could be this proud of – except you'.

Hypatia looked away from the stars above and saw two others at a much closer range; her father's eyes had turned into a pair of springs. Theon· was beginning to yield all the more to the empirical dimension of the phenomenal world, thinking he would soon depart to rejoin the One, which he gladly accepted, for he knew his offspring had become the woman he had envisioned ever since her birth. All he had had to do was provide her with basic skills that defied the world she lived in, enabling her to survive by thinking like a man, therefore avoiding intolerance and disrespect; her voice was bound to become an authority, immortalizing the name of her father before her, together with her own. This way, the House of Theon made sure a shred of light would still pierce through the stormy skies lingering above the Mediterranean, spreading their ever-growing influence across the desert, where Jesus of Nazareth himself had wandered for forty days and forty nights, resisting the temptation of God's once favorite angel.

'Why are you crying, Father…?', Hypatia innocently asked her old man, while grabbing his nightgown and making a fold on it by clenching one of her small hands.

Theon did not mean to scare the child by telling her bluntly that he felt his expiry date closer each day, for which reason he knelt as he leaned against the ornamental parapet, held the girl's visage and said, in a tone of comfort:

'It's all right, my dear. I'm just a silly old fool, losing the wits I was once sure to have about me. Now, getting emotional is an effortless task. I'm proud of you, Hypatia. I've never told you this before, and perhaps you should have heard it long ago, but it's never too late. You have all the necessary power to rule this world like kings, pharaohs, and emperors have done for thousands of years, now. I needn't look at the stars to realize History will remember you across its annals until humanity is no more. Having you for a daughter is the best gift a father could ever ask for, and the same goes for a mother. She's up there, watching us right now, and I know she shares my feelings, the greatest woman before you, embodied in your very flesh'.

Despite her young age, Hypatia found herself speechless for the first time since she had learned to talk. Her sight swiftly swept Theon's face, focusing on its every spot, dancing in-between his pupils. Without any prior rationalization, the little girl yielded to what felt like the best response to her father's words and held him around his neck. In turn, he placed his hands on her back, closing his eyelids and allowing the tears to cascade freely down his cheekbones. After a while, as Hypatia quietly sobbed, Theon looked back up to the firmament and smiled, assured his mission had been successful and his duty was done.

Chapter IV
In Nomine Patris et Filii et Spiritus Sancti

By the time the daughter of Theon of Alexandria supplanted the common target for infant mortality, ten years of age, the three reigning Roman emperors (Theodosius, Gratian, and Valentinian II) issued a new edict bound to replace Constantine the Great's legislation, which had been approved in Mediolanum sixty-seven years before.

Within the triumvirate (even though academics have never referred to it as such), Theodosius was the most prominent. He would be the last man to rule as sole Augustus of the entire imperial domain, but for the time being, his concern was the Eastern portion alone, governing his share from Constantinople, of course, despite his birthplace being Hispania.

Theodosius had no blood relation whatsoever with the royal family, but that did not make him less Roman, as he was the son of Theodosius the Elder, a military commander with whom he would eventually learn the ways of battle, having strived in the province of Moesia, in the Balkans, of which he was the governor, against the rebellion of both the Alemanni and the Sarmatians.

His father, however, fell foul, having been executed. Heartbroken, the successful soldier and politician moved away from the very grounds a great deal of Roman blood had been shed upon, especially in the neighboring province of Illyricum, and returned to the family estates in Gallaecia, just above Lusitania, which spread across the West and Southwest of the Iberian Peninsula. There, Theodosius became a quiet, provincial aristocrat for four years, therefore avoiding drawing attention to himself when a political crisis struck the Empire in three hundred seventy-five, following the death of Valentinian I. The latter's sons, Valentinian II and Gratian, took over for him as co-emperors of the West, as Valens, their uncle, took care of the Levant side.

In the year of Our Lord three hundred seventy-eight, during the Battle of Adrianople, Valens saw his demise against a Gothic rebellion, leaving his seat in Constantinople empty, for he had no descendants who could claim their right to the throne. The only solution in sight according to Gratian, who was alive and well in Rome in the company of his brother, was to invite someone from outside the family to serve as co-Augustus of the East. It was in that moment Theodosius's life changed abruptly, once he accepted Gratian's proposal – the both former military commander and local politician, living in exile for fear of persecution, was now royalty, an empowered man who had no problem whatsoever spreading the Western ideology of Christianity across the East, where Arianism was prevalent.

This doctrine, created by Arius of Ptolemais and supported by Eusebius of Nicomedia, the bishop who baptized Constantine the Great near the latter's death, claimed the Holy Trinity was faulty, for the Son was not the embodiment of the Father, but rather an independent creation, making Jesus Christ a primordial creation and a mere subordinate of God. It had already been defined in the First Council of Nicaea, presided by Constantine in three hundred twenty-five, that Arianism was a non-trinitarian heresy.

Soon after Theodosius began his reign, the purging of heretics, followers of Arius' teachings, became a necessity. Gratian, in turn, concurred with his counterpart and launched a full-scale hunt throughout his jurisdiction, in order to make Nicene Christianity the one faith across the Empire.

Finding himself in Thessalonica and once recovered from severe illness, Theodosius was baptized in the year three hundred eighty in Thessalonica by the city's bishop, Ascholius, and, together with Valentinian II and Gratian, he issued the Cunctos Populos Edict (also known as Edict of Thessalonica), addressed to the people of Constantinople, authorizing the followers of the Apostolic Faith according to Peter, disciple of Christ, to call themselves Catholic Christians. All others, branded madmen, were stripped of the «church» designation of their temples and condemned to both the chastisement of God and the Augusti, who enforced the infliction of a heavenly will as punishment.

Within six months' time, Theodosius began preparations for the summoning of the Second Ecumenical Council, First of Constantinople, which took place, precisely, in the capital city of the East, with the purpose of both bringing the Empire together as far as Nicene Orthodoxy was concerned, as there was still much disparity between its halves, and amending the original Nicene Creed of three hundred twenty-five, approved by Constantine. Around May three hundred eighty-one, it became clear the one faith was indeed trinitarian, which meant the Holy Spirit should not be discounted, as it was equal in divinity to the Father, proceeding from him, whereas Jesus was begotten of him, instead of made; this Third Person of the Trinity was the Lord and Giver of life, glorified together with the Father and the Son, the entity who spoke via the prophets.

Although Theodosius had been relatively tolerant regarding the coexistence of Greco-Roman Paganism with his own faith during the first period of his reign (inclusively appointing Pagans to public offices, such as the Praetorian Prefecture of Egypt, held by Eutolmius Tatianus), once the Nicene Creed was declared the official State religion, so did the persecution of Polytheism begin, which is obviously rather curious, as it is plain confirmation the board was sufficiently spun in order to entitle those who had challenged the Hellenic pantheon for nearly three centuries to evolve from prey to predators. A series of decrees that followed and complemented the Edict of Thessalonica dictated the fate of all men and women who renounced to the Church of Our Lord Jesus Christ, choosing to defy the new rules and stick to old habits, which were quickly deemed criminal for their brand-new proximity to witchcraft, probably the most cited felony in the history of Christendom and the perfect excuse to get rid of anyone popular enough to deviate the flock from the path of light leading to the shepherd. Pagan sacrifices and subsequent haruspicy were prohibited, the fire of Vesta (the Roman goddess of homes and families who was rarely represented in human form) was extinguished at the Roman Forum, polytheistic organizations and associations (such as the Vestal Virgins, priestesses of the aforementioned feminine deity) were disbanded, the Senate lost its Altar of Victory in Rome (which had been dedicated to the homonymous goddess), visits to Pagan temples were forbidden, all Paganism-related holidays became regular working days and, for the time being, any magistrates who refused to enforce laws against Pagans were marginalized and placed under arrest, if not executed.

In the year three hundred eighty-four, however, there was somewhat of a setback on account of Magnus Maximus, an army general who, to the likes of Theodosius, was originally from the province of Gallaecia. He was proclaimed co-emperor of the West by his own soldiers in detriment of the unpopular Gratian, whom he pursued with the aid of his troops from Britannia into Gallia, eventually murdering him (by the hand of Andragathius, Maximus's trusted Magister Equitum) and usurping his thrown, which could not be fully claimed by Valentinian II, for, at the time, the latter was just a boy aged twelve. His true intention, of course, was to also kill the child by chasing after him into the Italian Peninsula, therefore taking over the entire Western Roman Empire. It was thus up to Theodosius to prevent Maximus's full-blown territorial expansion, having sent an overwhelming force led by Flavius Bauto to his encounter. It was only after negotiations mediated by Ambrosius, Bishop of Mediolanum, that Theodosius officially recognized Maximus as co-Augustus of the West, handing him over the two provinces he already had under control, under the condition that Valentinian II's domain be left untouched.

For the next three years, Pagans were tolerated yet again, rising as distinguished public officials, free to perform their customary rituals, as well as care for their temples – a task that was exclusive to them. Nevertheless, and because ambition is the most common cause for falling from grace, Maximus still craved for the remaining Western portion of the Empire and endeavored to overrun Valentinian II once more, who joined Theodosius after fleeing for his life all the way to Constantinople.

From the capital city of the East, both Augusti campaigned against Maximus, who was defeated in Aquileia, in the Italian Peninsula, where he also surrendered; Andragathius and Marcellinus, Maximus's brother, were killed. The fact that the usurping emperor pleaded for mercy was of no good to him, for he was executed on the spot. The remainder of his family (his mother and daughters) was spared from the same fate, apart from his son, Flavius Victor, who was strangled in Trevorum, Gallia, by one of Theodosius's generals, Arbogast.

Following Maximus's defeat, Valentinian II reclaimed complete control over the West and reinstated Gratian's policies against Pagans, though a new issue had brewed in Northern Gallia, where Marcomer, a Frank Dux, had started an invasion. Still, it would not take long until his own defeat at the hands of fellow countryman Arbogast, who did not care much for the people he shared his roots with.

As for Theodosius, his battle against heresy moved on to a whole new level, sending emissaries instructed to destroy Pagan manifestations via temples and man-made representations of the Greco-Roman deities across both Egypt and the Levant, where a synagogue was also razed to the ground by a Christian bishop and his followers (in Callinicum, near the River Euphrates, to be precise). Apparently biased, the Augustus of the East reverted the situation, ordering that the temple be re-erected.

This decision, however, was profoundly criticized by the Bishop of Mediolanum, Ambrosius, who regarded the emperor as being Jewish himself for being so kind to the murderers of Christ, claiming they too had burnt down many churches that had not yet been rebuilt. In fact, the clergyman went so far on his attempt at influencing Theodosius's faith that he could not help but remind him that the Father had looked upon synagogues as houses of unbelief, having destroyed the Temple of Jerusalem immediately after the Son's crucifixion at Golgotha, the skull-shaped hill.

It was in three hundred ninety that Ambrosius held full control of the Eastern Augustus's resolve, right after the massacre of seven thousand people in Thessalonica, Macedonia, exactly where he had issued the homonymous edict a decade before, as a penalty for the assassination of the governor he had chosen for the region. The impious action was, in turn, punished with Ambrosius's excommunication of Theodosius, who was also barred from entering the Mediolanum Cathedral. The emperor had no choice but to repent and cry for the forgiveness of the Lord via Ambrosius, who only yielded after several months of penance and guilt, to the likes of King David, following his adultery with Bathsheba and the murder of her husband, Uriah, who was defending David's throne as ruler of Israel; profoundly devoted, Theodosius accepted his punishment before he was welcomed back into the Church of Christ.

Under the influence of Ambrosius, both Theodosius the Great and Valentinian II kept campaigning against all forms of heresy, witchcraft, and Paganism, which eventually became outlawed, as per the Theodosian decrees issued at the start of the last decade of the fourth century of the Christian Era, which meant that both Pagan-related property and sites were to be abandoned and closed, thus allowing Christians to seize control over the remnants of what had once been a part of Rome's identity, now bound to be crushed and replaced by holy temples and iconography, except for the representation of the Lord as a human being – the cross sufficed.

Nevertheless, in Alexandria, there was still a great deal of segregation between Pagans, Jews, and Christians. Pope Theophilus, the clergyman in charge of ecclesiastical affairs in the Egyptian province, whose capital city was the same the Ptolemaic dynasty had governed from for three hundred years, quickly took advantage of the ever-growing fight against the heathens and conjured up a plan that made sure his authority would only be second to the emperor's, even though Theodosius was represented by the Praefectus Augustalis, which was irrelevant to the Pope, as he seemed to be learning the ways of sacred persuasion from Ambrosius, ultimately intervening in the Augusti's political decisions, though it was enough for the Bishop of Mediolanum to puppeteer only one of them, Theodosius the Great; more than devotion, his extreme (if not fanatical) fervor and old age, which was now beyond the forty-year bar, were sufficient to cloud the mind of a co-emperor in his early twenties, that of Valentinian II. It was a short leap from Ambrosius's will to imperial legislation, naturally ignoring the Senate's vote, especially when it was still riddled with Pagan members.

And so, a holy war was progressively brewing in an urban center where tolerance reigned and religion did not make any difference at all among scholars, and that is the regal motive behind any imminent destruction of intellect, the one element that separates humans from beasts, which is to say that, when reasoning is no longer effective, the only road there is left to walk is that of conflict, no matter how many people are killed or knowledge shredded and burned in the process; there were already not that many papyri left in the harbor city, and the Great Library was now reduced to the much smaller Serapeum. Most archives were located inside the minds of scholars, the Pagan kind. Should their purge become necessary, Theodosius himself would easily back Theophilus; all the Pope required was an excuse, the perfect pretext to rile the Pagans so much into hotheadedness that there could be no coming back from their actions. Support from neither the imperial army nor the Praetorian Guard mattered; one of the perks of being a man of power within the Church of Christ was the ability to summon a personal army with no allegiance whatsoever to any order or vows. Their faith in the Lord was all the strength they needed to become brothers-in-arms and violently disband any visible threats against bishops, regardless of their commitment to tending the poor, the wounded, and the dead (those who shared the same faith, at least).

Theophilus's luck, however, would literally grow a lot more, for, in the vastity of the desert, other missionaries lingered, readying themselves to soon join the local militia.

Chapter V
Brothers-in-Arms (and Faith)

The brotherhood of the Parabolani had been founded fairly recently, under the papacy of Dionysius of Alexandria, just a little over a hundred years prior to Theodosius's reign of the Eastern portion of the Roman Empire, who placed them under the control of the province's Prefect, regardless of their despise for the imperial representative who, in turn, kept losing his authority once Christianity was empowered from Mediolanum to the entire State; whether there were still Arians, Jews, and Pagans to be dealt with, the truth was the Church of Christ was not going to give up so easily, neither in favor of a multitude of gods (and goddesses, which was worse), nor a handful of Pharisees, murderers of Jesus and, therefore, the Father himself, as per the Nicene Creed.

Because of their overreactive beliefs, the law withheld them from being present at public gatherings, including the theater – there was always an immeasurable risk rioting would take place, often against citizens who put their fate in someone else's hands other than the Lord and Savior.

After all, members did not really have much to lose, as they regularly originated from the lower strata of society including slaves, especially if it meant their freedom from the home of a polytheistic master. A lot of them did not care who they actually believed in, if anyone at all; cradled under the umbrella of a new and revolutionizing institution, the Parabolani were granted shelter, food (in the form of the body of Christ, mostly), and drink (his blood). In exchange, it was asked of these men that they stick to their original duty, which was taking care of the ill, just like when Alexandria had endured an outbreak of the great plague during the ecclesiastic leadership of Dionysius. In the official idiom of the State, being a Parabalanus meant nursing those afflicted with maladies, but because some of them were highly contagious and the life of these nurses was often at risk, the Parabolanus variation became a current vocable – the product of the Greek language's influence, as was natural in a formerly Ptolemaic city.

Direct contact with plague-infected patients was not necessarily fatal, but should the carrier parasites still be feeding off nearby rodents and jump from either mice or rats to the attendants' skin, then they would soon join their creator. Although they were not exactly spreading the word (not in a civilized manner, at least), dying next to a moribund patient was the same as heading into the light on account of faith, for, as Christians, it was their mission to help those in need, which meant they had everything to depart what the Pagans called the phenomenal world in the sanctity of martyrdom.

The planning for the city of Alexandria comprised a well-structured layout based on Hellenic architecture, bearing parallel streets of which two were ranked as the main routes connecting both the Northern and Southern walls of the urban center from the Great Harbor (between the Island of Pharos and the mainland) to the port of Lake Mareotis which, in turn, joined the Canal of Alexandria, outflowing toward Eunostos Harbor, West of the Heptastadion (designated like so because of its length of approximately seven stadia), the manmade passage connecting the Lighthouse to the agora. These two streets were named Aspendia (the most direct passage between the Musaeum, to the North, and the Serapeum, to the South) and Argeus (connecting the South exit to the Canal with the Macedonian acropolis, located on the outlet of the Great Harbor's Easternmost pier).

Though the city in general fit a great deal of quarters, the most important were a total of three – beginning with the center, there lay the Broucheion, reserved for the Pagan Greeks and their respective institutions.

To the East lay the Jewish Quarter, housing as nearly as one hundred thousand Children of Israel; their dead were laid to rest in the sepulchers on the outer side of the enclosing wall, made accessible via the Canopian Gate. These burial chambers were shared with Christians and, close by, there was also a cemetery dedicated to the Roman military.

To the West, where the Serapeum and the Temple of Serapis happened to be included, lay the Christian Quarter – a much more confined space in need of bursting its stitches for the expansion of the one true faith.

Until Theodosius the Great became the ruler of the Eastern Roman Empire, this triple segregation hardly ever inconvenienced anyone, for the city's inhabitants were free to walk around wherever they pleased and, as is known by now, Theon accepted in his Neoplatonic School all of those who craved for an academic education, regardless of any kind of creed his prospective students may have had within them. It was at the start of the fourth century's last decade, however, the turmoil rose because of the co-Augustus' decrees, stirring what, until then, had been a perfectly acceptable way of socialization between people who did not require whatsoever the marking of their territory. The problem was, bearing in mind the presence of religious symbology scattered over two thirds of Alexandria (Greek-Egyptian temples, representations of their respective Pantheon, synagogues, and Stars of David), together with the sympathy shown by Theodosius to the traitors of the Lord (despite Ambrosius's disapproval), Pope Theophilus took it to him that the only way there would ever be actual peace in the city was to ravish it to the opposite wall, counting on the imperial codex to relieve the infidels of their property and build churches in their place. As for the people, either they willingly converted to Christianism, or lynching might just become an impending penalty, the sort a baptized and passionate emperor wouldn't pose a threat to; on the contrary, it was likely he may even condone it, just like seven decades prior, during the good old days of Constantinian rule. One of the best means to this end rested in rhetoric and eloquence, two subjects the Pagans themselves taught everyone else; a convincing, conniving tone, along with words of wisdom channeled from the heavens to frighten the people, was infallible. Tell them what they want to hear, and their support becomes unequivocally short-sighted.

Every now and then, whether it was under direct orders from Pope Theophilus or simply of their own accord, the Parabolani did not hesitate to leave their nursing skills to the side, choosing to adopt those of wounding the people whose soul would not find salvation in the first place, once Judgment Day came, which is why mauling their bodies was an act of faith, seeking to rid the earth of its salt rather sooner than later.

Oddly enough, this is the part where another Christian group, perhaps even far more fanatical than the Parabolani on their own, becomes renowned in History for bringing that exact same mineral under their very soles.

The Nitrian Monks are a group of Christians who first flourished in three monastic centers of the homonymous desert located to the South of Alexandria, already within the Nile delta (Scetis, Nitria, and Kellia), where the first Egyptians had obtained sodium bicarbonate, essential to the process of mummification; under Roman rule, the alkali lakes were the main source for the production of glass.

Their choice to live in the solitude of individual cellulae, disperse across the vast arid plains, was regarded as a way of heeding the divine call, therefore excluding from their journey in the material world certain carnal-related pleasures, looking to achieve a different sort of ecstasy by not exerting a reaction at all, thus becoming stoic, accepting of the Lord's will.

The credit for the practice of this lifestyle is mostly attributed to Saint Macarius, who, in Scetis, around three hundred thirty, founded the first monastery where peace could be attained and spirituality disciplined; the fact the first to join him were already used to the quietness of the desert, living as hermits, was critical for the successful establishment of a few more shrines, which assembled men who shared similar lines of thought.

Of course, it is but obligatory to add that the pacific state the monks intended to grasp was only applicable to other people who believed what they did. No matter how either Judaism or Christianism appealed to communal respect and understanding, free will was never a question of choice. There were those who claimed to be empowered by God to play the role of shepherds and offer their guidance to the flock, and there were the sheep, whose purpose was none other than follow The Lamp of the Desert, as Macarius was frequently referred to, which you've been told before, close to the beginning of this story.

Another aspect that is not at all new either is the need to spread salvation as further as possible, meaning the only path an earthly vessel can take in order to guarantee its essence (the spirit) does not make a wrong turn toward eternal damnation in the fires of hell is the acceptance of Our Lord Jesus Christ as our only Savior. Should a step be taken while heading somewhere else (a different light source, perhaps), there would be no need for the interfering of Roman soldiers, as Theodosius the Great could simply rely on unofficial agents of public order and law enforcement to keep everyone and everything under control – a group of vigilantes (or the mob, bluntly put).

The most passionate of all the Nitrian Monks combined was, without a doubt, the young Ammonius, likely in pursuit of not just inner peace and self-discipline but, more importantly, sainthood, canonization (despite having taken vows of humility). Come to think of it, he had more of a Parabolanus side to him than that of a monk walled in his cell, in silent prayer. Being a Christian implied embracing poverty, a total distancing from the materialistic ideals (please excuse the paradox) hedonism had to offer, which meant that, to both Ammonius and other monks, who acknowledged in his personality the presence of a natural ambition toward leadership, staying under the Lord's watch was absolutely everything, for which reason none of them had anything to lose, in case temptation showed itself right before their eyes; they would easily recognize Lucifer was clearly behind the whole scheme, even if the devil's treachery signified attracting souls who willingly followed the Antichrist in the shape of imaginary deities associated to a human-like representation made by men themselves, given they were obviously under the influence of the devil's dark magic, thus offering these people answers to their ulterior doubts – something the followers of the one, true God would never question, to begin with.

Because the elder hermits were far too paced for his taste, Ammonius often quarreled vivaciously with those deemed as the wisest, though, to his misfortune, he could not pull rank, inevitably leading to imprisonment in his cell for weeks without a single breadcrumb to content his stomach – or so the Abbot and the Great Schema thought; other youths enthusiastically sympathizing with the Stavrophore (also known as Little Schema or cross-bearer, connected to divinity by the paramandyas, which is to say the yoke of Christ, metaphorically speaking) made sure their companion was given at least a few loaves, thus preventing the weakness of both his body and mind, in order to sustain the spirit still inhabiting his flesh, though willingly waived to the Lord's satisfaction.

Now, although the Church of Alexandria did not exactly comprise an unequivocal separation between the statuses of Rassaphore and Stavrophore, not all monks were seen as fit by the Abbot to immediately be asked to join a higher degree within the monastery. Some did not even aim that high out of humility, respect, and obedience, which were vows the men dressed in dark robes (as in dead to the world and entirely devoted to God) were required to take, following the tonsure in the shape of the Holy Cross – four locks of hair severed along with the enunciation of the words pertaining to the Trinitarian formula, subsequently burned. This did not mean, however, the monastic robe-bearers agreed with their superiors, in which case it would probably be best to abandon their ecclesiastic home; the only impediment was one of the vows was that of stability and moving from one place to another required the blessing of either the Abbot or the Great Schema. Failure to comply resulted in excommunication.

One night, prior to his watch of the monastery's perimeter, confined to his cellula and kneeling in prayer in front of his icon corner, where he kept his beeswax and the candle that would be lit for his funeral (God only knew when), Ammonius implored the Lord for a sign. He asked of both the Father and the Son that he be bequeathed the significance of his existence, that light be shed as to how he could more proactively serve the Trinity before abandoning the earthly realm in a chaos the upper class of the monastic hierarchy did not seem keen on acknowledging. The thought of murder was something that, for a short period of time, the monk took into consideration, but the sixth commandment inscribed into the second tablet surrendered by the Lord to Moses on Mount Horeb, in the Egyptian Sinai Peninsula, turned out to be a dilemma. Then again, Moses, raised Egyptian, though Hebrew by birth, was the first to lead a people, under the Father's instructions, from captivity to freedom across the Re[e]d Sea to the Holy Land, where fifteen hundred years later, give or take, the Messiah would only be regarded as a blasphemy in the flesh, as opposed to their savior. To Ammonius, both the Great Schema and the Abbot played the roles of Annas and Caiaphas, the original leaders of the plot to frame the Son. The fact they were Christians and not Jewish was irrelevant at this point. Something had to be done for those two men to stay out of the monk's path toward becoming a true servant of Christ, punishing, exactly like the latter had done, those who failed to see the light right in front of them, once he abandoned his body and joined the Father, sitting at his right hand. And so, Ammonius was given the answer he had been vividly looking for after parting ways with the vices of a land that was mundane and meaningless, when compared to the heavenly glow God was prepared to bestow upon everyone who took his eternal glory into their heart. Naturally, what the Stavrophore interpreted as the Lord's will could have perfectly been mistaken for the monk's own hatred, but, far worse than being cursed with blindness by some third-party was to cede to the darkness of wrath, one of the seven capital sins. This is how murder is religiously justified, regardless of faith or denomination – if it is for the greater good, then the Creator shall offer his pardon.

Ammonius, who was supposed to overlook the monastery's surroundings from the building's rooftops in just a few moments, was now prepared for an entirely different mission of sacrifice, but not necessarily his own. The moment he held his head up and looked at his personal shrine where a wooden cross, beeswax, and his burial candle lay, he arose, took the small container of secretion and, dipping his right thumb in it, crossed himself for self-protection, for he had embodied his resolve and was not willing to recede. As he mouthed his prayers, he grabbed one of the tapers illuminating the cell and lit his personal candle, whose diameter was much wider, thus increasing the amount of time required for the wick to burn through the wax's density. Whether Ammonius would die that night was a mystery, but as sure as the fires of hell was the fact he would be gone from the monastery before the Sun came back to circle around God's earthly plains.

The Stavrophore exited his cell wearing the hood of his cassock on his head. As he moved across the corridor where the robe-bearers took it to their sleep, his free hand covered the flame of the burial candle to concentrate the lighting mostly on his face. If anyone were looking at Ammonius from the wick's perspective, they would realize a stern composure, aggravated by the black, rugged beard linked to the sideburns, as opposed to his still visibly tonsured hair, especially in the temple areas, where silvery spikes were beginning to stand out. His eyes seemed to be sinking into their sockets, surrounded by black marks in the shape of uneven semicircles. One could almost say that was a dead man walking, with an apparently debilitated physique. At each step he took forward, quietly pacing his feet in worn-out sandals, the footwear of poverty (the counterpart of wealthy Greco-Roman apparel tradition), the candle's flame's dancing nuance, though protected by Ammonius's palm, eerily illuminated the monk's features. The temperature rose by the second, nearly boiling out his skin; the cross he held in his other hand, attached to the candle, almost reached a smoldering state at the center, as it also drove drops of melted wax, sliding down on his knuckles and in-between his fingers. It was becoming harder at every step not to release the slightest gasp for the relief of pain, but the discipline mirrored in the cross-bearer's visage came from within, forcing him to stay quiet. He did not even bother looking around to see if he had caught the attention of other monks, but with the doors slam shut, his lingering was hardly noticeable, whether they were sound asleep or profoundly focused in their vigil.

Once he got to the end of the cell hall, Ammonius reached the stairwell, choosing to descend, rather than climb up to the domed cupolas on the roof. After the last step, he found himself on the lower level, in the Northern extremity of the transept, a rectangular area that separated the nave of the monastery from the apse, located to the East, thus attributing the main building the shape of a holy cross or crucifix. In turn, the apse led up to three distinct apsidal chapels, each with an altar of its own; to the West lay the narthex (the main entrance), kept apart from the shrine area by an iconostasis. In fact, depictions of the life of Jesus Christ were something that simply could not go unnoticed, particularly the episodes of the Passion. The cross-bearer, now feeling freer to walk about, held his candle close to the mural decorations covering the mudbricks the walls were made of, in order to keep a cool environment and avoid the desert's heat, moving between columns along the aisles, as emotion appeared to take the best of him, from the Agony of the Lord in the Olive Garden of Gethsemane, to his being presented in front of Pontius Pilate, his flagellation, and his repeated falls while carrying the cross on Via Dolorosa, in the city of Jerusalem, on his way to Golgotha, outside the sacred walls. Tears came streaming down from Ammonius' bloodshot eyes, simultaneously hitting his chest with his incandescent cross – tearing his robes in sorrow for the death of the Lord would be a Jewish thing to do, something that could never cross his mind; the high priests had done the same a first time, following their accusations of blasphemy on account of the Son speaking the truth. The second time, their keriah manifestation had taken place in the shape of repentance, for they knew not what they were doing. Still, it is arguable whether pardon was indeed granted by the Father at the Son's request, as he lay nailed by the hands and feet, covered in dust, sand, and blood from both the whipping and the crown of thorns he wore on his head to his demise. Regardless, some of the live sparks from Ammonius's cross were transferred to his cassock as he beat his heart, quickly extinguishing themselves, though leaving both respirable and visible traces of smoke – suffice to say it was almost as if his core were on fire.

Headed South via the church-bay, after which he turned East, the dark-robed cross-bearer completed his tour of the shrine's aisles at the end of the transept opposite to where he had come down from. During his walk, he had slid the tip of his right hand fingers most of the time on the engravings, perhaps in search of a more powerful spiritual connection to the Holy Trinity. Straight in front of him were the doors leading to the ambulatory, encircling the choir and the apse, whose entrance was through the rood screen. For a moment, he considered walking over to the central altar, but that option was soon discarded. There was not much time left for dwelling. He had to move, and fast – how much more forgiveness can a man ask for in just less than an hour?

Along the hemispheric ambulatory, three magnanimous gates led toward the chapels – at that time of night, they were locked. In-between said entrances, however, were two less resistant doors, despite being ornamented atop by architraves into which both the «Great Schema» and «Abbot» designations had been carved in Coptic Egyptian; those were the chambers of the two highest ranking officials in the monastery, a crossing between cubicula and tablina – there they studied, wrote, read and lay in slumber. The pathway was illuminated not by lit candlesticks, but oil lamps.

As opposed to the apsidal chapels' gates, neither the Great Schema nor the Abbot felt the need to keep their personal spaces sealed, except during the day, should they be fulfilling their duties elsewhere in the building with the monks, who were not supposed to be out of their bedstead unless explicitly instructed to do so. It was but a mere question of discipline implicit in the vows these men took. Ammonius was, thusly, in a clear violation, as his guard duty did not comprise loitering about – not within the monastery's walls, at least.

Perhaps in somewhat of a short, though paradoxical moment, the Stavrophore debated himself which of the two clergymen would he pay a visit to first, having decided he should conduct his business in a descending order, meaning the first would be the Abbot, whose chamber door was to the left. Quietly merging the wooden cross with the candle again in just one hand, he drove the other to the knob, grabbing hold of it one finger at a time. With a gentle push, Ammonius turned the handle and opened the door into nearly complete darkness – a small recess in the wall covered with glass let the starlight in, just above the bed. As a man who had to set the example, formally inviting the monks to become unequivocal servants of the Lord and Savior, who deserved no less than the greatest respect from those made of flesh and bone to his own image, the cubiculum-tablinum was kept remarkably tidy. To the office side, where Ammonius swiftly moved, there were multiple bookshelves made of tamarisk wood surrounding the magnanimous desk, which, in turn, was made of sycamore fig-tree; these are two of the most common species in Ancient Egyptian flora, often represented in mural frescoes and bas-reliefs as part of quotidian scenes, particularly the latter, also known as nehet. On the resistant-looking desk were two lecterns. The one on the left-hand side was holding what seemed to be a complete version of the Good Book, written in Greek; atop the one on the right lay a half-finished manuscript the Abbot was copying in accordance to what had been defined as the ultimate biblical canon by Athanasius I in his Easter Letter, dated from three hundred sixty-seven – he was the third-to-last predecessor of Pope Theophilus, now in charge of the Coptic Orthodox Church. Apparently, the Abbot had stopped copying at Ecclesiasticus, chapter twenty-one, verse five, "A prayer out of a poor man's mouth reacheth to the ears of God, and his judgment cometh speedily", authored by Ben Sira, originally in Hebrew; it was his grandson who carried the book to Alexandria and translated it for Greek-speaking Jews. As far as Ammonius was concerned, the verse seemed somewhat ominously appropriate.

Without wasting much more time rummaging around, the monk turned to the Abbot's bedstead. The old man was sound asleep, apparently undisturbed, not a single concern weighing in on his chest, its motion in profound recycling. Come to think of it, it wasn't only until Ammonius drew his attention to the clergyman in charge of the monastery that he noticed how wheezy his breathing was. The cross-bearer stood there for a moment; he hardly blinked, thus reddening his eyes to a strain under which it was impossible not to tear, though he was not feeling like crying at all. Speaking of cross, the top of the monk's was yet again turning incandescent, becoming frailer by the second around the edges, given the wood's diminished thickness. The Stavrophore took it further and deliberately burned off the sides, softly landing on the floor already in ashes. Ammonius had just fashioned himself a murder weapon, sharpening the top of the cross like an incensed stake. One step forward… followed by another, and the Abbot was within range. Cast on the wall was the silhouette of a forearm and a hand firmly grabbing what looked like a dagger. Just as the monk had raised his arm to its full, possible extent, so did he bring it down to the old man's heart, furiously stabbing it with his makeshift pick, turned upside-down like Peter's crucifix, for he was not worthy of dying the same way as his Master. The clergyman opened his eyes and mouth to exacerbate the excruciating pain, but he couldn't breathe hard enough to make a sound as he bled out. The wrinkled visage of the priest suddenly transformed into the very face of Satan, for which reason only Ammonius could confirm, when the Abbot met his furious gaze, his soul about to depart the body, the monk turned the candle the other way around and let the wax drip all over the clergyman's face, focusing especially on the eyes, as if blinding him also on his way to the afterlife. Still in search of the slightest draught, the old man was not strong enough to throw the Stavrophore on the floor and call out for help. Overcome by a wrath he believed was the very ire of God, Ammonius dripped the candle's hot wax into the Abbot's throat, choking and silencing him permanently. His last words, concealed in an inaudible whisper, were:

'Dies irae…'.

By the time the monk finished reading his lips, the clergyman was already dead, but Ammonius still retorted for his own satisfaction:

'Kyrie eleison'.

The Abbot's damaged heart progressively reduced its pace until it no longer beat. His warm blood, gushing at first all over the wall next to what had become his deathbed, streamed down his chest, soaking the hay-filled mattress, dripping also on the feather-stuffed pillow from the open mouth. Because Ammonius left the cross in place after the final stabbing, there had eventually been some cauterization involved in the wounding, though it was naturally irreparable. Praying for his soul was all there was left to do; the question was – the Abbot's or the monk's? The Stavrophore did not appear to be concerned. His respiratory cycle was slowing down, despite the severity of both inhalations and exhalations, stretched to their maximum. He had done a necessary deed; there was no way he could avoid fulfilling the will of the Lord.

To the right of the bed, on the nightstand, was the Abbot's silver pectoral cross, symbolizing his statute as head of the monastery. It was lying on top of the thread the clergyman would put around his neck after kissing and crossing himself with the crucifix, early in the morning; Ammonius took it, holding the thread with his arm extended down his torso, while the candle, in his other hand, remained close to his face.

Perhaps temporarily dwelling in his subconscious, the monk left the cubiculum-tablinum and closed the door behind him. Now that half his mission had been completed, it probably wouldn't take him that long to run the final stretch. Ammonius walked in the ambulatory area to the left, passing the gate to the central apsidal chapel and into the Great Schema's bedroom and office, where he would often offer pastoral guidance to the monks who hadn't yet attained his level of spirituality. With respect to Ammonius, this man too was a pebble in the sandals of those who had chosen to devote their life to the Holy Trinity.

He was about to go in by surprise, when he was the one who was caught by an unexpected impasse – the doors were locked after all, making him collide against them quite noisily while dropping the candle. The monk feared he had given the Great Schema time to react and prepare himself for a possible overnight threat, but not a sound was heard; the echoing of the collision had already gone.

The candle's wick must have been incredibly resistant, for the flame had not yet once gone out. In fact, the wax cylinder was rolling on the floor, stopping only when closer to the doors. That was when Ammonius realized he wasn't going to go in at all; on the contrary, he would help the Great Schema feel safer by tightening the security, which is to say, twisting the silver thread between the knobs, making it difficult to pry the doors open. Walking just a few steps back, he saw one of the oil lamps illuminating the ambulatory. The monk took it and, nearing the cubiculum once more, threw it against the doors, now soaked and ablaze. As the fire rapidly consumed the wood, the amount of smoke blown into the cubiculum grew out of proportion. Inside and unable to ignore the build-up of a tragedy soon to come, the Great Schema began shouting as loud as he could before the fumes invaded his lungs, but the burning in the air made it difficult for him. The highest-ranking monk tried, nevertheless, fitting his key in the lock, but it was now incandescent; covering his hands with the cloth of his robes still made it impossible to pry the doors open. Should he throw himself against them, he would easily catch fire and burn on his own sooner than expected. Every chunk of wood, every spare bit of parchment, all was caught in the ravaging of the fires of hell. Unwilling to give up, the schemamonk grabbed hold of a chair and sought to force the blazing gates, but the wood the chair was made of was far thinner than that which the flames were feeding on. At each attempt, the silver cross shook, sliding on the thread, reddened and steaming. Ammonius couldn't figure out what it was the Great Schema was uttering, but whichever his words, they were beyond irrelevant. The other monks would soon arrive at the scene, once they smelled either the smoke or the nauseating odor of burning human flesh – it was therefore time to go.

Having left through the same door he had gone in, the monk made his way to the church bay and entered the narthex, stopping just once more to behold the baptismal font. Carefully walking toward it and placing his scarred left hand on the outer rim of the basin, he pulled back his hood with his right and immersed his head three times for as long as he could, cleansing himself – not from sin, for he had fulfilled the wish of the Father; it was the blood he had spilled that he wanted to wash off, even though most of it was merely figurative.

As the Stavrophore began hearing several steps echoing in the transept stairwell, together with cries for water, he put his hood back on, moved to the main doors of the monastery and left through the smaller entrance, shutting it as he saw the flames consuming every flammable material they could leech onto. Now, a long crossing of the desert awaited him until he could find signs of life once more.

Chapter VI
Dawn of the Wanderer

In a period of twenty-one years since the birth of Hypatia, daughter of Theon, many were the changes the entire Roman Empire had experienced, and the capital city of the Ancient World's complete knowledge, Alexandria, now with so many original works lost to the most assorted catastrophes, was no different.

The ever-growing tension between religious factions had become beyond unbearable, though not all hope for unity was lost – not at the Musaeum, anyway, where the former child prodigy, grown into a full-blown woman in the meantime, was the most popular professor of the Neoplatonic School, easily surpassing her father before her. At first, it was the novelty of a woman speaking her mind and teaching young men the ways of Philosophy that called upon the pupils' interest, but once they got their chance to learn with her what the world was like and the part each and every one of them played in the scheme of things, gender would cease to be an issue and arguments either for or against it turned out to be unfounded.

Theon, still in charge of both the Musaeum and the Neoplatonic School, couldn't be any prouder of who his offspring had become, and not only as far as intellect was concerned, but also with respect to the beauty Hypatia had inherited from her late mother; the fact a widowed father had a daughter to raise and provide for was neither a synonym of neglect nor renouncing to femininity.

Relying on the concept of a family with both a male and a female figure as parents and examples to be followed by children according to their biological nature, further contributing to an already deeply segregated society, was an utter, unequivocal fallacy, and Hypatia was the irrefutable evidence. Having just now become a matured adult, the daughter of Theon remarkably stood out for her looks, constantly bearing a genuine smile on her smooth face, simultaneously wielding a confident attitude (not to be mistaken for arrogance) that made her want to be helpful in any way she could, though, naturally, it was at the Musaeum she made herself the most useful, passionately discussing with her class the philosophy of Plotinus, mostly, and how it made sense when applied to the phenomenal world they all lived in, regardless of background or creed.

Now aged fifty-six, Theon had had to pace himself and slow down on his duties as Director, dedicating a great deal more time to his commentaries on Euclid and Ptolemy, jointly produced with Hypatia, whose role in this task was more of a revisor, correcting her father to the decimal; his health kept further declining and teaching, one of his most favorite things to do in an unusually long life, became all the more seldom, kept only for special lecturing occasions. His prestigious image as a pedagogue wasn't lost at all, far from it, which is why students and colleagues never missed an opportunity to listen to his eloquence... alas, keeping up with the daily rhythm of schooling was too much to bear, so, in order to spare Theon as much as she could, Hypatia would walk along the Brucheion, accompanied by a couple of slaves, to the Northwestern corner of the agora and into the Musaeum, allowing her father to make use of the chariot, should he desire to be present at the institution (considering he didn't always feel he could make it); he had to stand, of course, but the distance was quite short and the horse strutted along just quickly enough. As one of the most influential families in Pagan Alexandria, the House of Theon had access to a lifestyle not everyone could even aspire to graze, such as transportation via litter, requiring either two or four slaves to hold it, depending on the person's weight, but the truth is Hypatia was so inexplicably humble that she didn't care for flamboyance. She was a person, just like everybody else, so why should she flaunt her superiority? Still, and taking the age she was living in into consideration, masters and servants were a reality, and their coexistence comprised an unnegotiable hierarchy – the latter made the life of the former more comfortable at their own physical and psychological expense and that was it. Instead of bathing all by themselves, the wealthy would have their human property do it in their stead, also drying them up and oiling their skin to maintain it young and hydrated; the involvement of men servants in this task wasn't something to be regarded as awkward or embarrassing, on the contrary – it was as common as both genders sharing public baths, which begs the question: if there was no modesty out in the open, why should it be an issue in private?

All deviating aside, Hypatia's enthusiasm while playing the part of a pedagogue was genuine, regardless of the Thespian phrasing. The best time to teach was always in the morning, once the Sun began providing its irradiating energy, gradually spreading its arms from the Jewish quarter all the way to the Christian faction. The streets, quiet and upmarket, soon started being walked yet again for another day, as the Roman soldiers standing guard during nighttime switched places with those who had been asleep, permanently making sure public order was kept – especially in times as controversial as these.

From both the Aspendia and the Argeus avenues came the Neoplatonic School's pupils and academics, segregated among themselves, which is to say they stuck close to their own, regardless of sharing any time soon the same lecture hall. The Jewish, however, didn't take part as students of the institution; the Torah was their Good Book, explained and administered to them by proper rabbis. Judaism wasn't just a question of religion, it was a way of life with its own rules and laws; for a people who had broken free from the clutches of Pharaoh under Moses's guidance, returning to Egypt to be governed by either Pagan or Christian emperors and be cast astray from God's plan was not something they looked forward to, thus keeping to themselves, except when provoked, which was turning out to be much more frequent at each day that went by, though the Pagans had nothing to do with it – it was the Christians, supposed spreaders of peace and the holy word, who perpetuated the nearly daily verbal attacks.

Violent confrontations, while rarer, were

threatening to overwhelm the reality of a multicultural city, a key factor Ptolemy I Soter had always sought to sustain ever since claiming the Egyptian throne following Alexander's demise. Nevertheless, as intellectuals, both Pagans and Christians were still in unison with respect to not offending each other during lectures. That was the power of Hypatia, the ability to generate a consensus within a fastidious rivalry.

As per usual in nature, regardless of the species within the known fauna, there is often a prominent male (or female, depending on either a patriarchal or matriarchal regime, respectively) marking his territory in the most assorted ways, even if such conquest has nothing to do with mating rituals, but rather dominance, challengeable only via physical aggression to either death or the acknowledgement of the opponent's defeat, inevitably retreating, having to find elsewhere suitable for taking shelter and preying upon when both nourishment and replenishing are required; in the end, Humankind isn't that much different, and the present conflicts between religious groups make the strongest evidence. So, who is the alpha male among Hypatia's students? As far as the Pagan side is concerned, Orestes is the one to stand out; regarding the Christians, no particular disciple shone as the elected star. All we can do at this time is but dwell in speculation, and in taking that chance, it is likely this quieter demeanor had something to do with the lack of irreverence felt by a group of youths, when facing the fact the only trustworthy pedagogue in the most knowledgeable city of the Empire was indeed a Pagan herself. She didn't oppose anyone's beliefs, so why should her faith (if not way of life) prevent them from learning with the best there was?

Now, Orestes was a rather curious young man; he was about Hypatia's age and, just like his mistress, he had ambitions, though of a somewhat different nature – the daughter of Theon, as a philosopher, constantly sought truth in the science she taught, simultaneously developing her own theories on how the world had come to be, very much unlike her father, devoted to better explaining what was already known. Though slightly dogmatic with respect to certain subjects (which just seemed to be irrefutable, no matter how hard one tried to deny them), Hypatia was keen on aiding her students in the growth of their respective opinionated mind; as long as they could come up with enough evidence to support their theses regarding the topics of her lectures, the philosopher's heart would simply expand with pride, therefore perpetuating her inadvertent popularity – her being enthusiastic when teaching wasn't an act to the likes of those seen at the Roman amphitheater, on the contrary. The one and only Hypatia wore no masks whatsoever, nor did she require a man to play her part in the lecture hall of the Neoplatonic School, where forbidding women from standing on a stage and having men dress up to play feminine roles wasn't certainly applicable. Theon's foundation was definitely a unique haven for the blossoming of a female in a patriarchal society, progressively yielding to the teachings of the Holy Scriptures, which easily excluded dominant female characters, subjecting them to the will of men, whether or not married to one, attributing also the latter with the divine power to kill the former whenever necessary.

Orestes' ambitions, on the other hand, were of a political sort; he took a great deal of interest in social affairs, namely government. Naturally, as a Pagan, becoming a politician didn't present itself to be an easy feat, though, studying under Hypatia, whose influence spread each day to all four corners of the Empire, thus attracting disciples from the remotest of provinces, perhaps he could easily land his chance. In spite of the tension felt across the streets of the city, it was Orestes's hope there could still be some stability left, once he concluded his education; the Theodosian decrees, continuously promulgated over the course of the last three years, made it difficult for anyone who failed to believe in the Lord Jesus Christ as their sole savior, but, nevertheless, he felt such considerations should be dealt with when the time was right, without the need for anticipated anxiety. The youth's origins were commendable on his father's side, and his mother was too a well-respected woman. Like any other young man, Orestes aimed to become a respectful Roman citizen, deeply empathizing with the prowess of his mistress, with whom he kept both a genuine and ongoing friendship. Even though he realized the way Hypatia's remarkable beauty played a strongly contributing factor when other men sought to privilege of studying under her, he was intelligent enough to understand he and most of his classmates were far more attracted to her sapience, rather than the majestic physicality the gods had bestowed upon her. Come to think of it, who could be sure Jupiter hadn't sent Minerva down from Olympus to put men's carnal pursuit to the test? Would they ever dare violate the goddess' sanctity of celibacy, polluting the harmony and purity of her knowledge with a mundane misdemeanor? These were questions Orestes often thought about when observing Hypatia as she spoke to the class, and he was quite confident as far as the veracity of such hypotheses was concerned.

'Wouldn't you agree, Orestes?', Hypatia asked, addressing her disciple in search of his corroboration, though she noticed he clearly had something else on his mind and had not paid any attention to the lecture at all, therefore interrupting her class with the aid of peer pressure, whose eyes turned to the young man two by two.

Having brought his awareness back to himself, Orestes looked around, meeting his colleagues' gaze as he tried to decipher what the subject being discussed was, but no such luck was gifted to him, and that was the moment he averted his sight to meet Hypatia's, who was patiently waiting for an answer with a soft smile on her face, trying to figure out whether the shrewd pupil would find a way out of the cognitive mess he had just gotten himself into.

'Yes, Lady… by all means, I thoroughly agree with every word', Orestes said, able to somewhat juggle an eloquent statement with which to escape his own snare.

'So, Euclid's first axiom does apply to all of us, regardless of the nature of our faith', Hypatia continued, making sure the disciple shared the same opinion.

'Well… no, now that you have phrased like so, not necessarily. I beg your pardon, Lady. For a moment, my consciousness flew away and I simply lost track of what we were discussing – my apologies –, but no, I wouldn't say it does – not at face-value, at least. "Things which are equal to the same thing are also equal to one another", indeed, depending on who created them. That is precisely what divides us from them', he said, pointing to the Christian side of the hall as he spoke in a tone of disdain. While none of them made use of their rhetoric, their expression was far from being amicable.

'Please, Orestes, I have already asked each and every one of you to refrain from insulting when addressing each other. This is not the place for the brawling sort of argument, whether physical or plainly intellectual. Besides, you are contradicting yourself; if you agree we are equal to one another, how can you claim the existence of barriers between us?', Hypatia asked, simultaneously exasperating discomfort regarding the ensuing religious debate.

'It is quite simple, Lady. According to Plotinus, as you said yourself, we, as human beings, were created in the image of the One, the Good. Although this ulterior entity cannot be described (regardless of how the Muses may inflate the poet) or represented for our perceiving eyes to behold, it is an unquestionable fact we are the result of the demiurge, the energy passed onto to our bodies, afterward inhabited by our respective soul, awaiting to board a vessel of flesh and bone idealistically governed by the mind, pure intellect, that which provides such matter with purpose; were it to be otherwise, I believe there wouldn't be any point at all in being sent from the One to the phenomenal world and live a promising, fulfilling mortal life.

We might as well just inertly sit back and wait to perish, thus reincarnating yet another body as a second chance, though Porphyry believes the cleansing of our soul could take a great deal of time before dwelling once more in the lower portions of the world, unless it chooses to connect itself with the world-soul, refusing to accept any dead-ends whatsoever regarding the presence of the nous in the phenomenal world', he explained, bearing a smirk on his face showing just how proud he was of his discoursing abilities, patted in the back by his Pagan colleagues.

Because Hypatia was fair and wanted everyone to participate and have their say, she turned to the Christians and asked them what their thoughts were, without choosing a particular disciple:

'What say you? Does Orestes's explanation make sense to you, and, if so, how do you relate?'.

One of the students held his hand requesting permission to speak and, once granted via a quick nod from Hypatia, he shared his attention span between the opposite group and the lecturer herself, occasionally averting his sight in both directions to broaden his audience:

'It does, Lady. However, our origins are much clearer to us, leaving no room for doubt. First and foremost, «the One» our fellow Orestes spoke of is the Father, the Creator, who – and please excuse my redundancy – created heaven and the earth when the latter was still shapeless and untamable. We could be portrayed by our esteemed Pagan colleagues as sufficiently ignorant to state there is absolutely no evidence the Earth is an orb and insist on flattened claims, but even we Christians are aware that is not the case, as demonstrated by Ptolemy only a couple of centuries ago, evidently supporting the geocentric premise God transmitted unto Moses, for the cosmos was inexistent until the moment the Father's will was done and the surface we walk upon was erected from underneath the waters. Before doing so, however, there had to be light, which the Creator cast by naming it so, clearing away the prevalence of darkness and, therefore, bringing order to a generation yet to be completed and cleansed of chaos. Furthermore...', the Christian student said, presuming he was still in turn, though neither him nor Hypatia expected Orestes to interrupt the ongoing train of thought:

'With all due respect, Lady, I would like to ask my fellow classmate how his explanation is any different from what I said just a while ago, not as far as the form is concerned, but regarding the content, because it seems clear to me, and I believe I speak for the entirety of my side of the hall, we turn out to agree with the origins of the world as it is today, except the entities we credit for accomplishing such an achievement are different in number and name! Our Christian counterparts believe in an unnamed god of their own who created the Universe and all other sorts of emanations, just as we can counter-argue that same power was divided by primordial gods who, in turn, produced titans who, in their turn, produced an undefeatable Pantheon, as neither the Titanomachy nor the Gigantomachy resulted in their casualty. Honestly, and I cannot stress it enough, what is the point of all this battering between us, if our disagreement lies solely in a question of toponomy and anthroponomy (granted we were all made in the image of our respective creators and, still, we happen to be exactly alike)? It is but teleological, which is what drove Plato and Aristotle apart in the first place'.

Both Orestes and the Christian disciple sought feedback from their peers, ultimately focusing on Hypatia's gaze as if the Lady had just been proclaimed some kind of a referee.

'Haven't you just contradicted yourself there, then, Orestes?', the Lady asked the young man; having adopted a confused expression, the Pagan student stuttered for a moment, yet again mumbling his way out:

'I... but Lady, I... my apologies, but I am... I am at a complete loss for words... right now', he said, clearing his throat in the end, only to enthusiastically fuel Hypatia's philosophical commitment to harmonize an impending conflict:

'Let us walk a few steps back and remember

Euclid, "things which are equal to the same thing are also equal to one another". You, Orestes, told us all you didn't exactly see it that way regarding each other's faith, but please tell me – just how far away from the truth are either of you? You aren't, and that is the point! "Things which coincide with one another are equal to one another", Euclid's fourth axiom. Isn't that also what we have been talking about for the past hour? You see, no matter whichever your faith is, what you believe in or how you try to refute each other's assertions, the conclusion is always the same when it comes to the factors connecting both body and mind and where they hail from. If you care to take a look at an even more convincing piece of evidence proving just that, then remember Iamblichus, who organized all celestial beings into a hierarchy, including both angels and demons, present in Christianity. Evil didn't start out as an independent force in neither faith; there was simply a loss of enlightenment regarding the conjurers of chaos, Lucifer included, even though the name itself translates to bearer of light. Our domains are the same... there is a firmament illuminated by the stars, a ground to walk upon, and a sea filled with the most assorted creatures, exactly like the previous two. However, it is up to us all, having been offered the gift of nous, to help maintain order in the cosmos as the regents of our gods, for, without us, made to their image precisely, they would lose their purpose, their teleology, and without purpose, what is it we are doing here? Why were we placed in the world, and why do we bother rationalizing it? Should different explanations for the same cause become a reason to kill each other and seek prevalence? That is what makes life worth living, the ability to discuss ideas and yield every now and then to new possibilities. There isn't just one course Philosophy must follow; the truth can present itself in countless, different ways, and yet… why must one path turn out to be deceiving while the other is branded failproof? Where is reason in that? Why do we educate ourselves in various subjects, if we are not open to alternatives as valid as the arguments we first learned? Nothing can ever be taken for granted, gentlemen – if you choose to accommodate yourselves and give up on the link you share with the intelligible sphere Humankind was included in by God, whether we call him Serapis or the Father, deliberately blinded by a canon others chose in your stead, those who refuse to converse, then all of this will have been for nothing, and by all I mean the life of each of you, your very identity, your personality, your chance to make your sapience stand out and generations yet to come proud of how hard we worked, men and women alike, to improve their livelihood with the best blade ever forged, if you will – knowledge; it will instantly pierce and puncture the weakest spot of the human body, and that is the inability to show respect for the individual mind'.

From the very moment she began her speech, remarkably delivered by a twenty-one-year-old who seemed to possess extraordinary experience regarding the ways of life, often associated to wise old men, of which her father was an example, Hypatia brought her class together as if all those young men were family, marveled in unison at her eloquence and excitement when describing how powerful learning and thinking for oneself could be, thus posing a threat to those who played mind tricks on easily impressionable brains, ready to be washed with darkness and the consequent fear of divine punishment for choosing a way people of influence deemed as the only possible path to follow, for, according to them, it was the wisest of all, permanently leading to the one truth; any other «truth» would certainly have been the work of the devil. Luckily for these disciples, both Alexandrian and foreign, there was someone right in front of them to cast eminent light at the obscurity tyranny kept in its company.

As the Sun rose higher in the sky, indicating how close the day was to the end of its first half, penetrating the windows of the hall and metaphorically (to the likes of an epiphany) enlightening the disciples from head to toe, confirming some sort of celestial aura around them that protected every single one against the dogmatic shade, the Lady declared:

'Well, I believe that's enough fodder to feast on for today, so... I'll see you all tomorrow. Class dismissed'.

'Lady...! Forgive me, I... I'd like to say something before we leave, if both you and my colleagues will allow it', one of the Pagan students said, rapidly sweeping his eyes over the forum seating, just so he could focus on Hypatia quickly enough.

Judging from the curiosity that had just risen from the classmates, who ogled their counterpart in the most assorted expressions of surprise, the Lady only saw fit to give the young man permission to speak:

'Of course, Apollodorus. I'm sure we'd all be thrilled to listen to what you have to say. Would you like to join me and address the class from the stage?', Hypatia asked, both gently and genuinely smiling at the student.

Apollodorus felt like backing down from an enterprise he only realized was much too dangerous to handle after he had opened his mouth, especially with a surrounding audience picking up on every word, but it was exactly the pressure of his peers, together with Hypatia's transparently quizzical body language, that gave him no choice but to engage and finish what he had started, thusly stepping down from the tiered seating, as his colleagues made room for his passage.

The moment he climbed the single-stepped stage, Apollodorus turned around to face the Lady and his fellow apprentices, assuming a three-quarter position. Staring at the floor for a brief moment, the young man closed his eyes, took a deep breath, lifted his chin from his chest, reopened his gaze, meeting Hypatia's, and said:

'Thank you, Lady. I would like to…', he mumbled, clearing his throat for a boost to his self-confidence, 'I'd like to tell you, as my illustrious colleagues bear witness of this statement, that I find your purpose in the world we share to be magnanimous, harmonizing of all the obscure enough differences between us that could set us apart, but the truth is, Lady and gentlemen, within these walls there is nothing dividing us, no sort of barrier whatsoever, either intelligible, moral, esthetic, or simply physical, material, for Hypatia, daughter of Theon of Alexandria, founder and director of the very Neoplatonic School and Musaeum in which we stand, was sent down to earth to unite and spread peace among us, brothers, perhaps not in blood, but nevertheless equal. Behold, brethren, Isis in all her splendor, beauty, grace, and intelligence. I find you, Lady, worthy of being worshipped like the goddess inhabiting your flesh.

Only a divine being like yourself could show us the true light of wisdom through the Eye of Horus. Ever your servant…', Apollodorus concluded, simultaneously approaching and kneeling at Hypatia's feet, also holding her hand.

Despite her lively character and undeniable wisdom, as the student had mentioned, the Lady's young age made her falter for a moment, for handling compliments from the opposite gender was something she was used to ever since she had become aware of herself. Being wooed, however, inevitably made her feel some discomfort, not to mention whenever a crowd was watching. Looking to regain her composure, Hypatia met the static gazes of her incredulous students, after which she stared at her lap, reddened by embarrassment, saying:

'Thank you, Apollodorus. Yours were kind words, I appreciate it. I'll see you all tomorrow, enjoy the rest of your day'.

Hypatia remained in her seat as, one by one, the students bade the Lady their wishes, echoing her own. Once outside, they all reacted to Apollodorus's daring behavior, most of which resounded back into the hall, where the daughter of Theon remained pensive, intertwining her fingers against her lips as she leaned forward and supported her elbows on her legs; her eyes seemed to lose their natural brightness for a moment while staring at the void. Comments ranged from complimenting nods and laughter to reprimanding on the grounds of disrespect.

For what was likely the very first time in her short life, the Lady felt her intellect failing to respond to any stimuli at all, catatonically dwelling in an apparent state of peace of mind, though it was her, as opposed to her disciples, who had just been served an immeasurable amount of food for thought.

Chapter VII
An Ecstatic Parable

"Thou shalt not kill" and, yet, blood now taints his hands, as red and boiling as hellfire, contrasting with the darkness of the robes, so vividly stained. All he can do now is repent; only true sorrow will bring him forgiveness, but how can he be absolutely sure the Lord will break his fall by sending the angels his way? None of it is certain anymore. The rules are clear – "thou shalt not tempt the Lord thy God", but if the Father was the one to instruct his messenger, why is the latter to pay for his sins? Light may not be attained at all, for, with murder, and a double, at that, salvation is forever lost. Our Lord does not contradict himself; it is Man's distortion of the Scripture, mistaking his own will for the Father's, that leads to eternal damnation, as opposed to a sordidly poetic oxymoron.

His current whereabouts are uncertain; describing a full turn on his axis unveils the sort of landscape nothing can help differentiate – except for the Sun up high, which becomes more unbearable at each step of the way of this erroneous wandering through the burning sands of the desert. Dunes are the one chance to cool off, though such a relief cannot be made available at every hour. Also, the key to staying alive in the arid climate lies inside of a waterskin, which he had not reminded himself to carry, regardless of having washed his head in it after sentencing himself to become a possession of Satan.

Indeed, Ammonius had gotten it all wrong, or so he began to think, if thinking he was still capable of. Walking under the abrasive star of days cannot be eternally beneficial if shelter is beyond his reach; the dehydration process the monk was undergoing started making him paranoid, delusional, as his imagination kept tricking him into believing he was always finding that which he lacked the most, should God still have a plan for him – food and drink, and if the Holy Trinity was in fact to reward him for his actions, then the present situation was to become his trial. He would need all the faith he could find in the depths of his torn, corrupted heart to endure the loss of direction his earthly vessel required to prevent throwing himself into the fires of the underworld, where the common criminals lingered, along with the infidels; their purge had only just begun, and Ammonius had already contributed to the cleansing by preventing the Abbot and the Great Schema from tarnishing Christendom any further. It is but God's decision who to imprison in a cloister, not a man's – unless, of course, God chooses to act through that man, and that is what made him different from those he had lived caged with. He had been chosen, he had a job to do, a holy war to fight, for blood that is spilled in the name of the Lord will have been well spent.

As both thirst and hunger grew stronger, so did the Stavrophore's self-awareness shrink weaker. He could have been lost for hours, having walked no more than a couple of stadia, regardless of the monastery having disappeared from his visual range, just as much as he could have been dragging his sandaled feet for a couple of days, now. His cognitive abilities were still enough to make out it could not have been much more than that, or he would have certainly found the winged skeleton by now, whose mission would have been carrying him far away from that place – depending, of course, on what one's notion of afterlife is; perpetually bound to wander in the desert without resting, incapable of finding ways to satisfy his entrails, could have perfectly been the Lord's doing… it is a well-known fact he works in mysterious ways. In short, such was Ammonius's belief and faith in what the Father did that his will to survive somehow kept him awake. God would not have given him this grand privilege, were his devotion to be put into question.

Eventually, and though «mens sana in corpore sano» is the phrase of a Roman Pagan, the monk's body could not sanely proceed on an undernourished mind, that much was certain. As the Sun slowly twirled in the light-blue dome, closing in on its zenith, Ammonius tripped while raising his foot to step forward, falling face down on the warm sand, whose temperature was gradually rising. He inertly lay there for a while, just until his survival instinct forced him to turn his rugged visage away from the grains he was unconsciously inhaling, blocking his nasal airway. Frightfully for him, some of it had made its way down his throat, for which reason he strongly coughed and blew his nostrils separately, making sure no residue was left. An abrupt increase of his anxiety nearly got the best of him, regardless of his desperate attempt to live, which makes a rather confusing contradiction – one will do anything at all in order to stay alive, even when one's death is in plain sight; the result is either left to chance or, perhaps, to what has been moving this man ever since he was first mentioned.

Once he cleared his throat of the impending menace, the monk rolled over himself onto a dune and only landed at the very bottom of the steep descent, lying on his back as portions of sand cascaded all over his body, rendering him almost completely covered in it. Had it not been for the fact his diaphragm was still moving, he could have been deemed an unfortunate case of forgetfulness by either a scavenger, or perhaps a trade caravan, not only as far as his lack of water is concerned, but also a possible divine carelessness for this poor devil, the image of the fallen angel himself.

A great deal of effort was required of Ammonius to even open his eyes the slightest he could; his lids were much too heavy, and the clarity of day made everything all the more difficult. With his mouth just half-open, one could tell his lips were chapped in multiple sections, completely dried out. Incapable of enduring the present conditions, regardless of not letting go of his inner strength, the monk shut his eyes and passed out.

Yet again, time was not something easily measured; there were no indicators around that made any sense, but this was not about location, anymore – right now, the question could perhaps be phrased regarding all the noise heard in the distance, even though the ruckus was taking place right there, under some kind of screechy, unstable wooden surface, instead of an arid one, almost as rough as rock, which could easily inflict a flesh wound and pry the bloodstream open to a festering infection. In the end, it was likely that could have been the case, but Ammonius quite certainly did not find himself capable of confirming he had indeed withstood an injury. Together with the sound of the contraption, the monk could also hear voices in the distance; it was unclear what the people they pertained to were uttering, for which reason they could have been speaking a foreign language. Whatever it was, Ammonius's brain activity was still much too depleted to figure it out. His eyes sensitive to sunlight, the shadow that kept leaning over worked as an assistant to the struggle he was in, seeking to open his lids as much as he could, but he still could not make out any features at all on the misshapen visage staring at him. For a moment, the face came closer and whispered, softly:

'Steady, now. We're nearly there'.

The reassurance of both shape and content had been enough to relax the feverishly trembling young man, who had been once more cast astray from the main path; whether it was all real, a trick played on him by his imagination, or both somehow combined, he most definitely knew not.

After another lapse in the spacetime continuum, the monk effortlessly opened his eyes; it was as if he had just woken from the deepest slumber, literally jumping back into reality. As much as he tried, he could not find a suitable cause for how grainy his eyesight was... for some reason, it looked like it kept raining sand; rubbing his eyes did not make any difference at all. It was then Ammonius focused on his whereabouts – he was still in the desert. Now, despite the fact one of the synonyms for «desert» is «uninhabited», it appeared it was not so – at least, not in this case.

Craving both cool water and a loaf of bread since he could last remember, the former Stavrophore (as he obviously had no intention of going back to a monastery where blood had been spilt by his own hands, even though his devotion remained untouched) found himself somewhere near what looked like a garden of sorts, as he spun on his axis. He had heard stories about gardens flourishing at unspecified sites in the arid plains before, but he never thought he would ever see one in his lifetime. In fact, they were not even known as gardens, but rather «oases», as first described by the Greeks of an earlier antiquity. It could have also been a mirage, because of the distance the monk still had to travel, but the sight was much too clear to deem it a product of his imagination, even though the grains in his eyes had begun to deeply annoy him; then again, he had already spent so much time dawdling in the desert sand that perhaps it was something that could come to a stop if he washed the sordidness of his face and hands after first quenching his thirst.

Without another moment to waste, Ammonius began running toward the heavenly sight, having suddenly gained enough strength in his legs to surpass the friction the sand inflicted unto his feet and ankles at each step of the way. As he approached, the outlines of the palm trees providing shade for other flora became clearer and more static, without having their trunks waving about from the heat generating said optical illusion. Also, as far as audio was concerned, the soothing sound of running freshwater was deliciously exquisite to hear, which makes this synesthesia even more agreeable, not only to our eyes, but to Ammonius' ears.

The sand that held him captive at each of his attempts to move forward was no more; now he was able to experience what it was like to walk on soft, fresh grass again, whose last time he could not at all recall, as the terrain surrounding the monastery was a sheer mixture of sand and dirt – cultures could still be grown, of course, but the greenery made the environment a lot livelier, esthetically pleasing to both body and soul. Neither the Abbot nor the Great Schema had ever shown concern about that kind of detail... just because all those men had given up on their worldly life did not mean they could not grow a well-maintained garden and enjoy the peace of it. Why did all the riches have to be channeled to the building alone? Was the vow of poverty not relevant to the men in power? And there he was, Ammonius, who feared he had gone too far, twisting the will of the Lord from his own point of view. He did not mean to compare himself to Jesus Christ, obviously, but when the Son found out trade was being conducted at the Temple of the Father, his sense of humanity grew strong and a most ferocious wrath invaded his sacred heart, leading him to destroy with his own hands the majority of merchants' booths present at the site.

Delivering his mind into the palms of a well-deserved rest, the monk knelt by the shore of the streaming aquifer, pulled the hood of his cloak back and dove his head in the water as he swallowed a great deal of it, simultaneously cleansing himself once more (like he had done before leaving the monastery) while dampening back his lips, tongue, and throat.

His skin hardened by the Sun, he thought perhaps he should take a full bath, rather than just let the water slide down his sweat-soaked body, ending up absorbed by his sweat-soaked robes. Soon after pondering upon this newest idea, Ammonius emerged his head from the stream and recovered his breath. The intake of air was not painful, anymore; it did not burn like before. Protected by the shade of the palm tree canopy, taking a deep breath had never been more satisfying.

Looking around in search of anyone who could take a chance at disturbing his peace of mind, the monk unfastened his robes and took a dive, wearing nothing but his skin. The riverbed was shallow, though deep enough to cover the young man's lower half of his body while standing. Transparency could have constituted a problem, but, fortunately, he was all alone, which meant there was no modesty to be observed.

The darkness spread all across the monk's flesh and soul was being successfully washed away, flowing along with the stream. It somehow must have been an indigent of the Nile, one he had never heard of. Then again, the river in question was approximately thirty-six thousand stadia in length, so, in the end, his state of surprise was not surprising at all. What was legitimately curious, however, was the fact that water does not simply spring from an endless source as if it had just been placed there brand-new; on the contrary, it is constantly recycled, which is why a continuous pollution process of streams sooner or later begins to show, despite their unstoppable flowing – there is a limit to how much waste natural springs can take. In this particular case, said limit was far, far away from being reached, as no one seemed to frequent the harmonious landscape; still, what the parable here comprises is the return of both physical and spiritual dark matter within the cycle – by cleansing his inequities in the stream, Ammonius would only become repeatedly contaminated, especially the longer he bode his time in that small piece of earthly paradise.

Without the slightest awareness, resting assured by now no one would surprise him, the monk was being observed after all, only he could not hear much, as he was down on both his knees, facing the sky with his eyes shut and his eardrums submerged; in short, his senses were focused solely on the stream. There is, of course, some sort of an inexplicable impression one is being watched because of the amount of energy redirected from another's eyes to one's occipital region, which happened to alert Ammonius, rapidly pulling his head and upper torso out of the water, subsequently looking around in the angle of a full circumference in both directions. His heart began to accelerate almost to the crazed beat of a tympanum. He was a wanted man, now; others knew what he had done. It could have been a matter of time before he was caught, though his location was unknown, even to himself. However, and strategically waiting for someone to move or make a sound, no such event took place, meaning he felt calm enough to go back to his state of relaxation. Again, he knelt on the river floor and, just before immersing the posterior half of his head one more time with his eyes closed, his eardrums caught the vague sound of a hiss, forcing him to try to stand on his left leg while supporting the weight of his full body with the right, but the monk eventually lost his balance and submerged completely, involuntarily channeling water into his windpipe and lungs, the same water he had only just so desperately craved. Under the agonizing impression he was about to drown, the momentum generated by his sudden movements confused his sense of direction, temporarily unable to reassume the upright position that would lead him to salvation. Turning on his belly, however, proved crucial to his survival, as he could now lift his head and move his arms in circles from back to front in order to gain back the grip of his feet on the wet sand and stand once more, emerging yet again with extraordinary relief. His following impulse was to, in-between sharp intakes of breath, immediately inquire across the airwaves:

'Who's there?! Show yourself! I know there's someone here, I've heard you only just now!'.

Even though Ammonius said he knew there was in fact somebody in hiding, what he did know was he thought there probably was a person observing him while secluded, but, naturally, stating something with apparent certainty is nothing but a strategy to make sure others are convinced, together with the reality that it is too late to go on with the charade any further, therefore forcing them to cease and desist.

The monk looked everywhere he could from where he stood, still with a grainy vision deceiving his eyes – apparently, washing himself in the stream had not worked as expected, for the distortion was still there; not only that, he was severely struggling to regurgitate the amount of water that had taken a wrong turn down his throat.

The idea the slight hiss he had heard could have just been the wind softly blowing on the oasis's vegetation ended up relaxing his heavy breathing, along with his attention span. He took it to himself to put his hands together in the shape of a conch while still coughing a few drops to the side, making sure he had completely cleared his airway, and collected as much water as he could to rub his face with, looking to discard those annoying grains that would just not leave him alone. Rubbing as hard as he could, the monk then let go and held his hands in front of his face while blinking repeatedly, though to no effect whatsoever. Trying not to move his stomach and, thusly, generate ripples on the surface of the spring, Ammonius looked closely at his reflection, so as to figure out whether the sand in his sight was real. Eventually, he realized such an endeavor was pathetically useless – there was no possible way he could make out whether said maleficence was actually there; after all, he required his eyes to confirm both the accuracy and precision of his own reflection... otherwise, he would be as good as blind, much to the likes of the thief crucified next to Jesus, the one on his righthand side, speaking of which... it must not be forgotten that renouncing to his savior was only a way of inviting Satan to let the raven feast on the man's eyes. It is just something to think about.

Irate he could not get rid of his twisted vision, the monk, in a state of nature, struck his reflection in a fit of rage, despite hatred not being condoned by the Holy Trinity. Eventually frustrated, Ammonius supported his weight on his youthful arms and jumped out of the stream, staying down on one knee while washing away the remaining dirt on his robes, scrubbing folds against each other as hard as possible without, nevertheless, ripping the stitches apart; that was his only apparel and a man of God could not obviously wander about, pretentiously behaving like Adam in the Garden of Eden – the godly gift of innocence was something the first man to walk the earth had turned down the moment he listened to his female counterpart and ate a portion of the apple from the Tree of Knowledge, therefore desecrating the work of the Father and earning himself and Eve the expulsion from Paradise, where they were both protected by Providence. That could have been the only reason why women had no business becoming empowered within the several ramifications of the Church of

Christ – a woman, precisely, was at fault for leading a man right into the path of sin, even though the Father had specifically instructed both humans to leave the apple tree untouched; such was the power of women, now that the monk had begun thinking about it… the feminine wiles, the witchcraft, the innate aptitude to become enchantresses… that was how they forced men to worship them, making them passionately kiss their knees and firmly hold their shins to a point of no return from humiliation. It was all the work of the devil, who recruited women to join him and eventually break men's self-confidence, to say the least; worse than that was faith.

'Scum of the world!', Ammonius exclaimed out loud, embroiled in his washing task.

Distracted in the midst of his wrathful, misogynistic thoughts, the monk ended up tearing a slight hole in his apparel – had it not been wet, he could have easily set it on fire with all the friction. Luckily, the fabric was somewhat thick, which prevented said outcome. Besides, the orifice was barely noticeable. Sufficiently satisfied with the washing procedure, Ammonius considered hanging the robes nearby, as he was willing to wait for them to dry off. That was the moment he paid a wee bit more of attention to the flora encircling him, made of cereals just above ground and fruit trees whose height he was barely short of. There were figs, peaches, apricots, olives, an endless nat-ural market the monk could dispose of as he very well pleased; it was a sight literally created for sore eyes like his. All he had to do was walk across the field (which was rather small in length, demanding no more than just a few steps) and grab hold of the fruit of his choice. The canopy of the palm trees provided excellent cover for all these riches to grow and develop; everything was so carefully structured and planned that only God could have been the one behind such haven.

As he walked between grasses of wheat and barley, the cereals softly swept atop his legs' bare skin, swiftly traveling from the shins to the calves, left behind in a smooth dance provoked by the draft Ammonius' movements generated. It was, he would dare say, an extraordinary sensation, no doubt, but stepping through a field whose ground bore no distinctive marks could reveal itself to be treacherous to the untrained eye – "do not defile yourselves by any crawling creature; do not be-come unclean or defiled by them", the Scriptures say… but, should the creature be there, merged with, camouflaged by the surrounding environ-ment, how could one help oneself? How could one keep clear? Whichever the solution to said prob-lem, Ammonius most certainly did not possess it, as he felt his flesh being pierced by two fangs, just above his right heel. The attack had been so sudden that only moments later did his brain react to the acuteness of the pain, though not that of the bite, but rather that of the venom quickly tangling itself to the monk's blood; his screaming was spread by gusts of wind to the four corners of the world, including the latter portion – a wheezing of relief, also the sign of a decline in the power of his voice.

In a state of submission, the young man fell on his stomach and, because of the unexpected friction, the grasses of cereals unavoidably left scratches in several areas of his body; the more his subdermal tissue got exposed, the faster his blood had to travel to compensate the losses, no matter how small, running against time to induce coagulation and protect the body from infection. However, and regardless of how God had created Man to his own image, the Creator was the only one who could live forever; besides, the quote taken from Leviticus was unmistakable, even though Ammonius had not interacted with the slithering creature of his own accord.

Looking up in agony, his chin sliding on the ground with a bit of resistance, the monk could finally see a fig tree up-close; it was perhaps ten pedes away. It could have been his imagination, but the figs somehow seemed to be palpitating like a heart would. The reality of the scenario was getting more unclear by the minute; after all, having had its access clear to the bloodstream, the venom was quickly working toward coagulation, though of the blood itself, hardening the body's natural self-healing process. The monk's brain was already running out of oxygen, along with all other organs; there was not much survival time left.

With a vision now both grainy and blurry, making an effort to keep his eyes at least half-open, Ammonius could hear the same hissing sound he had heard before, while bathing in the stream. He was able to realize it was closer and all the more frequent. Whatever it was producing such noise, it slithered past his visage no more than a digitus away. At said distance, the monk unveiled the culprit – it was a snake, a horned desert viper, side-winding halfway between him and the fig tree, where it came to a stop, turning around to face the young man. His painful expression, while still there, was mixed with confusion, as if the beast knew exactly what it was doing. Its head was prominent in size, bearing a horn on top of each eye, which made a terrifying impression. In regard to its color, it bore a mixture of yellowish and brownish tones, making it easy for it to take advantage of camouflage on both sand and dirt, respectively. The tail was black-tipped, with a possible length of about twenty-four unciae all the way to the head. Amid his confusion, Ammonius was somehow beginning to understand that a creature bearing this combination of features simply did not pertain to this world, but rather the devil's lair. This was Genesis all over again, the Garden of Eden, home to Adam and Eve, the parents of Humankind, whose only living descendants had come to Noah's sons, Shem, Ham, and Japheth, survivors of the Great Flood. From there, one thousand six hundred and fifty-six years later, no more would God "curse the ground for Man's sake; for the imagination of Man's heart is evil from his youth; neither [would He] again smite any more every living thing, as [He had] done".

Temptation had led to wickedness, which, in turn, had led to the world's cleansing, had it not been for Eve's disobedience; there was only one rule to abide by, but the devil was far more persuasive than anyone could have ever imagined – perhaps even God himself.

It was then the snake erected itself to about a third of its body length, gently swaying as its eyes pierced Ammonius'. Supporting the weight of his head on his chin against the dirt, the monk stared at the viper, waiting for it to bite him yet again and perhaps finish the killing quicker. Instead, however, the hissing came to a stop and the muzzle adapted itself sufficiently in order to be able to speak like a human, uttering these words:

'You're dying'.

Ammonius was, to say the least, puzzled by what he had just witnessed, a talking snake, clearly addressing him in the nude. Damned him if he had not gone back to the beginning of time – the miracle of Creation, God's own pride and joy, but not in a sinful way, of course; claiming God was a sinner was like begging to be smitten.

'«Vade retro me, Satana! For you are setting your mind not on divine things but on human things»', Ammonius yelled as loud as his lungs permitted him, quoting Our Lord from the Gospel of Mark.

'You're much too far into the narrative, young man… are you comparing yourself to the Son of God? Would you be so desperately pretentious as to pretend you're Jesus? What of the olive trees nearby? Why don't you run along and agonize beside them, just moments before being seized by the Pharisees, tipped off by one of your own disciples? I swear, Judas is so sordidly treacherous he'll even kiss you while craving your forgiveness, and all for no more than thirty pieces of silver… pettily pathetic, in my opinion. But no, you're not Jesus of Nazareth, let alone the first man to walk the earth, though your present situation is quite similar to that of Adam, except he had a choice – just as much as Eve, to be honest; she could've simply ignored me and not taken a bite of that apple, but no, women never do what they're told. Some clergymen even think they're a part of a hypothetical army of mine, which, I must say, is not a terrible idea at all', the horned desert viper discoursed in a hissing manner, leaning its head to the side while seemingly looking into the void, almost as if it were actually considering taking that plan toward fruition.

Trying as hard as he could, Ammonius sought to support the weight of his upper torso on his forearms and elbows, despite his progressive weakness, enouncing:

'Please… if you're here to purge me from the world on account of my sins, then… then take me away with you to the fires… the fires of hell, where I belong', the monk whispered, losing his strength and falling on his face, coughing out the dirt that ended up invading his half-open mouth, as he ran out of air.

In a rather snarky response, the snake said unto him:

'Oh!, no… no, no, no, no, no…! You're not going anywhere! Well, at least not right now…! Your time on earth has yet to run out. You are, of course, right when you say hell is where you belong, you might as well get used to that, but it can wait. Let me just be straightforward with you and have you know the white-bearded man isn't interested in having you as a permanent guest. You can't be that rudimentary-minded as far as the reasons why are concerned, I mean… likening yourself to Christ, thinking murder was your only way of making the world a better place, spreading the good word by means of force… who do you think you are, the Angel of Death? I used to be an angel myself and, trust me, it's really not as fantastic as men make it out to be. There's nothing you can do without God's avail…! Everything has got to be the way he wants it to be, or you're pretty much done, you're over. Look at me now. I'm a rebel, I put an army together to overtake the heavens and ended up stuck below ground, where slum thrives by the thousands. Of course, I can come up here any time I want… I'm here now, aren't I? And do you know why I can decide when to resurface? Because of free will, which is something God sought to deprive men from, deliberately inflicting blindness upon Adam. If you ask me, it was all a test, you know? It's not just my opinion, it's the truth! Grabbing a rib of his and turning it into a woman just to keep him company, please… God wanted them out of Eden. He wanted me there to tempt them to lose their innocence. How else could his most fantastic creation be fruitful and multiply, just like he asked Noah's family to do? If it hadn't been for Cain, though, it all could've worked out just fine, but… ah!, well… as you would say, the Lord works in mysterious ways – an interesting excuse to justify an unplanned outcome and consequent failure. Why sow a Tree of Knowledge in the first place? He could've at least put up an ante; I just know I would've won that wager… but where was I? Ah!, yes, about you – your only salvation from the venom I injected you with is to grab one of these figs and take a bite out of it. They're garnished with the antidote that'll stop your pain toward complete paralysis. I bet you'd be swelling with honor, knowing you're so close to dying the same way as Socrates, poisoned by his own fellow countrymen, wouldn't you? If only you were a Pagan like them, undeserving of mercy and light… that is only for Christians to experience, isn't it? Too bad you chose a dead-end, boy… too bad. Now, drag yourself up to the tree behind me, hold on to its trunk and pick a fig, or you'll soon be gasping for air, even though neither God, nor I will take your barren soul. Is your faith as strong as you think that you hope will come to your aid, or do you deserve this punishment so badly that your suffering knows no bounds? Here's a hint: I would count on neither', the demonic viper said, concluding its ultimatum to Ammonius, whose only remedy was to follow the instructions.

His vision grainier and blurrier, his muscle strength rapidly weakening to a point in which he could not make use of his legs anymore, the naked monk dragged himself toward the snake, which, in turn, moved to the base of the fig tree, waiting for the young man to exhaust all the efforts he had left while closing in on the food source, while leaving a trail of elbows and forearms behind, along with the silhouette of a pair of fully extended legs and feet, though completely inert.

Every single intake of breath had turned into a struggle for Ammonius; had he chosen to stay the way he was now, his soul would only be trapped in a slowly decaying body, always a digitus away from a death that would never come, thus abandoning himself to a half-life. As he looked away from his objective, to the right, the monk was able to make out a few olive trees; regardless of the snake's previous jesting, he really was in a state of agony, now understanding what Jesus must had been through at Gethsemane, just before surrendering to the Jewish guards under the command of the high priest.

A few moments later, after battling his way against the ground's friction and resistance, Ammonius was able to reach the fig tree's trunk with a trembling hand; that was when the viper climbed up to the branches and waited for the monk to accomplish his goal, adding:

'Come, now, dear boy! You're nearly there! It'll all be over soon, just you trust me', it said, disgustingly smirking while simultaneously winking as a form of encouragement.

Pulling the weight of a fully-grown man's body was no easy feat, especially when the lower part was rendered useless, but Ammonius simply had to try and take hold of one of the ripe figs hanging from numerous branches. In the hope he might grab one of the lower branches as an anchor point while climbing further up, the monk engulfed the closest arm of the tree with both hands and inevitably fell, struck on the head by said branch once he hit the ground. Still, the whole stunt, while unequivocally dangerous, produced a positive outcome, for, as the piece of wood broke from the deadweight it was not strong enough to hold, it also flipped into a diagonal position in mid-air, knocking down one of the figs located in the far end of one of the upper branches. Toying with the dying young man, the snake congratulated him for fulfilling the most difficult part of the job; all he had to do now was carve his teeth into the fruit's texture, chew and swallow. God only knew what would happen next, or rather... Satan did.

Having fallen on his back, Ammonius now had to roll over and reach the bruised fig that lay a couple of unciae to his right. Fully extending his arm was no good, considering he needed to move just like the snake did to pull himself toward the piece of fruit; without the use of his legs, however, it was much harder to do so, which is why he clenched his right elbow against the ground as hard as he could and flipped his entire body within range of the fig.

The decline in his breathing ability was now

far severer than ever. His hand uncontrollably trembling, he grabbed the fruit and blurrily looked at it for a while in threes, maybe fours; his first impression had been right all along – it did palpitate to the likes of a heart.

Feeling he was close to passing out, the monk finally did it; he severed about a third of the fig, chewing it with massive difficulty. When the moment to swallow arrived at last, Ammonius choked; part of the bite he had taken got stuck in his throat, mandatorily having him regurgitate.

'No worries, boy. You've had enough to save yourself... for now. Until next time and... are you all right?', the snake said and asked in the distance, as the young man's body twirled and swirled through a celestial voyage from which the oasis, that earthly corner of paradise, had disappeared into the void; Ammonius felt he was being projected forward but could not hold on to anything, as if he were somehow traveling across the skies, with nothing but the darkness of night surrounding him.

At the end of the tunnel he felt trapped in, there was a source of light he was closing in on; its overwhelming brightness blinded him for a moment and, suddenly, he woke up from the nightmarish trance in desperation, now able to move the whole of his body. Two pairs of strong hands pressed against his shoulders sought to calm him down as a male voice said, echoing the serpent's last words:

'Are you all right? Are you all right? It's the fever, you're delusional, but calm down. The Parabolani will try to fix you up as soon as we take you to hospital. We're already near the walls of Alexandria, we can see them from here. We found you in the desert with fang marks on your heel, most likely from a snake, but you might be still in luck if we hurry. Lie back. You're on a trade caravan, you're safe'.

Merely able to understand part of the explanation, Ammonius's feverish state knocked him out yet again as he and the city's brotherhood were about to cross the gates of the Southern wall, headed for the Christian quarters.

Chapter VIII
Dissolute Worshipping ·

It was a fine spring morning in the Roman Empire's capital of knowledge and sapience, the third largest urban center in the entire territory. The general ambience in the urban center founded by Alexander, later cherished and maintained by the Ptolemaic dynasty for three full centuries, was calm and peaceful, just as it had been conceived in the mind of Soter, bringing interculturalism and diversity together, thus uniting both the Hellenic and Egyptian peoples, while simultaneously showing tolerance for other groups of inhabitants, of which a considerable part was of a Hebrew origin.

The present confrontation, as we have now entered the fourth century's last decade, is the result of a handful of men's imposition whose authority is even greater than that of those who are in charge de jure, as the first need not be extensively intelligent, but rather merely savvy enough on how to toy with the latter's beliefs, claimed as their own in the shape of an excuse to further extend their power over and across the majority of the population, for a good strategist never underestimates the shrewdness of having the people join their side; that is the mob's purpose – to divinely adore their human equals and pay their taxes under the penalty of being declared enemies of the State. Becoming popular by spreading fear turns out to be quite useful in a situation such as this.

In a solidly built tyranny, rulers and their representatives do not necessarily deprive minor citizens (plebeians and peasants) of an education (as long as they can afford it, of course), but such an instruction is obviously modeled the way governors and their peers (the clergy, in this case) find it suitable. It is much easier to convince a child to renounce to their underdeveloped cognitive process of thinking for themselves than anyone else who has lived beyond childhood and has, therefore, seen what the world is really like, a place where honor and merit are supposedly attainable concepts, even though they are nothing but ideals, hollow promises.

It has now been so long since a woman last sat

in the throne of Egypt, let alone one who actually forced men to turn their back on their own and kneel to her, so as to fulfill the desires of someone who, today, would have been deemed a witch or enchantress, setting her feet on God's creation only to disrupt the order he worked six days in a row for while making sure that it was good, that it was all good, exempt from chaos.

Now, despite Hypatia of Alexandria being a young woman of her own resolve, mostly independent ever since she became self-aware, learning so much from both her father and her own academic incurrences to the extent of surpassing Theon himself, especially when producing his commentaries on Ptolemy and Euclid's works, she also knew having that much intellectual power to overturn the thoughts of those who studied with her could quite possibly reveal itself to be exceptionally dangerous, but not so much to her; Christianity's attempt to erase her from History would only make a martyr out of her, for which reason they could not be that rudimentary. On the contrary, it was her students she was concerned for the most. Apollodorus's previous statement regarding the Lady's godliness, if not the incarnation of Isis herself, was troublesome. Her preoccupation had nothing to do with religion; one of the Christian students could have said she was the Virgin Mary, it would still not have made a difference (except, perhaps, if the word started to spread and reached Pope Theophilus). No, it was how her students, regardless of their faith, could get punished for making said claims, for which reason she had made her mind up to dedicate a few moments of her class to let the young men know about the seriousness of the problems they could get themselves into. If this is not a true pedagogical spirit, then what is? Pray tell us.

As each of the young men entered the Musaeum's lecture hall, Hypatia was consecutively bidden her good mornings, replicating them by either repetition or gentle nods, constantly bearing a serene smile on her visage while sat in a stool, her back hunching ever so slightly, her forearms and hands resting on her lap, though the latter were somewhat clenched, as if concealing a precious object in the safety of their palms.

When the disciples were finally seated, the Lady swept them all with her sight, one by one; it almost looked like she was conducting an examination process, as she analyzed the students' countless elements. The ongoing silence suddenly became heavy. Though a natural process for every known species in the world (whether fauna or flora), something as simple as breathing turned out to be challenging; self-conscious about it, some of the disciples rationalized it and sought to inhale silently, only to achieve the exact opposite – not to mention their exhaling, which sounded even more disturbing. Others were not so concerned about their oxygenation, but rather the inopportune noise they would make while either coughing or clearing their throat. The rest eventually started making tunes of their own while hitting their styli on their respective wax boards, unaware they were doing it in the first place. Only a few were able to maintain eye contact with the Lady without letting the awkwardness of the moment get to them; Apollodorus, of course, was a part of the latter group – whether he knew it or not, his facial expression bore a smirk. Lastly, Orestes just kept bouncing his eyes between his classmate and Hypatia, exteriorizing both tension and seriousness.

The Lady had politely responded to Apollodorus's greeting with a nod and eventually studied him, so to speak, together with the others, but it was not on him her eyes came to a stop; rather, she looked at the edge of the stage she was always on, except, perhaps, whenever her enthusiasm became quite effusive, leading her to stand, descend and move closer to her audience. Willing to put her students out of their misery once and for all, Hypatia inhaled and faced them all in general, feeling sufficiently prepared to both orate and articulate:

'Gentlemen, I'd like to begin today's lesson by offering my compliments to you and, by this, I mean to say I'm extraordinarily and unequivocally proud of each and every one of you'.

The young men's reaction to the beginning of the Lady's speech was static; no one could immediately tell what she was getting at, for which reason they remained silent, waiting for more stimuli before making any false assumptions, though Apollodorus did not seem to change his confident expression at all. Hypatia then went on:

'I'm in full admiration of what you've achieved so far under my tutorship… anyone can tell you've no problem whatsoever understanding and discussing the ideas and theories of our philosopher forefathers, inclusively proposing solutions of your own to theorems most would be unable to comprehend, no matter how hard they tried. As I've told you countless times before, the key to opposing those drunken with power is to retaliate through the use of words, thus reasoning with several factions, to the likes of a council in which you're… free to speak your mind. I was about to say, "you're allowed to speak", but that would've been wrong because, you see, when someone "allows" you to do either this or that, it becomes instantly implied that a person or people with authority over you – self-proclaimed, most times – must first give you permission, limiting your freedom just then. Let me be clear in advance that I do not condone any form of anarchy whatsoever – the world must be freed from chaos and put into order; it is the attempt, however, to induce said order by means of chaos that'll never justify the end, and it's exactly that which our home, its nationals, and us residents are traversing right now. Each and every one of you has the right to choose what to believe in, and so do I. Our sageness is a divine gift, no question about it, but whichever deity you choose for your own is your choice alone and must, therefore, not be imposed unto others. There is nothing new about this matter we haven't yet discussed so far, you needn't write anything down', the Lady adverted without directly ogling those who had begun taking notes, their styli scratching the wax surface of their boards. She proceeded:

'But let me tell you what I believe in – Philosophy. I was raised a Pagan, true, and I've everything to lose by admitting to such claim. Does it mean, nevertheless, you see me wandering about the streets of Alexandria all the way to the Serapeum, so I can show my adoration for Serapis? No, it doesn't. Have you ever heard me say I care for representations of animal heads attached to human bodies or the other way around? No, you haven't. It's likely you may be asking yourselves what it is, in fact and in the end, I'm getting at. Well, allow me to tell you – I needn't be seen in rituals to let everyone know whom my devotion is given to, nor should I be judged for attending these cults, because it's nobody else's business. Philosophy brings us all together, and the successive Christian patriarchs have known about this for a long time. Many discoveries made by Pagan philosophers have helped shape the Christian faith. Both the causes and the effects are explained in a different manner, absolutely, but don't all roads lead to Rome? The capital of the Western half of the Empire may have been converted in the last centuries, as was Constantinople (particularly under the rule of the incumbent emperor), but they certainly didn't start out that way; still, Euclid and Ptolemy are our principal references. If this Musaeum were to oppose and become unaccepting of any religious factions other than the Greco-Roman pantheon, would you, my Pagan disciples, be sharing this lecture hall's tiered seating with your Christian classmates? You most certainly would not. It has never been my father's policy, the founder of this house, to segregate those whose heart winces with the thirst for knowledge and truth. That is the purpose of our being here, to never quench such thirst with conformity; the more we drink, the more we replenish ourselves, and that is the road we shall continue to take, paving it with intellect at every step of the way, no matter the obstacles ahead. Theophilus may be taking advantage of the Augustus' decrees, but he does not have the power to toy with your mind, unless you want him to, Christian or not, and the same goes for Olympius, whether you're Pagan or not. The enjoyment he experiences in the public flaunting of his faith is not an appropriate demonstration of what it is to be a Neoplatonist, but, then again, that is my opinion and I alone am responsible for it. Such is the freedom I'd like you to taste – love your gods or don't at all; your choice. If I were to have Hebrew disciples, I'd tell them precisely the same. The problem, of course, is how creeds contaminate each other. Christianity is like an heir of Judaism – both share the same god, except the first acknowledges Jesus Christ as the begotten Son, the true Messiah, whereas the latter condemned him on charges of blasphemy and self-proclamation of being a prophet, a good enough pair of crimes to demand that Pilate crucify him, which he did for fear of the price to pay for a rebellion in Judaea – his own head, presented on a silver plate to Tiberius. Washing his hands over the matter was purely symbolic. This brutal assassination is the accusation the Jewish people have now been facing for the last few decades, just as the Pagans will, one day, when we fall (or so said Antoninus). The truth in plain is, had it not been for Jesus of Nazareth, King of the Jews, no new church would've risen, and as much as women can be stoned to death for adultery, so can men have innumerous wives. Christian men may not be taught to violate the sanctity of holy matrimony, but that doesn't stop them from being adulterers, does it? And once they're caught, who's to blame, if still not the women, for their wiles, product of witchcraft and enchantment? Apparently, we're the new Eves of this world. We're not "allowed" to be ourselves and must, therefore, obey the commands of our respective husband, regardless of his nocturnal strolls; some don't even care if it's night or day, they'll just do it in broad daylight. There's something about the taste for human flesh men are unable to control. You needn't question my creed, for I've already told you what it is, and I'm extremely proud of the values I grew up with, but siding with Jupiter's scandalous ravaging of what some of you may deem as… harmonious and beautiful, perhaps even divine… Venus surely didn't get away with it; god or gods forbid females from sharing the same rights as men, isn't it so? But never mind that; Apollodorus, won't you please step down and join me?', Hypatia asked of her student, after making it obvious to everyone she did not approve of adulterous behavior, regardless of being committed by either men or women, leaving her train of thought hanging by an ironic thread she felt there was no need to complete; after all, she had begun her speech by celebrating her students' intellectual abilities.

Due to peer pressure and excessive self-confidence, Apollodorus met the gaze of several of his classmates, still bearing the initial smirk on his face, now appearing to have become stuck. As the Sun gradually rose, the flame of lust and infatuation for the Lady he had ignited in his eyes became all the more vivid when daylight caught his eyes, as bright as a funerary pyre in the middle of the night. Supporting the weight of his upper torso on his hands, he got up on his feet and descended from the audience, placing himself next to Hypatia, smiling also, though in serenity.

'In honor of the words you delivered to me in front of the class not long ago, and as a token of my appreciation, I'd like to offer you this gift', the Lady said, opening at last her fists, producing in her right palm a wrinkled rag.

Hypatia herself took hold of her disciple's forearm and flipped his wrist up, unveiling the palm of his hand, in which she deposited the cloth. Seemingly confused regarding the weightless wrapping, Apollodorus averted his sight between the offering and the Lady, waiting for her to say something else, which she did, encouraging him to proceed:

'Please, do unravel it'.

Following her instruction, the disciple carefully held the edges of the cloth between both the index finger and the thumb of his free hand and unwrapped the rag, only to find its center vividly tainted in red, a kind of stain that had once been fresh and eventually dried out, thus becoming somewhat rigid. Utterly puzzled, Apollodorus sought feedback from his companions, though to no use, for they were as shocked as he was.

'Is… is this… blood? Are you offering me… blood, Lady?', the student asked, not so self-confident now; in fact, he was visibly shaken and trembling, his brow arched in doubt.

'Yes. Yes, it is', Hypatia candidly replied.

'I… I'm afraid I don't… understand, Lady…', Apollodorus stuttered.

'Oh!, but it's quite simple. You see, you claimed in front of your classmates I bore the harmony of a goddess, as if I were the incarnation of Isis herself. You deemed me admirable to the extent of publicly uttering your feelings for me, but let me ask you: do you really understand what love is? Do you realize what loving a body, a flesh vessel comprises? What you see is nothing more than a carcass, perhaps eye-filling for the time being, but oh!, how it'll one day grow old, wrinkly, and not so appetizing… not to mention the secrets it conceals within. Behold, you now have in your possession the blood of my cycle. You love this, O youth, and there is nothing beautiful about it, is there?', Hypatia concluded, her expression simultaneously listless and disapproving.

Incapable of showing a proper response (which he had no idea what it could possibly be) to the boldness of the Lady's rather intimate measure, as was the majority of his colleagues, the young Apollodorus gulped several times before turning his wrist to its natural position, leaving the menstrual rag to its downfall toward the floor. His visage rubicund with shame, the student walked away and left the lecture hall without looking not once at anyone. He had just realized Hypatia had put him in his rightful place, drawing an unbudgeable line not him or any other would even dare think of crossing ever again.

As she waited for the sound of the young man's steps to fade away in the distance, Hypatia had her eyes pasted to the floor, looking unequivocally stern and disturbed for having to take such a drastic measure; as affable as she was, commanding respect by choosing to be this strict was secretly corrosive to her heart.

She then resumed her lesson, moving on to Astronomy – Ptolemy's geocentric model, to be precise, feigning nothing at all had happened. The rest of the class did not risk uttering a single word, rendered idle by the most awkward situation they had ever witnessed in their short, yet promising life. Orestes, who usually did not care much for writing down the teachings of Hypatia, even though he always carried his wax board and stylus with him, was the first to open the notebook, just to avoid all sorts of eye contact, namely with the Lady.

They had all now been proven how powerful a

woman could be, as powerful as any man of noble rights given to him by birth alone. As a person of the opposite gender, Hypatia was no less a human being than the rulers of the patriarchy they lived in across the Empire.

Chapter IX
The Covenant

Having endured weeks of recovery in the Parabolani infirmary (located in the Southwest of Alexandria, by the catacombs), Ammonius, the former Stavrophore who had made his way across the Nitrian Desert all by himself, on the run from his fellow monks, if not God himself, was now danger-free after withstanding a bite to his heel from a desert horned viper, thus overcoming certain death by venom.

Throughout this indefinite period of time, he had barely remained self-aware, forced to eat and drink by the Parabolani nurses to help him fight off the toxicity in his blood and the increasing fever. The only way to save someone from a snakebite that was known to physicians was the process of bloodletting, which Hippocrates himself (the Father of Western Medicine) had been aware of, even though he did not necessarily condone it, choosing to administer dietary-related methods; however, other Greek (and later Roman) physicians eventually acknowledged the benefits of making a patient bleed, so as to rebalance the four humors of the human body, the best example of whom is Galenus of Pergamum, who lived up to his eighties (a rather heroic achievement as far as the average lifespan in the second and third centuries is concerned, though Hippocrates, having lived approximately six hundred years before Galenus's time, was still able to remarkably outlive the latter by another ten years).

Now, although Hippocrates recommended other medicinal approaches when it came to known ailments, he was indeed inspired, in regard to bloodletting, by women's menstrual cycle, which he considered to be a necessary purge of the feminine body in order to rebalance the humors and, therefore, restore it to its full health.

Long before Hippocrates' discoveries, nevertheless, the Egyptians had already been inspired by the bleeding of hippopotamuses – or so they thought; it turns out the red droplets seen on these exotic animals' backs were sweat, not blood. Still, and considering the beasts scratched themselves to the extent of inducing wounds for the sake of pain relief, the Egyptians eventually adopted the same practice, though they created specific instruments for the task.

Of course, and bearing in mind the life of Hypatia and all other characters took place in Alexandria, there is absolutely no way of moving on without mentioning the important fact that yet another Greek physician, Erasistratus, together with Herophilus, founded a school of anatomy precisely in the capital of the Ptolemaic kingdom, having both achieved extraordinary discoveries, though at a cost – a great deal of dissections were performed on the bodies of living people; the fact these men and women were criminals was the only excuse required in order to complete the pair of physicians' enthusiastic research, which led to a better understanding of both the brain and the heart, consequently having them discover the nervous system (subdivided into sensorial and motion) originated from brain matter (instead of the outermost membrane, the dura mater, between the brain itself and the skull), and that veins carried blood to the sanguineous ventricle, whereas the pulmonary vein (an artery, to be precise) penetrated the pneumatic ventricle, respectively, therefore carrying not blood, but rather air to the entire body.

Furthermore, Erasistratus, in particular, was convinced a plethora of diseases were precisely the cause of overabundances concentrated in the blood, for which reason he advocated physical exercise, sweating, reduced food intaking, or even provoked vomiting, if necessary, for the blood does not circulate and must, thusly, be diluted, so as to not become intoxicatingly stalled in the extremities of the body.

Herophilus, on the other hand, suggested bloodletting was a far more practical and efficient therapeutic approach, later condoned by Galenus, who confirmed arteries were in fact filled with blood as well, though its circulation was out of the question, which is why an entire bloodletting system was developed by the anatomist according to several factors regarding both the patient and their location, including, on the one hand, their age and build and, on the other, the season and the weather. The most common symptoms of overabundances in the blood are fever and headaches; the greater their intensity, the greater the amount of blood must be let. As far as localized pain is concerned and depending on the organ in question, specific blood vessels were designated by Galenus for small incisions; the alternatives to bloodletting are induced vomiting via emetics or induced urination via diuretics.

In short, whichever the cause of the malady and the prescription of its respective treatment, if there was one thing Galenus had no doubt about, it was that the blood was the main conveyor of concentrated toxicity, therefore contributing to humor imbalance, which is why, when it came to fevers, the higher they got, the greater the amount of blood to be let.

The humors in question (which are in fact bodily fluids) are as follows: blood, yellow bile, black bile, and phlegm, granted blood contains all other three; each of them is related to a primordial element – air, fire, earth, and water, respectively. Not just that, they are also connected to other features, namely age, seasons, environment, texture, organs, and feelings.

Starting from the beginning, blood is associated with infancy (which is to say spring), it is moist and warm, its source being the liver – it bears a person's approach to others, as far as being social and enthusiastic is concerned.

Regarding yellow bile, there is a much closer connection to those of a younger age, meaning summer; warm (yet dry), its target is the gallbladder, just below the liver, and, as one may guess based on language, the bile-related temperament is choleric and irate.

Black bile, on the other hand, is linked to adulthood, when health begins to decline under the influence of fall – the reason why it is dry and cold, attacking the spleen with a fit of none other than melancholy.

Finally, phlegm represents old age and it is

quite unavoidably tangled up in the wintery part of the year, therefore being cold and moist, affecting both brain and lungs, bringing no more than apathy to the ill, a kind of stoicism that is prepared to, sooner or later, welcome death.

Now, despite this theory being purely Hellenic, dated from Pagan origins, Christianity did not despise every single aspect of the Greco-Roman culture powerful Christian men wished to see become obsolete, and that is why the medical and philosophical Humorism treatment method eventually saved Ammonius from what appeared to be certain death, regardless of the visions he had experienced in the desert, which, at least as far as he was concerned, were quite real.

Having come to his senses on a leather-bound stretcher, to the likes of a great deal more patients stranded inside the catacombs, the Nitrian monk half-opened his eyes to the solidly hanging stalactites. Needless to say, it was somewhat of a risk placing people under those rocky, sharp-ended needles. Alexandria was known for its frequent earthquakes and it was simply impossible to figure out when the next trembling would occur; standing on the surface was already much too dangerous, let alone lying right underneath it. Of course, Ammonius had only just recovered, so this was really not an immediate concern of his. Healing at open air would have actually been worse, as that was where the lepers were sent to in exile – the hypogea, to be precise, where society left them to die in the company of their own, for, regardless of being family or not, they all had one thing in common: one of the most contagious, deadliest illnesses known to Man; sharing the same air was a great enough risk, let alone actual touching of the skin. It was the Empire's way of controlling an epidemic. Depending on the ruler, the diseased were either trapped and set on fire, burning alive with their parasites (just like with the plague), or confined to the outside of the urban center, where only a fool would dare go, were they in perfect health. Given the fact these hypogea were of Pagan use and design, created for the practice of polytheistic rituals, the Parabolani took advantage of Theodosius' decrees and turned the underground chambers into a center for disease control.

Inside the city walls, however, Christians had begun building their own catacombs in the Epsilon Quarter, a place for both rituals and nursing the wounded and ill. Supported by strong wooden structures along the way, both the ceiling and the walls were held in place as the tunneling continued under Theophilus' orders, though without the knowledge of the general citizenry; not only were the underground caves a place of worship and healthcare, they also provided shelter in the event of a natural disaster or a prolonged, catastrophic siege. A fourth purpose had too been conceived in the mind of the Christian Patriarch – the creation of a tunneled network for the sabotaging of Pagan structures and memorabilia, along with the pillaging and ransacking of treasury, in order to fund the demolition and rebuilding of temples deemed offensive to the one, true faith, posteriorly converted into churches.

Slowly regaining both his physical and humoral strengths, Ammonius could not help but feel dizzy, frequently blinking and rubbing his eyes, making sure that grainy vision he had experienced before was gone for good, and it was. He also felt compelled to further examine his body, in search of any missing limbs, but they were all intact. As he slid his right hand atop his left, however, he noticed a lint-based dressing which, by now, had absorbed quite an amount of grease and honey – the first working as a barrier to pathogens and the second as an antibiotic; that was the place from which his contaminated blood had been let, where an underlying vein took the principal humor to the spleen, its natural filter, incapacitated because of the venom's superior toxicity. A similar bandage could be found covering the monk's right heel, where the desert horned viper had originally struck. Had he not been found in time, part of his leg, to say the least, would have become necrotic and, therefore, in need of immediate amputation;

otherwise, the infection would have limitlessly spread across his body, festering to his vital organs and slowly killing him – there might have even been a chance he could have been thrown in the middle of the lepers for fear of contamination.

As he sought to sit upright on his stretcher, Ammonius tried to firmly set his right hand on the leather while boosting a bit more strength to his arm, but the hand slipped and his upper torso, already halfway up, eventually yielded, making him fall on his back, just short of hitting his head on the stretcher's wooden frame; there is no telling whether he would crack it open, having lain down so abruptly, which is why a man in black robes walking by approached him and said:

'Careful, Brother! You don't want another bandage on you, do you?'.

The monk stared at the man for a few moments, allowing his sight to properly focus on the outlines of his visage, replying with a couple of questions of his own:

'Hmm... who are you...? And where... where am I...?', Ammonius inquired, clearing his throat, in need of dowsing.

'It's all right, let me just get you a cup of water – you must be thirsty from all that talking in your hallucination', the man told the monk.

'Hallucination...?', Ammonius whispered, his mind spinning much too quickly to dare rise from his resting position; he could barely keep his eyes open, as it would only worsen his sickness (besides, the sight of rotating stalactites felt uncomfortable to his spirit).

'Here you are, drink', the man in the black robes told Ammonius, as he sat down in a stool, keeping him some company; as he watched the monk struggle to hold the cup without spilling the water all over himself, the man promptly rose, gently lifted his head and drove the hand holding the cup to his lips until the very last drop.

'Oh!, thank you… ugh… thank you, I'm… I'm still a wee bit dizzy', Ammonius said, resting the palm of his right hand on his forehead, as if he were holding his brain in place.

'Don't worry about it, I can tell', the man jested, placing the cup on a nearby makeshift table.

'So… could I bother you for… for some enlightenment concerning my questions…?', Ammonius asked, noisily exhaling through his mouth.

'Oh!, right. Yes, of course. I'm Peter, named after Our Lord's favorite disciple. I'm a lector at the masses presided by Pope Theophilus, as well as an aid to the Parabolani. Some call me Peter the Reader… I guess they find the rhyming funny. You're in the Christian catacombs of Alexandria. As far as I know, a couple of merchants found you in the desert and brought you to the city. You probably don't remember much, but I assume that's perfectly natural – your fever was so high your flesh nearly combusted. However, the Parabolani spewed the venom from that snakebite in your heel in time and you're going to be just fine', Peter explained.

Ammonius, who had been listening to the best of his ability, repeatedly tried to reassemble the syllables of the brotherhood's designation Peter had mentioned twice, but could still not memorize it:

'That name you said... what was it, again? «Palaborani»...? Who are they?', he asked, trying as hard as he could to keep his eyes at least half-open.

Peter let loose somewhat of a chuckle that faintly echoed across the rock walls and repeated the name for the monk's understanding:

'No, no, no, it's Parabolani, not «Palaborani». It's Greek, Brother. It means they're nurses risking their lives to save others. They're also the Pope's bodyguards, but never mind that part now; what's important is they're a brotherhood any Christian at all can count on. It's not like they're an order taking vows, or anything. They simply protect Christendom by any means necessary from provocations made against our faith, and a lot of them have been taking place for the past few months, I'll tell you that much. A new order is rising in Alexandria, Brother – heed my words. Soon, the Jewish murderers of Our Lord will be gone, and those damned hedonistic Pagans will follow – just wait'.

Now, either Ammonius was still delusional, or the words he had just heard could have quite possibly come from an angel in disguise, for he had never heard anything as holy as Peter's preaching; no wonder they called him "the Reader", and it was not just because of the rhyming, either. In fact, he was more than just a lector – he was perfectly aware how to interpret the meaning of the Holy Scripture and pass it on to his listeners, who, to Theophilus's great joy, immediately became followers of the Church, thus opposing anyone who dared speak against the Trinity, for an insult to God was an offense to the Emperor, who, in turn, would authorize patriarchs across the territory handle these issues accordingly, even if unaware of these men's puppeteering.

'So, tell me, what's your story? What were you doing roaming in the desert all by yourself, anyway? Oh!, but first I should probably make your acquaintance', Peter bade the monk.

'Ugh... of course. I'm Ammonius and... well, let's just say I was paying penance, somehow', he replied, slightly stuttering.

Contracting his eyebrows, Peter looked Ammonius in the eye and asked:

'Why is that? Were you at such fault that you just had to cross the sandplains hoping you'd die in absolution? Because the Lord doesn't take the soul of a suicidal, I trust you know that'.

'No, I do, of course I do!', Ammonius quickly told him, adding, 'I wasn't looking to die in the middle of nowhere and rot there forgotten, I simply felt like I needed to be punished for what I did…'.

'Which was what?', Peter insisted, bearing a stern expression on his face.

Surreptitiously gulping, Ammonius disguised his guilt with a veil of words, so as to avoid falling foul of the lector, yet assuming on his visage a look that could be easily mistaken for candid repentance:

'I violated my vows of obedience as a Stavrophore Monk in the Nitrian Desert. Both the Abbot and the Great Schema kept limiting my dedication to God, his begotten Son, and the Holy Spirit on the grounds of much-needed discipline, which I often failed to show because of my fervor. One day, I couldn't hold it in anymore and left the monastery overnight, severing my ties with my brothers… it was almost as if I'd abandoned the Holy Trinity. That's why into the hands of the Father I commended my spirit while crying out to the heavens to be reborn and find the path of light and righteousness once more'.

Paying close attention to the monk's words, the moment he finished telling his story, Peter leaned toward him while remaining seated and took hold of Ammonius's right hand with his own, simultaneously placing his left on the monk's shaven markings still visible on his scalp, lowering the volume of his voice as he looked him in his eyes and told him these words:

'Ammonius, Brother... wanting to actively spread the Good Word instead of being confined to a cellula day and night in quiet prayer is no sin to the eyes of God. Those who tried to stop you are the ones who should've gone to the desert to die of thirst and starvation. What purpose is there in accepting the faith if you don't intend to do anything about it as far as spreading it is concerned? That's the war we're fighting here, and it's holy, a holy war! The entire world must be purged of anyone or anything stopping us from achieving supremacy. He was one of them, Ammonius – Our Lord Jesus Christ. He was the King of the Jews, even Pilate and his men knew it, regardless of mockingly crowning Him with thorns. He was the Messiah, the incarnation of God Himself, and yet... they called Him a blasphemer, a liar! Our Lord, a liar! The nerve of those people... claiming their God is the same as ours, though they refuse to recognize His human form. My soul is in pain, it bleeds... they simply didn't kill Him right in the spot because of Roman law, and not even the blood He spilled as payment for their sins was enough for their satisfaction. "Crucify him!", they yelled...! Believe me, Brother – the Jews have been paying for betraying God even long before He revealed Himself to Moses as the Burning Bush, and that is their perpetual curse, one that cannot be lifted: persecution and annihilation for millennia to come, all the way to The Final Judgment. Just you remember the words of Matthew: «When the Son of Man comes in His glory, and all the angels with Him, then He will sit on His glorious throne. Before Him will be gathered all the nations, and He will separate people one from another as a shepherd separates the sheep from the goats. And He will place the sheep on His right, but the goats on the left. Then He will say to those on His left, "Depart from me, you cursed, into the eternal fire prepared for the devil and his angels. For I was hungry and you gave me no food, I was thirsty and you gave me no drink, I was a stranger and you did not welcome me, naked and you did not clothe me, sick and in prison and you did not visit me". Then they also will answer, saying, "Lord, when did we see Thee hungry or thirsty or a stranger or naked or sick or in prison, and did not minister to Thee?". Then He will answer them, saying, "Truly, I say to thee, as thou didst not do it to one of the least of these, thou didst not do it to me". And these will go away into eternal punishment, but the righteous into eternal life». The others won't last long themselves, the non-believers'.

As Peter spoke, the monk genuinely started to

cry in silence, something he did not remember doing in a long, long time; it was as if a new flame of fervor had been lit in his eyes, giving him his strength back. In the end, Ammonius heard at last the words he craved for the most:

'Deinde, ego te absolvo a peccatis tuis in nomine Patris, et Filii, et Spiritus Sancti. Amen'.

'Amen, Frater', the monk whispered back in tears, grasping Peter's hand in excitement.

'Now come with me. I'll take you to see the Holy Father. I've full confidence he'll let you stay with us', the lector said.

Holding his forearm to the likes of a greeting, Peter pulled Ammonius out of the stretcher and helped him stand on his feet. The monk then wiped his tears off and gladly followed the reader along the lamp-lit catacombs, as if walking down the path of light once again, toward salvation. Regardless of having been delusional or not, he was now certain (once again) God did indeed have plans for him, and not the likes of those described by the demoniac desert horned viper. It would not take him too long to show the Father just how useful he had yet to become.

As both men kept walking across the entrails of Alexandria, about a third of the way, to the right, miners seemed to be undertaking yet another breakthrough in the building of these catacombs, for the rock wall was getting thinner at each strike of the several pickaxes. One of the miners gave it so hard a blow that eventually tore a hole in the wall; it was merely the size of a clenched fist, but enough to take a peek and try to realize what was on the other side. The man in question quickly demanded he be given a lamp to illuminate the naturally concealed room, but there was not much to be seen.

'Here, hold this!', he told one of his fellow miners, 'I need to widen this crack. I think I may have found something interesting', he concluded.

At this point, we believe it is fair to say faith can honestly revive a man's spirit and body, for it did not look like, judging from the vigor with which the man blew the wall into smithereens, he had fulfilled half a day's work at all. This whole excitement on the miners' behalf immediately drew the attention of both Peter and Ammonius, the first of which exclaimed and enquired:

'Whoa! What goes on, there?'.

The moment he heard him, the man responsible for the discovery started to reply between strikes:

'Peter… come quick! I think… there's… a hidden… temple… on… the other… phew!… side… the Pagan… kind!', he said, finally dropping the wooden handle from his calloused, blistered hands, the iron piece echoing across the tunnel as soon as it hit the ground, like a clapper inside a bell when it is time to call the flock back to the shepherd's home – a church, in this case.

He had done it; the miner had made the orifice wide enough for a full-sized man to walk through. Peter approached, followed soon after by Ammonius. Focused on the innumerous shapes hidden in the dark his eyes could only just make out, Peter twisted his wrist and held out the palm of his right hand with his fingers bent like a hook, indirectly issuing the man holding the lamp the order to hang the artificial source of light in that exact spot, safely clenching it between his knuckles. The lector cautiously took one step forward, making sure the ground was stable, also quickly illuminating both sides of the newly-carved entrance, for fear of ancient mechanisms built by the Ancient Egyptians as a means of keeping intruders out – or in, rather, thus avoiding the spilling of either the tomb or burial chambers' secret location to the outer world, which could only end in unavoidable pillaging and ransacking, possibly along with the rape of the mummy; the same had happened to the body of Alexander himself, seized on its way from Babylon to Macedon by Ptolemy I Soter, three hundred and twenty-three years prior to the birth of Christ, transferring the honey-filled golden sarcophagus to Memphis, whence it was afterward relocated to the heart of Alexandria by Ptolemy II Philadelphus.

It was not until the ninth of the Ptolemies,

known as Lathyros (officially Soter II) that the original sarcophagus was replaced approximately two centuries later by another made of glass, so that the Pharaoh could melt and turn it into gold coins. Once Egypt became a Roman province, Dictator Perpetuo Julius Caesar and Octavius, the first Augustus, visited the tomb themselves; an infamous Caligula is believed to have taken part of Alexander's armor for his own purposes – the breastplate, to be precise. It was only under the rule of Septimius Severus, about two hundred years following the coming of Our Lord to this world, that the tomb was closed, and Alexander was finally left to rest undisturbed, but possibly not for much longer. Both the burial and possession of the King's body were a royal prerogative, thusly legitimizing its proprietor to rule; even though Alexander's conquests were eventually divided into three kingdoms and one empire (which included the vast majority of the Asian assets), keeping his body in the Ptolemaic Kingdom somehow made Soter's dynasty far more superior. Moving the remains to the Kingdom's capital, founded by none other than Alexander himself, was without a doubt the equivalent to setting the Ptolemies' legitimacy in stone.

The tomb's precise location, however, had now become unknown for nearly two hundred years. Severus's heir, Caracalla, was the last to visit the tomb; whether it was indeed in the very heart of Alexandria (as in «its center») or somewhere else was a question left unanswered. As far as we know, it could have been secretly moved yet again to discourage any digging on the behalf of graver-obbers.

Having checked his passage into the newly un-covered room was harmless, Peter took a few more steps forward and raised the lamp above his head, spreading as much light across the uncharted space as he could. He silently signaled miners carrying lamps of their own to come in and increase the power of the illuminating source; one of them, try-ing to make out the shapes of the objects present, kept shimmying across the room without even no-ticing where he lay his feet, eventually tripping over a fetish representing an ancient Greek deity, now broken in half. Needless to say, everyone jumped in fear, including fearless Peter, who shushed the man immediately, signaling everyone else to estab-lish a perimeter in order to determine the size of the room. It could not have been any wider than fifteen by ten pedes, and the reason why it proba-bly looked so small was the fact that it was filled with idols of all sizes (the most prominent of which the twelve Olympic deities), together with riches – most of them fashioned from gold. Generally in ru-ins, it was the center, however, that looked far more well-preserved. Once again, in a silent man-ner, Peter instructed miners carrying their lamps to focus on the object set upon a pedestal – it was undoubtedly a sarcophagus, but a rather unusual one for Egyptian standards; instead of encasing the carcass of whoever the dead person was inside of a marble-like, gold-made, or even wooden coffin (to say the least), the ark was made of an apparently fragile source of material, though it was somewhat thick and completely opaque, as if worn-out by the hand of time. It was also chipped in certain areas, most likely due to the sporadic earthquakes that took the city by surprise every now and then.

'Ammonius', Peter whispered, 'come take a look and see if you can tell what this thing is made of'.

'Why does it have to be me…?!', the monk enquired too in a whispery tone, feeling shivers running down his spine.

'Don't you want to make a good impression on the Holy Father? We might've found something important, here! Go on, touch it', the lector said.

'I was the one unearthing this room', said the miner that had broken through the wall in his deep, regular tone, 'it should be me reporting the news to the Pope, not some outsider we barely even know', he concluded, ogling Ammonius from head to toe.

Peter, who did not care for the man's misdemeanor, stared at him for a while, deemed him expendable (should any incident take place), and eventually agreed, saying:

'All right… when you put it like that, it's only fair that you do it. Blow the dust away and tell us what you see'.

The miner, suddenly dropping his stern expression, arrogantly approached the sarcophagus, pushed a couple of his fellow workers out of the way, and slid his hands on top of it, trying to get a sense of what its creators had used to build it. As he traveled from the upper torso to the head, the palm of his left hand got caught in a fault, resulting in a flesh wound that began to bleed from the sudden tearing of his skin's upper layer. Annoyed by the incident and in pain, the man cursed the corpse entombed in that odd-looking involucrum and repeatedly struck it with his already injured hand in a fist, ending up cutting his knuckles and splattering blood on both the sarcophagus and the floor, where shards of all sizes also fell. It had now become clear the sarcophagus was made of glass. What was even more curious, however, was that, from the inside, dark crystals had begun pouring on the ground, causing everyone to step back, including Peter, who ordered the men not to move by looking at them alone. Shortly afterward, the cascade came to a stop; no one moved, except for the enraged miner, who picked up a handful of crystals and smelled them, sensing, nevertheless, no scent at all. He did not want to taste it, either, so he threw it all on the floor and started rummaging around with his right hand, in search of something other than that crystallized grain. Already weakened after having been struck, part of the sarcophagus's right side broke and the pouring resumed. It was only after a while that a different compound emerged from the weird sand. Still no one moved or uttered a sound under the lector's command. The miner, now more confused than irate, put his undamaged hand inside and dug up a rather moisturized object – it felt sticky, even. Puzzled, he grabbed a lamp from one of his fellows by force and shed some light on his source of disgust – it was a half-decayed head missing its nose, the exact place where the man had introduced one of his fingers; part of the hair was still visible, darkened by the crystallized matter engulfing the whole body. Horrified at the sight, he screamed in terror and literally jumped back, fatally stabbing and piercing himself with the spear of Pallas Athena's life-sized statue, placed behind him and held as if the goddess were going for a throw. The miner still had enough strength in him to lift the lamp up to his chest and see the blade coming out of it. His lungs collapsing, he exhaled his last breath before inertly dropping his head forward and the lamp on the floor, spilling its burning oil. The reader was quick to react, telling the men to put out the fire before it uncontrollably spread.

'Drop your robes if you have to, now!', Peter yelled, but the men were much too afraid of being caught in the flames and combusting.

It was then Ammonius got his nerve back and, undisturbed by the death of a potential brother, he pulled the body off Athena's spear and made it roll on the floor by kicking it, thusly circumscribing the fire to the corpse, which quickly began consuming it. He then joined both hands and piled a considerable amount of grain from the sarcophagus, sprinkling it over the burning robes and flesh, extinguishing the flames at last.

Visibly disturbed (now that he had let his violent impulse once again take control of him), Ammonius started to breathe heavily; defiling the body of men who shared his faith was apparently becoming a habit, something he did not at all appreciate.

Peter, of course, was no fool – he could tell from the monk's effort at keeping his composure together that he had met death before, most likely at his own hands. It was precisely this sort of ruthlessness he wanted to be able to rely on; all he had to do was keep convincing the monk of the importance of his work as far as the Christian cause was concerned. Were Theophilus to back him, the lector would soon become second-in-command, which, come to think of it, he pretty much already was, but making it official felt even better; in turn,

Ammonius would become his lackey – it was the perfect plan.

'Don't feel bad, Brother… one man dying for the safety of his brethren makes him but a martyr. He's now joined Our Lord in eternal glory, praised be His name. Requiescat in pace', he said, blessing the cadaver, telling the others, 'take his body away, wash the blood off the floor and don't let anyone else in; Ammonius and I will go get the Holy Father. Something tells me the Lord chose this to be the day of our deliverance, but only Pope Theophilus can confirm it. Come, Brother – let us carry the good news to Saint Mark's!', he concluded.

'What of the pile of sand that fell out of the sarcophagus?', one of the surrounding men asked.

'Leave it. We may need to put it back in to preserve the corpse. Whoever this is must be utterly important to the Pagans and that might just be the leverage we need to squash them for good like scarabs', Peter replied.

Now, despite the ease with which «Peter the Reader» bossed the Parabolani around without even considering himself to be one of them, there were, of course, those who did not appreciate him much for it. It is not like he commanded extraordinary respect for the brotherhood to blindly obey him, but rather how he fell under the holy umbrella of Theophilus; were it not for the Patriarch, the lector would have probably already become a target needing to be taken down. The downside of a plot such as that would be, without a doubt, the loss of favor with the Holy Father, who had both the authority and the influence necessary to enquire each and every Parabolanus where his loyalty lay, thus imploding the brotherhood by turning them all against each other, quickly suppressing a possible rebellion without letting a single word reach the ears of the Praefectus Augustalis. And so, for the above reasons, and no matter how much some of them wanted the lector out of the way, the Parabolani focused on their contempt for the non-believers, together with the Hebrews, thus fortifying their bond, instead of giving the Roman officials more reasons to have them disbanded.

As for Ammonius, well… let us just say he was torn apart between the sense of guilt he was now so familiar with and the excitement he felt for meeting the Patriarch of Alexandria. According to Peter, the Holy Father would not oppose anyone willing to make the Church of Jesus Christ victorious over any other faith – by any means necessary.

Chapter X
Engaged to Philosophy

Hypatia did not necessarily take pride in the need to admonish people in general, let alone one of her own students. Even after carefully and repeatedly considering whether or not she should have gifted Apollodorus a cloth stained with the blood of her cycle, especially before an audience, the attitude per se had likely been the result of hot-headedness, something the daughter of Theon did not at all regard as a virtue, but rather a foolhardy fault.

She had always known how to maintain her composure and, yet, it crossed her mind she simply should not have done it; then again, there was the question of commanding respect, and her opinion regarding this matter was quite practical – being that she was the mistress, it was expected of her disciples they behaved properly. Not only were they grown men (therefore capable of restraining themselves), the fact Hypatia was a woman was also to be regarded as perfectly normal; there should not be any special treatment, thus making the biological differences between her and the young men nothing to worry about.

While it is true a generalization was made as far as women being more delicate and fragile than men was concerned, the philosopher surely did not see it that away, for strength was not found in the width of biceps brachii, but rather in intellectual ability, something the creator of Humankind (despite each person's faith) had not gifted only to men, thus making it possible for everyone to acquire the necessary knowledge to understand the ways of the world (though there still was, of course, the social stratus question – whereas Theon's household was considerably lucky for having learnt to write and read from Hypatia herself, other slaves were undoubtedly not as blessed; in fact, some of the masters lacked the same two basic skills required for the absorption of knowledge as much as their own property).

There was, nevertheless, an aspect Hypatia was willing to accept when it came to differences between both genders – women did indeed have it in their nature to be a lot more sensitive than men, but emotion was also something the latter were perfectly capable of understanding without compromising their manhood, position, or sense of honor; come to think of it, questioning the integrity of either these three elements or any others on account of being able to exteriorize feelings was preposterously nonsensical. In fact, parenthood was one of life's stages that definitely promoted a change in both men and women with a more rigid sort of personality, for having a baby to take care of (regardless of all the help from the household, when existent), an innocent human being requiring constant care and attention, miraculously produced from a bond between a man and a woman that is supposed to be a great deal more than plain physicality, changes absolutely everything in one's perspective of life, and there is not a better example than Theon, who had devoted most of his life to academia until the moment the loss of his wife became his greatest grief, though eventually made up for through the survival of the daughter they had in common, generated in her womb, but a successor to and bearer of features from both.

Despite all of this, while respect must be commanded at first, one must work on earning it thereafter. Should anyone in a place of power abuse their authority, shielding themselves from the inevitable consequences with aspects such as influence, riches, land, titles, et cetera, then they will sooner or later be relieved of their command or entitlements, which is the most common result of failure to earn, more than their subordinates' respect, their trust; the moment someone's trust is put into question, it hardly ever comes back, thusly doubling the effort (granted there was at least a shred of it to begin with).

In Hypatia and Apollodorus' particular case, there had not been an issue of insubordination, but rather a question of crossing the line, transposing certain boundaries we all set for ourselves, assuming their violation will never take place – until the very moment it obviously does. So, in the end, the Lady eventually comforted her spirits and put an end to her internal conflict. During the following lessons, Apollodorus had proven to understand the pedagogue's message and the subject was never again spoken of (not even among the students, whether before or after class).

As for the punishment in its whole, rumors were spread like wildfire concerning Hypatia's "indecency" and, when questioned on the streets about it, she showed neither denial nor sorrow; after all, why should she? The act had been exclusively conjured for academic purposes, and even though not everyone necessarily saw it that way, a menstrual cycle is but a natural process for a woman; deliberately sabotaging it was the actual danger, not the other way around. Then again, the reactions very much depended on the people reacting to the event, with elements such as education, gender, and strata splitting both explicit and implicit opinions into several groups; amid these three primordial points of view there were naturally other variables, as being learned could mean being the disciple of the Catechetic School, the Neoplatonic School, or perhaps even both – whether a student felt comfortable about discussing natural phenomena such as this was entirely up to the teachings his mind related to the most; as far as gender was concerned (and in somewhat of a generalization, despite it being a philosophical fallacy), it was common for most men to rebuke (if not feel disgusted toward) women for about a week every month, therefore avoiding physical contact at all costs, an attitude which, in turn, has been ostracizing menstruation into a multitude of conversation topics that ought to be kept private at all times and, from here, we approach the social strata question, as slaves bathing their mistresses obviously knew at what stage the latter were in their cycle – needless to say (even though we eventually keep mentioning and explaining what we apparently need not say) it was mandatory for the slaves to keep quiet and not discuss these matters amongst themselves, let alone with their mistresses (and most certainly not with their masters, either).

Female slaves also endured it and were well aware they should not go on about it. Now, about the choice of the word "endure" – may it be borne in mind menstruation is not a disease; in fact, as one may recall, Galenus had based his bloodletting treatment on the cycle, precisely. If we actually bide our time thinking about it, bleeding was the womb's process of rejuvenation and humoral balance (in short, self-healing) by shedding its own linings, which could turn out to be more or less painful (hence the endurance) – there really was no way of setting a pattern, and it continues to be so. While the several reactions to menstruation can be influenced by a series of criteria established by each individual, the women experiencing it were not a subject of choice, regardless of their place in society. Every now and then, however, there were cases of late blooming or no signs of menstruation at all, and that was indeed abnormal, as it often led to infection, resulting in a severe illness that sooner or later revealed itself to be fatal.

Hypatia did not mention the episode to her father, considering she had decided not to face it as a problem (and even if it had been the other way around, she simply did not see the need to talk about it), but Theon was bound to find out anyway from none other than Olympius, a man the Director of the Musaeum's daughter shared some philosophical views with, but certainly not the necessity to publicly preach divinity to the audience gathered in the agora or take part in theurgic rituals at the Temple of Serapis, next to the public square. He was what Hypatia called a «demodidaskolos», a sort of gratuitous professor who taught the poor and the weak-minded to believe the power of adoration and magic while making himself look divine, in permanent contact with the gods, chosen as their messenger (which is to say, «High Priest»). Theon's daughter did not differentiate her students based on faith, but social background and wealth were aspects to consider – she was, after all, a member of the aristocracy; we know she did not mind answering the most assorted questions asked by passersby when walking on the streets, but her disciples were unmistakably a part of the Alexandrian elite. The Ptolemies' funding had come to an end long ago, for which reason a source of income was necessary if the Musaeum was to stand; the only choice was, therefore, the charging of tuition, as counting on the Augusti (Theodosius, especially) to pay for a Pagan institution with taxpayers' money was out of the question.

Still, and even though Hypatia had little empathy for him, both the Musaeum and her home were ultimately the property of Theon, for which reason she had no right to bar Olympius from visiting, which had just so happened on a certain evening out of sheer surprise (a walk-in sort of visit, so to speak). When she arrived through the front door from her walk under the peripatos the skies cosmically provided, having reflected and talked to herself about a great deal of subjects, including the episode with Apollodorus (now far more infamous than famous), she was told by a slave that Theon was tending to a visitor in the triclinium facing the peristylium, where both were dining. Having asked who it was the Master was with, the same slave enounced the man's name, a sound that revealed itself to be quite distasteful to the Mistress' ears, if such a reaction is possible (which it is, should one season one's discourse with a pinch of synesthesia).

'Thank you', Hypatia told the slave, who, in turn, respectfully bowed to her and set off to complete whichever task he had been assigned to do.

Now, morally speaking, eavesdropping is, of course, a rather rude attitude to engage in, but still, the Lady simply could not resist overhearing what Olympius had purposefully gone to her home to tell Theon.

Aside from his exacerbated devotion and self-entitlement, if there was one thing Hypatia was under the impression of, much to her dislike, was Olympius's jealousy of her intellect. She did not deny the existence of the gods, quite the contrary, but it was all the fuss he made about hubris and its respective retaliation through divine vengeance (the sort he "discussed" himself with the Pantheon in order to "reason with them") that used to make her blood boil for a considerable amount of time; she obviously refused to give him the satisfaction, for which reason she undertook the undeniable effort of being affable, pleasant toward him, thus constituting yet another moral dilemma – losing her transparency, having to fake emotion. Though provocative, Olympius' attacks were impeccably disguised in good manners, preventing Hypatia from irately retorting not even once, for, if she did, she would be the one deemed unreasonable, giving men (including those directly involved with the preservation of the Musaeum as a reputed academic institution and, therefore, part of Theon's staff) the perfect excuse to forcibly exclude his own daughter from a place conceived for men – despite the etymology of its designation, which meant very little to said academics in practical terms («Home of the Muses», nine demigoddesses – or nine divine women, to put it bluntly, the same group that had been inflating and inspiring men to mirror sublimity on the works they produced, of which Orpheus or Homer are but a couple of examples); having women get themselves an education was simply unfathomable, let alone one woman who claimed the right to stand on the same side as the remainder of the Musaeum's professors and educate her own disciples. Interestingly enough, Hypatia's students were, in fact, willing to pay extraordinary sums to study under her; plus, not all of them had Alexandria for a hometown, which meant a great deal not just to the Lady, her father, or the institution, but rather the city as a whole. Such popularity bothered Olympius (and possibly others, though he had the gods' protection to freely speak his mind, attributing his statements to them when needed), which is why the menstrual rag situation was a blessing as far as his purposes were concerned.

Hypatia quickly made her way across the atrium and in-between the tablinum, to the left, and the culina, to the right, rushing by the peristylium straight to the corridor between the triclinium and the exedra (a garden room), allowing herself to listen in on the dialogue with better precision.

'But seriously, Theon, don't you think it's well overdue…? She's not a little girl, anymore – hasn't been for quite some time, now. It's obviously got nothing to do with a lack of suitors, I mean… I've only just now told you about the latest news traveling through the streets and there's absolutely no stopping it. I could even realize she didn't bother to tell and provide you with an explanation within reason for the taking of such an attitude… at least I'm glad you heard it from me, if not her. Gossip is much too sordid to deal with, especially when it concerns aristocrats such as ourselves', Olympius said.

Both Theon and Olympius were having dinner in the customary Greco-Roman fashion, reclined on the lectus innus and medius, respectively, with a lovely view to the peristylium, right in front of them. The table, set with food and drink, was only a few unciae away, close enough to be reached without either of them having to adopt an uncomfortable posture. Such was the common layout, u-shaped, lest we forget the lectus summus, in which people from lower classes lay, unable to properly address the hosts or the honorary guests, let alone ogle the peristylium.

As Olympius discoursed (at least pausing while chewing), Theon kept averting his eyes between the cup of wine he was holding and stirring with his free hand and his guest, sort of replaying Olympius' recommendations in his mind, while preparing a reply. When it seemed like his guest was done for the moment, Theon then spoke:

'My dear Olympius, when my lovely wife died twenty-one years ago, I made her a promise I always refused to break, regardless of the circumstances or the times we were and are yet to face. I told her, "our baby won't be like any other, condemned to perpetual silence and a mind placed under arrest. I shall raise her to become the honorable woman her mother was, hopefully surpassing the wits of her father", and that is precisely what I've done. The lineage of my family now depends solely on Hypatia's production of an heir, and, in order to do so, she must, indeed, just as you've implicitly suggested, find a husband, but the truth is that… so far, my daughter hasn't shown any sign of craving for my approval as far as a young, strapping lad asking her hand in marriage is concerned. Not only that…', Theon said, about to add another argument to the discussion, though Olympius quickly intervened without, however, intending to be rude or disrespectful toward the host by interrupting him:

'I understand your point of view, my good friend, and I am perfectly aware of the promise you made your wife, but wouldn't you agree that perhaps Hypatia could spare you from this sort of impulsive reaction and consequent tainting of her own honorable father's name? By Serapis, prancing her blood around like that for everyone to see? Have we gone back in time to Caligula's depravity, one knowing no bounds…?! She needs a husband to pull her reigns for her and you know it. If she doesn't find one of her own accord, then you make the choice, just as it's always been done'.

As both men's gazes met in both direction and proximity, given their lecti were close to each other by the head, Theon tried not to pass a momentary intention of piercing Olympius' eyes. Hypatia, while leaning against the wall just by the corner of the room, kept talking to herself inaudibly, weirdly praying to the gods that poor excuse of a man would just go away with a padlock through his lips. It was not in Theon's daughter's nature to condone brawling, but she did realize she was human and could not always help it. Still, seeking to keep his mouth under control, her father pleasantly replied to his guest:

'Olympius, my daughter is not a mane to have her reigns pulled'.

The man sensed he had spoken too much, possibly because of the wine's tongue-loosening effect, for which reason he paradoxically tried to explain he had meant no offense, but Theon was already silencing him with his index and middle fingers raised from behind the cup, proceeding like so:

'If you please, I'd like to return to the beginning of my argument. Neither has Hypatia shown any interest in love for a man, nor have any men approached me to ask for her hand in marriage, and even if they had, I'd quite simply be incapable of ensnaring my own daughter in such a trap. She'd have to choose a husband for herself, not me. We've known each other for years, Olympius, and you're perfectly aware I've always been much too rational… only when I lost my better half did I realize what I'd been missing out on. Hypatia hasn't yet committed herself, there's no one waiting for her right now, no damage has been done to anyone's heart. She enjoys her freedom in every sense of the word – speech, thought, association, teaching... in short, a potential husband would only incarcerate and drive her to madness. My little girl's education is that of an aristocratic boy; it was the least I could do for my own child – instruct her in her father's «trade», if one may call it that. I'm aware times are changing, my friend. Society was already intolerant, and now it's getting worse each day, indeed it is. There is a great deal of bachelors who wouldn't mind bargaining with me to marry Hypatia and put a stopper to her discourse. Even if there were some sort of love in the beginning on the husband's behalf, it would soon become clear to him it was nothing but infatuation, after all; claiming obedience and respect from her would easily turn into a priority which would inevitably result in her torture, if not death straight away. All Philosophy aside, such is the world of men, one in which women are all but disposable – especially one gifted with an intellect superior to theirs. If one cannot reason with another, what is the best way to deal with the impasse, I ask? One kills. We've been doing it for thousands of years; beasts have no understanding, so if we can't break them, we get rid of them. Man, on the other hand, is dominant; «man» – singular, which means one cannot threaten the other's rule... isn't that how Rome was founded? Romulus wasn't too keen on Remus's pitching, so he struck him down, his own brother (not to mention twin brother). You, my dear Olympius, are asking me to sentence my daughter to her death. Even if her body should remain immaculate at first, I'm sure her spirit would not; she'd be manacled to earth by flesh and blood, whereas her mind would be long gone; is that what a woman's life is to become? One of complete subservience? If virility and manhood are to be challenged, then I leave it to Hypatia to do so. Once I'm stranded on my deathbed, I'll happily depart reassured I taught her well enough for her to make the difference'.

As Theon completed his train of thought, successively adding fresh, new arguments as they popped into his head, his guest gulped innumerous times without even sipping his wine, his eyes focused exclusively on the host's, uncontrollably shimmying from left to right and back, acknowledging defeat at a debate he had started himself. Theon, on the other hand, felt his mouth was dry from all he had exposed and eventually turned the cup's bottom up, placing it on the table very quietly, afterward making himself a lot more comfortable while pasting his eyes to the floor and intertwining his fingers, almost as if he were in a state of introspection.

Hypatia's sensitivity eventually ruptured the dam blocking the tears in her eyes, allowing them to freely flow in a stream over her rubicund cheeks.

She was not as cold as some might think; quite the opposite, she had the most profound admiration for one particular man, and that was her father. She did not feel the need to tie the knot into a wealthy family, like all the other aristocratic young women aspired to; she loved her father, and that was enough. As long as he lived, he would be her sole protector, and once he died, she would take care of herself, making Theon and her unknown mother proud of their child.

Having nothing else to add, Olympius abandoned his half-eaten food on the dining plate and carefully positioned his half-empty cup beside it, directing his hands to a bowl of water in which to clean them, as he merely bade the host his good-byes:

'Well, then… ahem!, right… I… I'd best be going. It's nearly dark and I shouldn't want to wander the streets at night – not this late, anyway. Thank you for having me over, Director'.

'Oh!, it was but my pleasure. Do come by any time', Theon told him without a sarcastic inflection whatsoever, lifting his eyes only to see the back of Olympius's head as he rushed into the peristylium.

Hypatia had no desire of confronting the philosophically beaten man, and so, by the time the guest crossed the entrance to the triclinium, she had already disappeared into the darkness of the closest cubiculum. With tears still in her eyes, all she felt like doing was going in the dining room to hold her father tightly; such a demonstration of affection would have only satisfied Theon, but, then again, reason erupted once more, forcing Hypatia to restrain herself, as she would cynically have to conceal the fact she had listened to a great deal of a conversation which, while regarding her for at least the last part, was not supposed to take part in her knowledge. The daughter would just have to save the gesture toward the father for the morning, so as to not arouse any suspicion of something as impolite and unpleasant as eavesdropping.

Chapter XI
Rise of the Downfall

Being the twenty-third Pope of Alexandria, Theophilus held his seat as Patriarch of the See of Saint Mark, one of the Four Evangelists whose gospels are thoroughly described in the Good Book's New Testament; Mark himself was the one to pen down the sermons of Peter, first Bishop of Rome, for whom he served as an interpreter in the beginning of Claudius's rule as Augustus in the capital of the newly-formed Empire (less than a century old), around the year forty-two, just a little over a decade after the crucifixion of Our Lord; between the years forty-nine and sixty, Mark finally arrived in Alexandria, becoming the first ever man to spread Christianity on the other side of the Mare

Nostrum. There, he founded the Church of Alexandria, completely surrounded by Pagan temples in honor of Isis and Saturn, which were, of course, fully legal back then. Despite the struggle to convert Greco-Roman Pagans to Christianity, Mark was in many ways successful, performing miracles which already attested his sainthood, but in a predominantly Serapis-devoted urban center, during a festival held in said god's honor, the population grew tired of him, put a noose around his neck and dragged him across the streets to his death in martyrdom, thus confirming his canonization; Mark was later interred below the modest building which would posteriorly become a cathedral from where Christendom in Egypt irradiated its light to the likes of the Sun around the Earth, progressively piercing the barrier imposed by Grecian heritage.

The Holy Father was definitely not looking to deal with the impasse much longer, especially when he had the Emperor on his side, which was the same as commanding Law itself; now completing six years into his papacy, Theophilus was determined to subjugate the whole of the Egyptian province, through its capital, to his authority, which implicated either chance or a flawless plan to change the tide and avoid being found out – even though Theodosius was not fond of the Pagans himself, he could certainly and easily be coerced into easing on the non-believers on account of their intellectual shenanigans, obviously constituting a snag as far as the Pope's intentions were concerned. Fortunately for the Holy Father, however, he was in for a stroke of luck.

Peter the Reader and Ammonius the Monk, having traveled across the undergoing subterranean network more conveniently connecting the Christian Quarter without the risk of running into a street quarrel, finally resurfaced near the Kibotos, perfectly protected and secluded from the public eye, whose access was granted only to those the Patriarch and his Parabolani deemed as undeniably trustworthy. From there, both men walked down Meson Pedion to the East, with the agora and the Temple of Serapis to their left, whence the Musaeum could also be seen. Whereas Peter did not care for the sight, keeping himself focused on the news he was to relay to Theophilus, Ammonius, on the other hand, would have turned his head a total three hundred and sixty degrees as he paced forward, if only he could – the magnanimous manmade representations of false deities exposed like that, out in the open, were a provocation against Christianity on their own, much like spitting right in a believer's face. Unknown to him, the approximately one-hundred-pes-tall, long-haired and long-bearded man was Serapis, wearing, as usual, the modius on his head; Ammonius considered the whole statue to be delusional, ridiculous, especially the «vase» worn for a crown of some sort. Just a wee bit behind Peter, the monk rushed to meet the lector's pace and asked him quite loudly:

'Peter! Peter, look at that display over there, to the left! What in God's name is that thing?! Is a plant supposed to grow in the pot, or something of the kind…?! Good Lord…!', he shouted, but the reader was quick to react and pulled him away from the center of the street against a wall, diverting the attention the monk was drawing upon them both, violently whispering:

'Hold your peace, Brother! We're in the Broucheion, now – it's Pagan territory. Now, I find that statue as laughable as you do, but we're "slightly" outnumbered right now to pick a fight with these people. The time will come, I promise you; it won't take long, now – be patient. First, we warn the Holy Father. Then, he'll decide what to do, but we must gather every single man up to the task before we launch any raids, do you understand?'.

As the lector spoke, looking Ammonius in his eyes, so did the monk meet his gaze, which seemed to have somehow been lit by the wrath of an exotic beast to the likes of a lion; feeling cornered in every sense of the word, the monk nodded, appeasing the irate Peter.

'Good', the reader said, 'now come along;

Saint Mark's is just around the corner'.

'On Pagan soil...?', Ammonius asked, readjusting and wiping grains of sand off his garment while catching up again with the fast-paced lector.

'It was Christendom's first victory in this sin city, Brother, and we all owe it to none other than the Evangelist. These animals killed him like an inferior, when all he did was fulfill the mission entrusted to him by Our Lord before His Ascension to the Heavens. Mark was the one purged, not them... inconceivable, isn't it?', Peter said, condescendingly grinning as he tried to control his own rage, adding, 'still, it's holy ground, now; his body lies underneath the thriving piece of architecture his modest church has become – his spirit travels within us all'.

It was only a few pedes away that the former Nitrian monk saw at last the façade of Saint Mark's Cathedral in all its splendor. The structure was somewhat similar to the monastery he had lived in until not so long ago, the main entrance being the Southern tip of the crucifix whose shape most Christian buildings had adopted. Unlike the structure in the middle of the desert, however, and as the official residence of the Patriarch of Alexandria, Saint Mark's Cathedral was the object of constant renovation and expansion, clearly overcoming the simplicity of the Pagan temples regarding visual impact – yet another demonstration of the

Church's power over the old traditions and customs, eliminated stage by stage in a process of trial and error.

A smaller, rectangular door was embedded into the magnanimously arc-shaped wooden gates, opened only for the celebration of mass and other official affairs, naturally involving the Pope. It was through said door both Peter and Ammonius walked into the narthex, immediately cooling off the two men from the arid environment hanging in the air on the outside.

By the altar, in the apse section, was Theophilus, getting ready for the afternoon prayer, already dressed in his phelonion and omophorion; only the camelaucum, the cone-shaped headwear, was missing. A few Parabolani were aiding the Bishop in the preparation of the rites.

It is hard to describe how exactly Ammonius felt the moment he saw the Holy Father. As we have come to know for some time, now, there is only one true faith for the former Stavrophore, and someone on the mundane paradigm simply had to have the power above all to command salvation from the Father, his begotten Son, and the Holy Spirit as one entity alone. Whereas the long-bearded Serapis was the imaginary patriarch of the Pagan population, the old curl-free, long-bearded wise man flipping through a manuscript of the Holy Scriptures at the altar was right there, in the flesh, able to transmit unto others the will of God without resorting to witchcraft, which was precisely what the so-called "high priests" responsible for the cult of a statue of a man wearing a flower vase did. Pope Theophilus was a proactive servant of the Lord; everything Christianity had conquered up until then was still standing thanks to him and his devout aides. This was the sort of resourcefulness Ammonius had been looking for all along, impossible to accomplish under the strict rules of a devil-riddled Abbot and his Great Schema ceremonial puppet.

Peter noticed the monk had been struck by the sageness and confidence emanating from the mere sight of the Pope, allowing the young man to admire the credibility of their previous generation in action. Shortly afterward, the lector put his hand on Ammonius' shoulder and said:

'Come… he's a better sight for sore eyes from up-close'.

The monk smiled and, feeling shivers being sent down his spine, he walked side-by-side with the reader across the nave. At some point, Theophilus noticed the presence of both and turned to them; he discreetly signaled a young Parabolanus with a snap of his fingers, implicitly ordering him to place the camelaucum on his head, which he rushed to do. The Bishop's presence was now one of full empowerment. He curiously ogled the stranger walking aside Peter, focusing soon after on the latter, already extending his right hand for the lector to kiss it as a sign of subservience.

'Peter… my good Peter', the Pope said, having the reader replied:

'Bless me, Father'.

Theophilus obliged and subsequently asked:

'And who might you be, young man?'.

The Patriarch extended his hand yet again, hanging in the air for a moment as Ammonius wiped his own hands on his robes to hold the Pope's.

'Ammonius, Holy Father. My name is Ammonius', the monk promptly answered, kissing the Bishop's hand and adding afterward, 'bless me, Father', which Theophilus kindly did.

Peter took care of inflating the monk's story with a bit of detail, so as to bring the Patriarch up to speed – one we already know a lot better than any of the two men. It was the ending that was different and became rather important:

'And because he felt he didn't belong in the apathy of the monastery, Ammonius left and paid penance by crossing the desert and enduring a snakebite. Luckily, he was found by a caravan and brought straight to the catacombs, where the Brotherhood nursed him back to full health and I took the liberty of absolving him from his sense of guilt. I hope my actions may please you, Father',

Peter concluded.

'I trust you completely, Peter, which is why I granted you the authority to do as you saw fit, not only in this particular case, but every other you've come across with so far, granted either I, my nephew, or both of us are absent', Theophilus said.

'Those were the circumstances precisely, Father', Peter assured the Patriarch, bowing in reverence to him.

'Good, then that's settled. Pray tell, Ammonius, have you found yourself a place to stay at while in the city?', Theophilus inquired the monk.

'Erm… no, Holy Father, I have not, and that's what I'd like to-', the former Stavrophore began to say, but he was incisively interrupted by Peter the Reader:

'Ammonius would like to join the Parabolani, Father, but he's a bit too shy to say so without stammering all the way through it'.

'Well, but of course you can join the Brotherhood, young man. Peter himself was the man you had to ask. You didn't need to come for my approval', the Patriarch said.

'Well… yes, Holy Father, I understand. Erm… thank you, by the way! I just felt I should re- require your blessing… is all', Ammonius told the Bishop, nervously pulling his hand to kiss it yet again as a sign of gratitude. Pulling his hand back again, Theophilus told him:

'All right, all right, the Lord be with you, my son…'.

'Speaking of His good name and definitely not in vain, Father', the lector began, 'we also came to your presence to convey rather important news regarding the progress made on the underground network', Peter hinted.

'Oh?… What have you found, exactly? Any Pagan remnants?', Theophilus asked, looking him straight in the eye with an apparent newly-ignited flame in his own gaze.

'Indeed, Father. However, I think we may have found something even bigger to the non-believers among the several heathen treasures.

'You have my attention, go on…'.

'The place we unearthed is a tomb. It contains a sarcophagus fashioned in a paganistic style, although the material it is made from was rather… how would one put it? Peculiar, for lack of a better word'.

The Patriarch slowly turned his face about three-quarters, implying he was waiting for the lector to get it over with and tell him what could be so important to the Pagans to be kept hidden from everyone's sight, unlike all other demonstrations of adoration for false deities.

'Keep going, boy! What is it made of?', Theophilus impatiently asked.

Peter put his hands behind his back, cleared his

throat, looked down for a fraction of a second and then faced the Patriarch once more, withholding no more secrets:

'Glass, Father. Hardened glass. One of the men, erm… accidentally broke the area where the head lay and we saw that it's half-decayed, probably the result of its preservation from the crystals that began pouring on the floor'.

The Pope's signs of an impending wrath threatening to befall on the lector because of his sense of cheek with the actual Alexandrian clerical authority soon began to evade the old man's expression. He drove his left hand to his mouth, covering it in incredulity while leaning on the altar, supporting his weight with his right hand and lower back; his eyes rapidly shimmied, though they were pasted to the cathedral's floor.

The monk, fearing the worst, took hold of Theophilus's arm and asked him:

'Is everything all right, Holy Father?!'.

The Bishop uncovered his mouth and signaled Ammonius that he was fine, though he still did not look up, asking himself soon after:

'Could it be…? Have I been finally blessed by God Almighty with the sight I've longed for all these years…?'.

Feeling at ease again with his paternal figure, Peter asked of Theophilus:

'What, Father? Do you know the meaning of

our findings…?'.

'I'm still not quite sure, boy, but one thing's unequivocal – the Lord does work in mysterious ways…', the Patriarch stated, lifting his head to an upright position, his eyes accompanying the ascent all the way up to a side window ornate with alabaster contained within small wooden frames, making the whole piece look like patterned stained glass.

Both Peter and Ammonius looked at each other, bearing a puzzled expression on their face. The lector even went as far as to discreetly shrieking his shoulders in confusion.

'I need to see this for myself', Theophilus said, fully standing back on his feet, ordering one of his aides to bring him his crosier – and fast.

The Parabolanus quickly ran to the ambulatory section of the cathedral and came back moments later with the Patriarch's staff, leading the latter to enquire:

'What took you so long, boy?! Can't you see I'm in a hurry? The Lord has granted His true followers with a brand-new Ark of the Covenant!'.

The young man was rendered nearly speechless, stammering his apologies to Theophilus, but the Pope had already turned his back on him, rapidly walking down the altar to the crossing section, vigorously hitting the lower tip of his crosier on the floor at each couple of steps, loudly reverberating his movement across the entire cathedral, having come to a full stop at the crossing section just before the nave, where he looked back at Ammonius and Peter and frantically asked:

'What are you two waiting for?! Am I too fast for a couple of children in their supposed prime?! Come along!'.

Moved by the strength of Theophilus' words, the newly-made Parabolanus and the lector rushed to keep up with the Pope, walking behind him side-by-side, still somewhat puzzled by the channeling the Patriarch seemed to be making of the Holy Spirit itself. Peter, nevertheless, fully recovered from the earlier admonishing and earned back his confidence, resting assured he had found indeed something of great importance for the Christian cause.

The Parabolani guarding the gates did not even require the Patriarch of Alexandria to signal them the respective opening; they simply pulled and turned the magnanimous structures on their hinges the moment they saw Theophilus fully dressed in his clergy gowns, accompanied by his pastoral staff adorned with a blood-red cloth around the upper cross (meaning the shepherd was ultimately responsible for the blood of his entire flock), thus clearing the path for the Pope and the two men accompanying him.

Regardless of the fact Saint Mark's Cathedral

stood primarily on Pagan territory, Theophilus obviously did not care for his personal safety, as he had always figured Pagans would have to be much too idiotic to attempt an attack against him. Not only would they immediately face the brawling features of the Parabolani, but Theodosius the Great himself would have them all killed, for which reason the Bishop refused to run through the backdoor like a cowardly criminal, choosing to walk all the way to the entrance of the catacombs overground, instead.

As was typical of powerful men, nothing was left at random, subjected to a gambling-like demeanor; on the contrary, by walking down the streets of Alexandria, Theophilus was quite aware the people would join him by the hundreds, as if a parade were taking place, demonstrating of the Pope's superiority. He chose for his itinerary the transversal avenue leading to the cathedral itself, thus avoiding going anywhere near the Musaeum, the agora, or the Temple of Serapis, so as to not be disturbed by a sense of provocation experienced on the Pagans' behalf.

As he headed down the Beta Quarter, followed by Ammonius and Peter, all the more Christians began joining their leader, asking one another what was going on or what the occasion was; even though no one was capable of coming up with an actual answer, that did not halt their unknown purpose, for if Theophilus was involved, then the Lord sure was too.

Running all the way through Aspendia and then turning East while crying, "Uncle! Uncle!", there came the Pope's nephew, staying clear from the ever-growing crowd in order to easily meet up with his father figure around the second-to-last Southern street. A couple of the Parabolani who had joined the Patriarch in the meantime to protect him were having difficulty recognizing the fourteen-year-old boy with all the dust engulfing him (the result of his racing), which led them to believe a Pagan surprise attack was inbound. As they prepared to unsheathe their swords, Theophilus himself, having heard his nephew's cries, realized his sister's son was in danger, stopped and struck the two Parabolani on their heads with his crosier, tainting the red-blood cloth with considerable spatters of the actual humor-carrying bodily fluid. Though the Pope did not kill the aforementioned couple of bodyguards, their blows to the head had been sincerely severe, leading Peter to immediately react and instruct three other members of the brotherhood to take them away without ever letting them know who had struck them once (and if) they recovered.

'What happened, Uncle...? What did you do to them?', Cyril asked, visibly scared.

'Don't you worry, my dear boy', Theophilus

responded, bringing the young adult close to him, 'they're fine; it's just that, sometimes, you can't make people realize the stupidity they're about to engage in without showing it to them, instead of just reasoning, which is far more civilized, but come along, now', the Bishop of Alexandria concluded.

'Where are we going?', the boy inquired.

'I'm not sure yet, but I think I have a pretty good idea and oh!, my dear nephew, if I'm right, the Lord might've just delivered us all from the clenches of the heathens', the Patriarch responded.

Instructed to never question his superiors (his Uncle most of all), Cyril rested assured Theophilus had done the right thing, moving on with him and the remainder of the crowd, turning West on the last street before the city's South Wall, headed toward the Christian catacombs. The boy, who was originally born in Didouseya, about sixty-two leugae East-southeast of Alexandria, and, as we already know, was the son of Theophilus' sister, had always benefitted a great deal from the proximity both him and his mother kept to the clergyman; of course, once he was elected Pope, his education became even richer – proof of that is he was about to reach completion of Grammar school, soon to become learned in Rhetoric and other humanities under his uncle's careful and dedicated watch. His passion for Theology would still have to wait its turn, until he was old enough to entirely grasp the Bible's teachings.

Even though the Patriarch had initially avoided walking across most of the Pagan territory, it was practically impossible to walk around the Serapeum, as it lay close to the entrance to the Christian catacombs. It seemed to be some sort of an apparent, interchangeable truce between both factions, as Saint Mark's Cathedral was located mostly on Pagan soil, just South of the Broucheion. Both academics and Serapis-devotees walking in the vicinity of the temple did not take too long to grow suspicious of a parade led by the Christian Patriarch, its edges covered by a self-proclaimed brotherhood whose fanaticism was of the utmost concern; one of them was Olympius, the High Priest serving the god the Serapeum itself had been built in honor of.

Noticing how heavy the Pagans' gaze upon them had become, Peter spoke to both rows of Parabolani in a low voice, saying:

'They're onto us; tell the Brothers behind you to keep pacing forward and do not make any sudden or threatening moves until the Holy Father instructs us what to do, are we clear? Spread the word, but no fuss'.

And so they did – the Parabolani forwarded the message to each other back-to-back, though, with so many people following Theophilus, the brotherhood could protect but a handful of the entire crowd. No threatening ogling was deployed on behalf of the Pope's bodyguards, and neither did they drive their hands toward the pommel or grip (the hilt section) of their swords, whose blades were sheathed in their respective leather scabbards. Still, fearing there might be yet another uprising (probably of epic proportions, this time), Olympius reached out to those praying with him and gave them the order to collect as much weaponry as they could, relieving any caravans of their merchandise, if needed, in order to prevent a full-scale attack from a group of hooded demons claiming their violence was commissioned by their god, one who should be on the lookout for peace, just like Serapis and the remainder of the Pantheon. Anyone willing to fight was to be at the ready; those physically debilitated would simply have to surrender their slaves – other than that, there could be no exceptions (apart from women, girls, and small children in general, of course, as the adolescent males were already strong enough). Still, the alarm had to be triggered silently. So far, the Christians had not shown any signs of aggression, for which reason the Pagans would certainly not be the ones to engage in provocation, thus proving their intellectual and civilized superiority by not entering a brawl for no motive at all.

It may seem by now the Prefect nominated by

Theodosius to maintain imperial order in the Egyptian Diocese, Evagrius, was completely irrelevant as far as these disputes are concerned, and the truth is an assumption of the kind would be unmistakably appropriate. Neither the Roman military, nor the Prefect's personal security detail intervened in Alexandrian riots, unless, of course, at least one of them were at risk, if not already and suddenly dead. With Christianity centralizing all the more power in the higher officials of the clergy, disputes between different religious or even political factions were hardly resolved by the Augustus-nominated magistrate – Roman Law was Christian Law, for which reason the Scale of Truth and Justice could not be balanced like in the old days, when Osiris presided over the trials of the dead, having the purity of their hearts weighed against the ostrich feather of Maat. Now, whether it was true or not, it did not matter, as all was to be played for, and everything was at stake.

A short walk later, the Patriarch of Alexandria, sided by his nephew Cyril and followed by Peter the Reader and Ammonius the Parabolanus, had finally reached the entrance to the catacombs, where even more members of the brotherhood were tending the ill as nurses, instead of militia.

Those with sufficient physical ability knelt and bowed to Theophilus, for he was, yet again, regarded as having a great deal more authority than the Prefect. In three gestures of signum crucis, the Pope blessed everyone from left to right, saying to each group, 'the Lord be with you', to which they all responded with, 'and also with you, Father'; the unison of their reply echoed across the rock walls like in a genuine mass, sending fervor-riddled shivers down the men's spines, a synonym of the Holy Spirit's very presence in each and every one of them.

Turning back about three-quarters, the Patriarch caught Peter in sight with his peripheral vision while pointing out to a heavily guarded makeshift orifice in the rock just a few pedes away with his chin, asking the lector:

'Is that it…?'.

'It is, Father', he responded.

'And who made the discovery?'.

While it is true Peter wanted to claim all credit for him, he still did not want to push the authority the Parabolani acknowledged in him; plus, Ammonius was certain to hold somewhat of a grudge against him, so he soothed the situation with the following reply:

'It was… sort of a collective effort, Father. We all put our muscle down to it'.

'Very well… a wondrous job – all of you', the Patriarch remarked, sweeping the audience with his sight, immediately averting it back to the entrance to the tomb.

Lifting his blood-tainted crosier while leaning its lower tip forward, the Pope began pacing in the same direction, headed toward the discovery. Without requiring anyone's instruction, the men guarding the secret room stepped aside as Theophilus progressively went in. Everything was now well lit, and no signs of an earlier struggle were visible anymore, especially the pool of blood.

Though the Patriarch briefly gazed upon the several representations of Pagan deities, they were of little importance to him – for the time being, at least; his focus was now on the sarcophagus, still pouring crystals every now and then, but at a slower rate than before. The decomposed visage of the deceased in the funerary container offered no doubt, let alone when Theophilus looked at it up-close. The flames that both Peter and Ammonius had seen just a while ago in the back of the Pope's eyes had once more been ignited, this time accompanied by a maleficent grin. Without looking elsewhere, the old clergyman rotated his head another three-quarters and called out:

'Cyril! Come in here, boy! The Lord is definitely on our side, today!'.

The young man swiftly moved in-between the Parabolani lurking on the outside, quietly shoving each other for the best peeking spot. When he saw the dead body, the Patriarch's nephew drove his right hand to the cross he bore around his neck and exclaimed:

'God Almighty...!'.

'Do you know who this is, son? Do you know where we are, right now?', the boy's uncle asked.

Cyril looked around and quickly realized the tomb was merely the end of a possibly more complex route built centuries ago, eventually caving in on itself after it was left abandoned at the hands of the desert sands, taking back their rightful territory. Now that he had a pretty good idea, the boy decided he should let his uncle know his thoughts:

'I... I thought it was only a myth, but... this is the Rhakotis...!', he said, facing Theophilus, who was still waiting for the best part.

'Which means...?'.

That was when Cyril gazed at the tomb, opposite his uncle, adding:

'Which means...', the boy gasped, 'this is the tomb of Alexander, Alexander the Great! We found him!'.

'Yes, we did! What did I tell you?! This is all we needed to put an end to the ridiculousness of Pagans still among us! Now, we crush them, and the One Faith will spread like wildfire! We are triumphant!', Theophilus shouted, hitting the floor with his pastoral staff as if he were parting the waters of the Re[e]d Sea, freeing his people from the slavery of non-believers running the city founded by the very man whose body the unfaithful would do anything for to claim back their right to sovereignty, just like in the good old Ptolemaic days.

'«Iacta alea est» – let the fight to the death begin! For God!', the Patriarch proclaimed, appropriating himself of the words of none other than Julius Caesar.

Joining him, everyone echoed his victorious spirit across the catacombs with the same vivacity as the followers of the Dictator Perpetuo had when traversing the Rubicon:

'FOR GOD!'.

Chapter XII
Alexandrian Cravings

With his orders being carried out and relayed from one Pagan home to another, all the way up to the Broucheion, Olympius walked as fast as he could while holding the folds of his garments, choosing to deliver the news himself to the Director of the Musaeum and Head of the Neoplatonic School, Theon.

Most streets in the Epsilon Quarter were up-market, which was convenient for a Pagan passerby to quickly move toward the agora and the Temple of Serapis, but not necessarily good for anyone included in said faction, for the only conclusion left to infer from this was obviously the enormous gathering of Christians near the Serapeum, the only standing building originally connected to the Great Library of Alexandria. Now, as we know, while most of its destruction was mainly due to natural causes, it is no great risk to say human action was also involved at times, and a new version of this nightmare could seriously be in sight, which is precisely what Olympius had taken upon himself to avoid at all costs, though he had to be sure there was a good enough reason for an attack on the Christians; turning the Nicene Creed into the Empire's official religion had made it a lot more comfortable for the Church to progressively obliterate any remnants of a millennial culture and its ways of life – the very last stronghold was at stake.

Facing the agora was the teaching institution founded by Theon, where he happened to be as a guest lecturer for his daughter's class, not only caving into Hypatia's persistent wish (one he could not resist to), but also into how proud she was of having him for a father. Under discussion was Ptolemy's 'Almagest', now bearing the corrections of both parent and child, making it more precise and easier to understand. After all, Hypatia shared with her disciples an approximate age, for which reason she might have gotten a better grasp of how to pass on Theon's commentaries to a new generation of intellectuals, a breath of fresh air for the Alexandrian academic world, not yet fully smothered by the Church's dogmatism; the fact there were still Christians studying under her was the necessary proof to keep Theon's offspring exactly where she belonged – the lecture hall and definitely not at home, playing the role of both a silenced and obedient wife.

The ambience in the room was even more enthusiastic than usual – Hypatia was only a little girl a while ago, becoming, in the meantime, a living legend, but to have her own father join her in class was like a once-in-a-lifetime opportunity that quite simply could not go to waste, something every single disciple was well-aware of, regardless of their personal interpretation of who the Creator truly was.

Both parent and child sat in the center of the pedestal next to each other while in a three-quarter position inward, thus inviting all students to feel included in the conversation, allowing them to ask any questions crossing their mind. As Theon spoke, Hypatia bore a candid smile on her face (the kind involving eyes and lips), resting her hands and forearms on her lap, facing her father with admiration, sweeping the audience with a serene, yet happy gaze.

Suddenly, from the entrance corridor there echoed the soles of sandals in an unsteady racing pace, mixed with wheezing outtakes of breath and mild clouds of dust left behind at each step – it was Olympius reaching the lecture hall, leaning against the doorframe while holding his chest in pain the moment he made it to the spot. All eyes in the room were averted to the source of the commotion, having Theon been the first to rise and address the man:

'Olympius! You look as if you're about to draw your last breath…! What happened?!'.

Acknowledging the High Priest was in distress, Hypatia rose second to her father and ran to the old man, bringing him back while holding his arm, so he could safely sit in her stool without faltering on his way to the pedestal.

'Come', the Lady said as she sat him down, 'rest here'.

The disciples were beginning to grow restless each moment that went by, waiting for Olympius to catch his breath again in a more silent fashion.

'Water… somebody… please get me… a bit of water', the old man whispered.

Theon promptly yielded and ordered one of his own slaves to find some sort of container, wash it at and head for the well in the agora; the servant, present in the room, grabbed a dusty silver bowl from the table in the back of the lecture hall and ran as fast as he could. Shortly afterward, the servant came back in walking quickly but steadily, seeking to avoid any spillages whatsoever. As soon as he heard the sound of freshwater cresting against itself, he turned to the slave, extended his arms and told him:

'Give it here, quickly'.

'But sir, I haven't found you a cup yet...', the servant responded.

'Never mind', Olympius retorted, 'there's no time for subtlety'; he then took the container from the slave's hands, leaned his head slightly backward and poured the content of the bowl down his dried throat – need we add it was not just a mere bowl meant for soup, but a rather large one for hand washing, and still the old man nearly drank it all. After he was done, he dropped forward still seated, and though he let go of the container close to the floor, the precious metal it was made of echoed through the hall like a bell ringing in everyone's ears, which showed massively in the students' faces.

'Argh!...', Olympius cried in relief, 'thank Serapis'.

Confident he was of no further use for the time being, the slave withdrew himself from between the pedestal and the audience, returning to the side.

'Are you all right now? Why did you come in here running like a madman, anyway?', Theon asked of the High Priest.

'Because we're in danger, Theon! The Christians marched past the Serapeum led by Theophilus, protected by those Parabolani hoodlums! One could sincerely argue it almost looked as if Caesar were triumphantly marching across Rome, followed by his treacherous lackeys!', Olympius exclaimed in exasperation.

The Director met his daughter's gaze for a moment with his mouth half-open; Hypatia too looked worried, crossing her arms just below her bosom. While Theon picked his stool to sit closer to Olympius, the Lady averted her sight to her disciples and confirmed their restlessness and twitching were beginning to grow, as Pagans and Christians, already sat apart, as usual, whispered among them as both factions progressively turned their back on each other, widening a gap that was a great deal more than figurative.

'But have there been any disturbances? Did they do any damage, launch an attack on the people?', Theon inquired.

'Not yet, but I'd say it's rather likely – wouldn't you, Director? I've given the order to prepare for battle, but we're all still waiting for your confirmation, which is why I came running all the way from the Serapeum as fast as my old legs would allow me. The call is yours – what are we to do?', the High Priest asked, looking Theon straight in his eyes with genuine concern, also pushing him to give the order.

Resting the palms of his hands just above the knees, his elbows pointing outward, the Director of the Musaeum gulped, looking to Hypatia for her counsel, who, in turn, looked at her disciples and saw nothing but rupture – whereas the Pagan side kept whispering among them, the Christians remained in a silent frown, feeling intimidated by Olympius' suggestion of engaging in a casus-belli response to what was yet to be confirmed as a provocation, and even if that were the case, violence was certainly not the sort of retaliation the Lady had in mind; it never was.

* * *

Meanwhile, back in the Christian Catacombs, where both the Rhakotis and Alexander the Great's tomb had just been found, Theophilus had indeed something up his sleeve, but he was not willing to make it look like the Christians were at fault; whichever the result of his endeavor, the Emperor was certain to receive word of it, and even though the Patriarch was sure to obtain Theodosius' sympathy toward him, his flock and their communal cause, the concern for the Pagans' intellectual features remained, for which reason the Pope had to make sure he was simply abiding by the law enforced by the Augustus himself – the fact the Serapeum and other temples were still standing was a violation of the Theodosian decrees enacted this year precisely, three hundred ninety-one, anno domini, and that was enough.

After carefully revising the tomb in search for treasure and other sorts of valuables, the Patriarch of Alexandria gave the order himself that his Parabolani pick up the several idols surrounding Alexander's sarcophagus and distribute them by the accompanying citizens, thus igniting an exposing march that was to begin at the entrance to the catacombs and flood the streets immediately leading to the agora, where Pagan citizens were sure to dwell, especially when the Musaeum, the Temple of Serapis, the amphitheater, Cleopatra's Needles (or obelisks), and the Caesareum were so close to each other, riddled with even more Greco-Roman imagery – might we add the latter structure had been originally commissioned by Cleopatra in honor of Julius Caesar, though it was not completed until Octavius's victory over Mark Antony and the last of the Ptolemaic dynasty; as Caesar's appointed heir, the first Augustus of the Roman Empire eventually transformed the temple into a cult center for his own adoration by the subjects of the Egyptian province, erasing all traces of the former triumvir's presence in the capital city.

And so, all across the Epsilon Quarter, both the Pope's bodyguards and the Christian people started a procession headed North while holding relics sacred to the old customs and polytheistic faith, simultaneously mocking and ridiculing how the false deities were portrayed and represented, though it was all but a distraction, for the one element in the parade that would definitely boil the Pagans' blood would be the carrying of Alexander's broken sarcophagus, whose location remained unknown and greatly coveted even to them.

Theophilus, along with his nephew, would walk ahead of it, claiming the body of the city's founder for the exclusive keeping of the Church; whether an army is made of actual military equipped with weaponry specifically conceived as warfare or rioting folk bearing domestic utensils, morale is of grave importance and must be considered at all times, which means that, if there is a good enough reason to make the enemy believe they have nothing to fight for and win the battle (let alone the war), then everything turns out to be much easier than ever. Of course, fighting to reclaim the remains of Alexander is likely to trigger a violent response, but without any coordination or planning (not to mention the outnumbering factor), what chance of success can possibly lay ahead for the heathens? Such were the thoughts of the Patriarch, confident in the triumph on behalf of the Holy Trinity. Those who had not joined the march toward the catacombs were now present on both sides of each street, either standing and waiting to take their place among the crowd or just leaning on their windowsills, ogling at the unraveling of the events taking place.

Aspendia Avenue was the widest of all paths leading straight to the agora, which made it a great deal more comfortable for Theophilus and Cyril to be surrounded by Parabolani in a square formation, swords at the ready, followed by other members of the brotherhood placed in a rectangle carrying the sarcophagus with the help of thick wooden beams over their shoulders, collected from a pile by the entrance meant for the expansion of the structure preventing the catacombs from collapsing. There was populace on both ends of the Pope's parade encouraged to keep shouting and shaming the idols found in the tomb – an excellent strategy whose purpose was to protect Theophilus, the boy, and the body, as the people would make a good enough shield for the first blow, allowing them to divert to Saint Mark's Cathedral as soon as possible and stop anyone else from going in.

From the agora, the main square where everyone spent some convivial time and the merchants sold their goods, thus preserving a millennia-old cultural and architectural tradition, the day-to-day commotion seemed to be clouding (along with the glooming sand) the ominous layout of people marching with a threatening look on their faces while inconsistently yelling, though, given the distance between both factions, it was still impossible for the Pagans' eyesight to make out what it was they were mouthing or the objects they were holding and shaking above their heads, as if damning them all to the consuming fires of hell.

A few moments past, the entire agora's attention was at last caught and drawn toward the streets leading up to it, flooded with an insurmountable mass of Christians who, led by the Parabolani, stayed in formation much to the like of a professional army, engulfing the Pagans inside the square, keeping them from reacting to the surprising event, let alone leaving; the brotherhood gathered up front, staging a safety perimeter. It was then they all discovered the horrific truth – their idols were being defiled by the very touch of the mob's hands, together with the insults uttered against them and the undergoing mutilation they powerlessly withstood, such as severed heads, phalli, or full bodies, split in two halves; the most fragile artifacts simply turned to dust, once their destruction was attempted, even if just to scar them, which was especially the case with earthenware depicting important historical events set in stone by not only mythological heroes like Hercules, Perseus, or Leonidas, for instance, but Alexander himself.

Their tears streaming down their shocked faces, cascading similarly to waterfalls, the cornered Pagans were rendered speechless and inactive; it did not matter whether those treasures had been hidden all this time or where they had come from… every single object destroyed in that frantic fit of both rage and laughter constituted a piece of cultural heritage now lost forever, but the worst was still to come.

Near the mouth of Aspendia Avenue there opened a corridor of people to the like of a strong wooden gate, except the doors were well alive and responsive, cheering the coming of their leader, Pope Theophilus of Alexandria, bringing behind him and his faithful nephew, Cyril, the ultimate Pagan treasure, the very reason that city existed – the founder, whose body was supposed to have been kept preserved inside the original sarcophagus, instead of toyed with for its value, along with other unique pieces (namely, his armor). Marking his self-empowered pace with the lower tip of his crosier, the Bishop walked into the square, stopping soon after to face the trembling Pagans like insects he could squash with his own feet, putting an end to their damning plague once and for all; bearing a condescending grin outlined by his long beard, Theophilus kept being enthusiastically cheered, walking over the broken pieces of the Pagan treasures laid to rest by Alexander's side, somewhat satisfying his impulse to crush everyone else, purging hundreds of shards into thousands, headed for the stairs of the Temple of Serapis, whose entrance was perpetually watched over by a magnanimous stone representation of said deity. As he climbed one step at a time, depending a great deal on the pastoral staff to make progress, the old man's enraged gaze met the stony void of Serapis' eyes, iris-free. The height of the statue was no match for the magnificence given to the Pope by the hand of God himself, for which reason he whispered, gnashing his teeth amid the continued yelling, his eyes bloodshot:

'You don't frighten me, buckethead. The Lord shall have His victory… today, tomorrow, it doesn't matter – through me, His glory will be made eternal across this land, and others shall follow through with it after I'm gone', he concluded, striking the step above his so vivaciously with his crosier that the marble sustained a slight chip; not just that, he spat as far as he could toward the statue's feet out of outraged spite.

It was then the Pope turned around and faced the public square, deliberately ignoring the shock mirrored in the contemptuous eyes of the Pagan crowd, signaling his security party to bring and hold the broken, opaque glass sarcophagus in line with him, now able to look upon the corpse from a powerful vantage point, exerting the superiority of the Church through his very patriarchic figure. Cyril was quick to join him, standing just a couple of steps below his uncle, allowing Theophilus to quench a thirst of grandeur he had been struggling with for years. The Bishop opened his arms and reached for the sky, feeling illuminated by holy light, as if God had finally decided to give his representative the floor, canonizing him while living still, just over twenty years in advance. Both Ammonius and Peter were nearby, though not so close as to be ruled intrusive in one, new covenant the Patriarch was presently signing with the Lord; the newly-made member of the Parabolani brotherhood could not restrain himself with the same discipline the reader did – a Christian Moses was coming to life right in front of him, rendering him unable to hold back his joyful tears as the Sun revolved West, pointing that day's last beams of light toward God's servant at the Lord's own will.

Feeding his lungs the necessary strength with a deep intake of breath, Theophilus cried out loud, his voice ranging to all four corners of the agora:

'People of Alexandria, listen to me now! For centuries, the Shepherd's flock have had to run for their lives, communing with their Lord and Savior in absolute secrecy, under penalty of death, thrown as fodder to and for the circus lions to maim them to the like of lesser human beings, animals – but no more! The gift of civilization we take part in based on a glorious Empire led forward by Theodosius the Great, chosen as legitimate ruler of our Holy Land by the hand of God, has at last delivered us from the fear of being caught in flagrante delicto, when the crime is none other than preventing us from begging the Almighty Holy Spirit to cleanse us of our sins every single day, so that we all may seek salvation – even you, resistant non-believers! "The truth will set you free", the Lord saith! Thou art still in time of yielding to thy deliverance! May the blood of Christ fall upon thine eyes and heal thy blindness away, as it did your fellow-Pagan Longinus's! Come forth and allow yourselves the cascading of water over your head from the baptismal font in the home of Saint Mark, viciously swept away from his life by your ancestors. Peace can be attained, but not without sacrifice... too many have spoiled these grounds with the shedding of their blood, both Pagan and Christian. Join us and put this nonsense behind you', he said, pointing the top of his staff to Serapis' statue without even looking back, adding, 'the one, true God does not linger about inanimate representations such as this, carved from stone; He lives inside each and every one of us, and it is precisely up to ourselves to embrace the light shone inside our heart, thus pledging allegiance to salvation, for these are nothing but sorry excuses to stay in touch with falsehood, so tell me, now, Alexandrians – is that the purpose of the Philosophy you so proudly preach? To make you believe in the sins of untrue adoration, witchcraft, heresy, poisoning of the youthful mind with stories of incest and other abominations punishable with fire and brimstone?! You claim to seek the truth – well, then… you'll never find it that way; looking up to demonic entities like these will only cast you astray to the lifelessness of useless pieces of rock. "Thou shalt not tempt the Lord"… do so, and forever will your souls hang in the limbo for failing to look forward; continue to choose to look back, and you shall become as passive as this vase-crowned man, for you'll have salted your spirit and nothing will be able to grow and flourish ever again – not in this world, not in the next'.

The surrounded populace was utterly helpless; ogling them with a threatening tone were the Parabolani, ready to spill as much blood as necessary to prevent the survival of those people's creed, thus annihilating the persistent weed for good to the like of the salting of Carthage, once destroyed. Silence prevailed as the words of Theophilus were carried by the wind to anyone listening.

Failing still to address the broken sarcophagus and the body inside it, immersed in crystallized honey, the Patriarch held his crosier in front of him, struck the marble one more time and told the crowd, now looking the several faces in their eyes:

'The time for absolution has come – kneel on your own or lose your feet to the blade and crawl'.

* * *

Hypatia: Empress of Alexandria

As in every sociopolitical movement, whether it may be rashly radical or considerably thought through, regardless of the end to which the means aim, not everyone blindly agrees with said movements' policies; apart from the obvious opposition, those who one thinks would subscribe to the ideals at hand may show some reluctance in the aftermath, having become displeased with what was once regarded as a necessary enterprise to achieve the best for the people. Believing tyrannical enforcement will eventually be given up once order is reestablished is but an illusion; in fact, the concept of order usually depends (even though not entirely) on the views of government bodies claiming extra powers to reinstate control and, just like that, the Church of Alexandria traveled through four of the five political regimes Plato himself had conceived in his 'Republic', naturally skipping the democratic degeneration, jumping, therefore, straight from oligarchs to tyrants, for a man of democracy, without any priorities to his name (apart from the imprisonment of freedom in a world of equality, attainable by all), is much too dangerous to be allowed undisciplined cravings, granted superiority is one of them after a considerable amount of time living in an egalitarian society. Such was the new content of a lecture conducted by Hypatia, as she saw fit speaking not only to her disciples, but both Theon and Olympius – the latter especially, given his proposal of retaliation against the threat of power-seizing Christians.

'Can you not see what's happening? At all...?! Are we not in the Neoplatonic School? Your suggestion, my good Olympius, is completely sophistic and utterly fallacious, which has just rendered my argument moot because of this unnecessary redundancy. Plato described this precise situation over eight hundred years ago. What does the eighth book state? The politeuma of the politeia – a continuous breakdown of the perfect policy, thus resulting in the decay of our community's situation. You're no different than Thrasymachus. Measuring your own strength with that of Theophilus won't help you out of the trouble you're getting us all into, preaching your wisest counsel to my Father as if he were no more than a silly Glaucon to you', the Lady discoursed.

Olympius's visage could not mirror any more outrage, even if he wanted to, which is why he was prepared to put Hypatia in what he felt like was her place, though Theon prevented him from standing all the way up, regardless of his being worn out, never averting his gaze from his daughter's, allowing her to continue; it was clear that any decision the Director was bound to make had to seek its constitution in flawless philosophical advice. With respect to the students, they all felt the reverberation of an actual debate in which their very fate was being discussed, nervously looking at each other, though unwilling to dare say a word.

'What do you suggest, Hypatia?', Theon asked of her.

'Father, you know how it began... Rome was founded as a Monarchy by a king who hadn't even completed the city yet and had already murdered his own brother. There was no wisdom whatsoever in the mind of who was supposed to be the Philosopher-King with a soul of gold, overlooking his personal interests on behalf of the people's welfare. Romulus's hunt for power tainted every chance he had of being a just leader, for his idea of good became hollow the moment he confounded what was good for him and the populace, warping both the first and the latter into a unilateral state of things, thus beginning the cyclical war of king-overthrowing, because, in the end, wealth and lust will move every man in a suiting position to the most criminal ideologies – precisely what happened with Tarquinius, having provoked and promoted assassination to legitimize his rule. The aristocratic kingdom, though reliant on public consultation, was nothing but absolutist, and every time the majority becomes discontent, labored to their death to quench an incessant thirst for wealth, an uprising is inevitable; plus, should the perfect pretext rise via concrete actions, then there is nothing left to do, and that's why Lucretia's claim for justice to be done, prior to sacrificing herself as a call for help, once she tasted the abuse of Tarquinius' son, was the last straw to call on for a Republic – nearly five hundred years of it! But of course, the aristocratic premise of placing souls of gold in representative seats lost its way, diverging what is still called «The Senate and People of Rome» toward corruption and, therefore, Timocracy. Gold and silver souls matter not anymore, which will give bronze (if not iron) fists, a chance for the Plebeians to grow into Patricians, seeking to build a secluded wealth of their own in detriment of the benefits of an artful and reasoning education, allowing them to own properties and other sorts of riches; from there, the path to Plutocracy is easily laid down like road bricks, enforcing the protection of such assets with an increasing military power. The government of the wisest turns into the ruling of the wealthiest; there is no other way of making an Oligarchy this obvious – the road to enlightenment is now clouded with the incompetence of the rich man, preventing thinkers and do-gooders from bringing back the aristocratic haven we include ourselves in. The coveting of a military campaign, whichever its purpose, won't easily succeed, for the minor governing body will not so lightly give its defensive strategies away, favoring an uncontainable rebellion of the people, who you'd think would finally be free to split the spoils of the dead, exiled or both in an equal manner, and the taste for Democracy ensues, but does letting the people choose what's best for everyone without a clash of classes appeal to an imposing nature? Everyone here knows the answer to that – no, it does not, and there you have it, an Empire of both legitimate and illegitimate succession whose failure to adopt a firm hand results in assassination. So, in the end, how can the masses be controlled and taught what to think, avoiding, therefore, a hypothetically deviant plan of yet another overthrow? Put fear in them, force them to keep quiet and mind their own menial lives, if alive they indeed eager to be. An Emperor is no different from a King. It's still a Monarchy – aristocratic, timocratical, oligarchical, absolutist, militaristic, and falsely autocratic, for the official ruler is but a puppet in the hands of a theocratic entity with whom an alliance grows strong at each sunrise. The fear of excommunication from something an iron-spirited man highly believes in without ever questioning its sources will bend and break him to the will of the clergy, who will make use of his apparent authority to strike down opposing forces, admittedly stripping one faction of their powers in favor of another. Politics is but despotism and nepotism; while qualities and qualifications are still important, the weaker their presence in oneself, the stronger the remainder and its consequent distribution across relatives and friends, no matter the amount of stupidity they wear on their heads like a crown. You're as dogmatic as this, High Priest, but you're outnumbered; yield to what may seem to you a sense of honor and your actual pride will have you and many others killed, for which reason I say unto you – count me out, as I shan't take part in a bloodbath out of sheer, masculine arrogance and assertiveness based on unfounded Philosophy. Say what you will, tell me my discourse was blank and rhetorical, paradoxically filled with nothing but void; perhaps it doesn't make us that different, after all'.

A disturbing wave of silence plummeted toward the ground the moment Hypatia's voice rested after her long statement. The Lady sat back down, rested her elbows on her legs and dove her visage into the palms of her hands, hiding it in exhaustion.

Whereas Olympius's face was riddled with incredulity, his eyes unwavering of the first woman to ever defy his innate male authority (let alone that of a High Priest), Theon was set to ogle the floor, switching every now and again from the cold, lifeless marble surface to the pulsating, ardent eyes of his daughter's disciples, who found themselves back in a chronical situation in which the more they tried to breathe silently, the louder their respiratory tract wheezed. Though quiet and adopting of a shut, inaccessible posture, Orestes's mind was not at all at ease; ambition was a feature of Man that was not so easily describable, as it could either lead to greater things on behalf of everyone, preserving the freedom of those entitled to it, or viciously transform a change for the better into personal convenience, abandoning the collective to their own fate, granted they would still keep working to their death for the benefit of their unthankful governors. A scenario such as this in the minds of the elderly was promising of tempestuous times ahead, but when pictured by a young man with so much to accomplish, still learning to tell right from wrong, using a weather-related metaphor was sure to grow no further than the usual limitations of a euphemism.

Disregarding of Theon's hierarchic superiority, the servant of Serapis rose and confronted the former's daughter, bearing a wrathful tone beyond measure:

'How – dare you speak to me in such a fashion?! For far too long you've been taking advantage of your father's name and position to do however you may please, forgetting and going further beyond yourself each time! A mere child, a little girl, branding me a sophist, and in public, discrediting my reputation, both philosophical and sacred!', Olympius vociferated.

Hypatia was quick to retort, making use of her sharp mind:

'Oh!, you don't need me to throw you in discredit. You did that to yourself long ago. "How dare you?" isn't a question for me – I've never claimed divinity or a subsequent ability to commune with the gods and force unto others their will, preaching on the streets like a madman or the common soothsayer; a real philosopher asks questions and is never content with explanations pulled from under the folds of their garment or the soles of their sandals – sheer improvisations justified with what you claim is a divine conjecture, unsupported by any reasoning whatsoever', the Lady responded, simultaneously rising from her seat while confronting the old man.

Olympius turned around to seek support from Theon, but the Director kept fixating the floor; in a way, and as her father, he had always known this was what he had raised Hypatia to become – independent and able to speak her mind without the backing of any man, something the High Priest had already found unsettling when paying the Director a visit after the menstrual cloth episode. Although he chose to omit that part (as he deemed recalling it utterly unfit), Olympius moved on to pursue the fact that Hypatia's immeasurable insolence would have been contained long ago, had she been forced into wedlock:

'You believe your pedestal to be so high that you needn't pay the gods their due reverence...! It's you who'll turn out to be the downfall of the little heritage we still have in our possession, left to us by our ancestors, as if we hadn't lost enough of it over the past centuries! You should've never been allowed the freedom to strut around like a man, pretending to be one of us by wearing the pelt of a world-class academic. Had I been your father, you would've stayed home, where women belong, learning the craft of housekeeping, instead of letting you meddle with the affairs of the stronger gender! And these young souls, ever-content for "studying" under you, merely deluded by your feminine wiles while hoping to win your heart in exchange… what can they possibly "learn" from a woman who doesn't even know when to do something as simple as minding both her business and place?! Do you mean to defy the laws of both men and gods so you can take charge? A female leader, well…! That'll be the day! I warned your father… you're much too outspoken… nothing a husband wouldn't tame out of you'.

The Lady was ready to retort when, suddenly, from the tiered bench rose one of the youths attending what was no longer a debate, but rather a profoundly shameless argument, unworthy of philosophers and, in his opinion, the weak-minded, of which Olympius was the crudest of examples; the old man had mentioned them all the moment he indirectly accused Hypatia of being a courtesan, and although he knew she was capable of fending for herself, his outrage had become uncontainable and needed to be let out, for which reason Orestes thundered:

'Enough! That – is – enough! Have you completely lost your mind?! Haven't you offended enough people as it is in no more than just a moment?! Telling the Director how he failed in his difficult parenting by humiliating and belittling his daughter, our Mistress, on account of being a woman who, according to you, is only capable of keeping us here out of sheer, carnal attraction…?! There is more to Hypatia that you'll never understand, no matter how long you live – beyond her unquestionable outer beauty, there lies a brilliant mind, the product of her father's upbringing, which was already herculean enough, having no one else by his side to come to his aid, relying only on servants, and still, did they do a poor job? Did they?! This woman is capable of doing what no man has successfully done so far – she's brought us all together, never pointing out to any of us what to believe in, or… telling us whether we were right or wrong to look up to one deity or another. Hypatia is a cornerstone of this city… she's kept it from tearing itself apart ever since her father believed in her intelligence and refused to oppose her being here. No matter where we come from, how we were raised, or who we go to in a moment of desperation and need, we have our Lady to thank for showing us the light we'd have otherwise failed to see, had we listened to the likes of you or Theophilus. Coexistence is possible through Philosophy and Reason. It's the fear of damnation the clergy so passionately seeks to embed in our souls that will eventually backfire and bring you all down – Pagans, Christians, Hebrews... no matter. Every time someone in this world threatens another's position for being better skilled, it's imperative they be taken down... why? Why, I ask you? It's the amalgamation of different cultures that throw us back into the course of evolution as a civilization, allowing us all to exchange customs and traditions, thus improving our knowledge of the Universe and how it all works together in harmony. Not everything is subjected to legislation. Being Serapis's High Priest doesn't give you the right to banish Hypatia from her position. Would you like to know why she's much more popular than you ever have been? She does not instill fear into the people by threatening them with Pluto, the Duat, or even Hell. Being herself is the sole secret to her general praise from the people – no mysticism required'.

Exalted on account of his fierce statement in Hypatia's defense, Orestes sat back down, glancing at Hypatia at first, looking at his feet afterward, his forearms resting on his knees and his hands loosened. One of the Christian disciples, vividly staring at his colleague in admiration, began clapping, soon followed by others; «Pagan» and «Christian» were designations that, for that short moment at least, meant absolutely nothing, as those young men had one common cause – keeping their mistress safe from fanaticism, whichever the root. Multiple cries erupted; "hear, hear!", the lads claimed, bringing a smile to both Theon and Hypatia's faces, while casting Olympius away from the lecture hall, vexed by the reaction to his outburst, whose outcome had backfired, indeed – a premonition he had apparently failed to observe.

Just when the old man was about to leave in a fit of rage, someone else walked in from the entrance hall. It was one of Olympius' followers, whom he had instructed before to gather all available weaponry and every foot soldier physically able to fight. As the young man approached the marble platform, he bowed to both Hypatia and Theon, then immediately addressing the High Priest:

'Sir, I urge you to follow me; there's an uproar taking place in the agora as we speak'.

'What's happened?', Hypatia asked him, just as Olympius was about to utter the same query; too tired to prolong the argument, he annoyedly rolled his eyes while facing the youth and waited for his response, bearing a stern expression in the meantime.

Hesitating ever so slightly on who to face while responding, the youth dodged his gaze between the High Priest and the Lady, making the whole effort rather unsettling:

'Theophilus has rallied his Parabolani and other Christian citizens in the agora. Our people in the marketplace are surrounded and he's just threatened to cut off their feet to make them all kneel and accept Jesus as their lord and savior'.

The moment they realized their Patriarch's public behavior had become outspokenly inhuman, resourcing to bellicosity, the Christian disciples in the lecture hall felt somewhat betrayed and most definitely outraged. The bonding with their Pagan counterparts had just been reconfirmed and shaken once more, though not because of their direct action, something they hoped their colleagues would understand, for neither Theophilus nor Olympius spoke on behalf of every follower of one faith or the other.

The High Priest then turned to both Hypatia and Theon, furthering his contempt for the family after smiling on Orestes' speech:

'Am I still the like of this beastly Bishop?! Am I, girl?! Have I ever forced the old customs unto the Christian folk with a blade pointed at them?! Never! Advocating violence in the name of a Hebrew, a people he and the others despise, a people who begged a Roman prefect to have him crucified, carrying the deadweight cross of his demise on his chastised back, suffering beyond reason in the name of Mankind, a man who supposedly paid for all their sins, and this is how these animals honor him, with the Emperor surely backing them up! Have I ever told anyone we should retribute like-wise?! You mock me, but I'm done figuratively bowing to you. I've only done so these past few years out of sheer respect for Theon, but even you smirked at me after that boy insulted me with his bewitched oratory!', he ardently exclaimed, point-ing at Orestes.

'Olympius, you're beside yourself. If we stoop as low as Theophilus and engage in battle, we'll only be granting him his one wish for our complete annihilation; not only that, we'll be making it clear for everyone it's all right to kill indiscriminately in detriment of our values as a civilization, and just because others don't agree with our own view-points. We must address this issue with a reasona-ble approach. He's sure to listen if we offer him terms of endearment toward peace. I beg of you – do as I ask', the Director calmly told him, making somewhat of an effort to stand.

Having known each other for so many years, the High Priest held Theon in the uttermost esteem and was, therefore, unable to completely throw away every single shred of respect he had for the

Director of the Musaeum; it was what the youth had not yet shared with the audience that was bound to leave a craterous dent, perhaps pulling both men apart for the rest of time.

'Director, if I may...', the young soldier resumed, 'there is something else – both the Parabolani and the mob brought a great number of artifacts with them from what we think might be a tomb somewhere in the vicinity of the Serapeum, and...', he gulped, 'most of it was thrown to the ground and made in pieces'.

Feeling they were all as part of the conversation as the Director, the Lady, and the High Priest, Orestes spoke on behalf of all the disciples and asked:

'What...? A tomb? Whose is it?', and the lad replied:

'We're not sure, but... they brought the sarcophagus with them and made it the center of all the attention. It doesn't look like a regular sarcophagus, however... it's as if it'd been transparent, once, worn-down with age. It seems to be broken and crystals keep pouring from it'.

As if a spirit had returned to the earth from the Underworld, bound to haunt the living, so did Olympius's visage reflect said effect. Turning to Theon yet again, the High Priest saw both horror and grief showing in the Director's facial expression – they were now both perfectly aware of what was happening. Speaking to the audience in the lecture hall one last time, the old man looked at Hypatia's Pagan disciples and eerily uttered:

'Gentlemen… our very identity as a people is at stake. Everything our forefathers left us as heritage may very well be razed to the ground before nightfall. If you're willing to risk your lives as descendants of Hellen, now will be the time to follow me and find yourselves a blade. Did you collect as many weapons as possible, like I told you?', he asked his follower.

'Yes, sir. We're ready to strike as soon as we're given the order. Also, more men would be appreciated. The numbers don't look promising'.

Before leaving the hall on his way to the agora, accompanied by the youth, Olympius looked Hypatia in her eyes and genuinely told her:

'You may yet turn out to be the last of us, soon enough. Live long and preserve the memory of our people'.

Usually aware of what people meant every time they spoke and accustomed to explaining it better, the Lady was now clueless regarding what had sounded like the old man's last will and testament – everyone was, except for Theon, who had no choice but to clarify the meaning of his ghoulish disorientation, especially after failing to support his own weight, which made him sit back on his stool, nearly tipping it over, had it not been for three disciples who immediately ran his way to hold him as Hypatia's visage turned white from fear.

'Father!', the Lady cried, kneeling beside him while holding his pale face with both hands, asking him afterward, 'are you ill?! What's all this?! What's happening?! Please, tell me everything…!'.

The three strapping youths made sure Theon had regained his balance before letting him be, stepping back to give him and his daughter some room, and though he was physically stable (or so it seemed), his emotions appeared to be taking the best of him:

'Oh!… never had I thought it would come to this!', he exclaimed, tearing as he placed his right hand over his heart, threatening to burst through his ribcage.

All the more concerned, the Lady insisted, fearing the worst:

'What?! What is it, Father…?'.

'Alexander…', Theon whispered as his voice broke, 'Alexander…!'.

'I think he said "Alexandria"…', one of the boys beside him suggested.

'No…!', Theon replied almost inaudibly, 'not Alexandria… Alexander!'.

'Alexander?! Is that it, Alexander…?!', Hypatia asked him, which he confirmed with a slight nod of the head.

'Alexander who, sir?', someone asked from the bench.

'Well, Alexander the Great, of course! Who else do you suppose?!', the Lady acidly retorted, gazing the student with despise before turning back to her father, now holding both his face and the hand he was covering his heart with, adding worryingly, 'what about him? What about Alexander?'.

Breathing heavily and wheezing much louder than he could speak, Theon looked Hypatia in her saddened eyes, gleaming with tears, and managed to summon the little strength he had to tell her:

'His body… Theophilus has found it… he's got his body… our heritage is no more… the Church has won… all these years I've… I've fought for diversity and inclusion… the preservation of our past… gone… all gone… darkness lies ahead…'.

The ominous environment that had already befallen the agora was now spreading to the Neoplatonic School to the like of an infectious disease; unaware up until then of the events unfolding in the public square, both lecturers and disciples felt the seams of their hearts being ripped by all sorts of emotions – listlessness, sadness, helplessness, confrontation, idleness, confusion. Sharing her father's pain, Hypatia the Philosopher, regarded as one of the most rational people of the time, could not help but lay her head on Theon's lap, looking into the void as tears of grief sought to cleanse her eyes of the sordidness her spirit had just been polluted with; still holding his heart with one hand, the Director drove the other to his daughter's hair, stroking it softly in an attempt to calm her down, even though he could not help being distraught himself.

Given that in the room were only warriors of the mind, nobody considered not even for a moment going outside to witness the crumbling of the city for themselves; Alexandria was already split in half like the trembling ground during an earthquake, for which reason the disciples would not widen that gap any further, rather choosing to get up one by one and encircle both father and daughter, holding each other's hands in a protective communion far stronger than any other promoted by either faith, for they could not afford the loss of the most valuable people alive in the whole of the Roman Empire, the very symbol of what it meant to be a true descendant of Ptolemaic Egypt, instead of just another forcibly homogeneous diocese.

* * *

Outside, after having just threatened to sever the Pagan population's lower limbs to enforce his authority, Theophilus was definitely not planning on relinquishing a triumphant moment such as this; it was merely a matter of time before the whole of the Brucheion bowed to the magnificence of the Holy Trinity. As for the Jewish populace, the appropriate moment would come, considering they did not constitute an eminent menace, for they were already cornered in the Delta Quarter, against the Northeastern city wall; not just that, they were more than outnumbered.

Bearing an enraged look on their faces, the Parabolani began moving their hands toward the pommel of their swords under the subtle instruction of Peter the Reader; the blades were still sheathed in their respective scabbards, but now that the Pope's real intentions were finally on the table, there was no point in insisting on stealth.

Unless they become affected by an ailment of the mind, it is a part of a proactive living being's nature to never forfeit, under any circumstance, their survival instinct, which means that, when looking death in the eye, they will either retaliate or, soon after recognizing the only possible outcome is defeat, yield to the victors in order to avoid the likeliest consequences, such as physical torture for the sordid satisfaction of the detaining agents, eventually culminating in execution; even though Jesus Christ lived through a horror only the begotten Son of God could have endured (with the purpose of ultimately sparing men from a similar fate), that did not stop his self-proclaimed representatives in the earthly world from engaging in sickly pleasures under the pretense of soul purification. And so it was – the trapped Pagans chose not having their blood spilled all over the agora, kneeling one by one as they looked at each other, seeking support from their peers, lowering their heads once they reached the ground, but not necessarily in reverence to God; the true reason behind their bowing was grief for the loss of their culture, coerced to renounce a far more ancient identity-defining tradition which, up until then, had roamed freely across the world's capital city of knowledge.

Nearly everyone was down on one knee in the agora to the Patriarch's delight when Olympius, accompanied by the youth that had gone in the Neoplatonic School to warn him, was just walking past the latter's front door, momentarily freezing as he witnessed the revolting scene, confirming indeed it was the remains of Alexander the Pope's bodyguards were holding up high. Utterly enraged and beside himself, the High Priest told the youth following him to remain unseen and wait for his signal to move quietly and warn the others; he then stepped forward and addressed the crowd from the top of the stairs in a high volume, where he leveled with his Christian counterpart:

'What is the meaning of this?! Have you all gone mad?! On your feet! On your feet, I say! Stand up – right this instance! I will not allow you to surrender your faith in Serapis to this "Trinity" nonsense! Stand for what you truly believe in!'.

The moment Olympius began questioning the crowd with his rhetoric, everyone present in the square immediately turned their head and sought the source of the only voice to oppose Theophilus's attempt to take Alexandria for himself, as no Roman soldiers were in sight (let alone the Prefect) to break it up. It was also in this instance the trapped Pagans hoped the High Priest would somehow set them boundless, but until they saw his plan in action, it was still much too hard to start feeling safe.

As for the Patriarch, obviously rendered upset that he had been interrupted in his communion with God as he was about to turn goats into sheep for the expansion of his flock, he lowered his arms, gently set his crosier down and turned to his right, whence Olympius had come out, condescendingly addressing him:

'Well, well... look who's decided to show up – the man who claims he can talk to the urn-wearing demon', he said with a smirk on his face, figuratively stomping on Serapis's name to the delight of the surrounding Christian populace and uncontrollable laughter of the Parabolani, looking at each other under peer pression for the approval of perpetuating their demeaning chuckles.

Experiencing some difficulty hiding his rage, the High Priest was still able to innocently slid one of his hands behind his back, take advantage of the general distraction caused by Theophilus's boasting and gesticulate to the concealed youth, instructing him to leave and tell those in hiding to start closing in on the Christian mob and await his order to attack at the designated moment. Making sure no one could spot him, the young man waited for the raptors to turn their faces away, including the Patriarch, who was laughing together with his sheep, and set out to fulfill his duty; only the entrapped Pagans were paying enough attention to see him running, as they could not take their eyes off of Olympius, praying to Serapis the High Priest could rid them of the trouble they were in.

'Well, isn't it remarkable listening to you, my bearded angel friend...', Olympius cried Theophilus's way, 'it is only ever so enlightening how your jaw clicks and wags the most astounding pieces of knowledge, brought to you by none other than the god who is far too important to show himself and take physical shape. Say... now that we're at it, how would you describe this deity of yours? Do you base your own appearance on him? I ask this of you because, last I heard, being a Christian was synonymous with poverty and, judging from the looks of you, it's not just fish you crave, is it? Also, you do enjoy dressing up, am I not correct? Your lackeys, on the other hand, wear but raggedy cloaks of darkness and, I'm willing to guess, shadows and death, because there's no such thing you preach that doesn't include that glorious notion that it is to die! What of life, Bishop? Must we all be miserable and bow to this invisible "Lord" through you, spending a lifetime in fear of legitimate ambitions as are prospering or learning? Because that is what Serapis, a true god we can literally look up to, wears on his head – a modius, the very symbol of abundance! This land has only borne fruit up until today on account of divine effort distributed by an entire pantheon; who does your god claim to be to have created the entire world in six days, all by himself? And again I ask – why does he hide from men…? Is "he" afraid?', the High Priest concluded in a rather provocative tone.

It is naturally no wonder to report that the Patriarch was growing upset at each piercing argument come forth from Olympius' lips, but his willing to be merciful as God would eventually cooled down the fire in his heart, just before yielding to the urge he felt to sprinkle it with brimstone. Playing along and still bearing a smirk on his face (though somewhat warped), Theophilus took a couple of steps to his right, facing and baiting the High Priest with a lower, yet audible voice register:

'The Lord is our one, true Creator. He made us to His own image to bring order to the world on His behalf. We needn't build any fetishes of Him, for He lives inside each and every one of us. What could He possibly be afraid of?'.

He had done it – Olympius had peaked the old man's interest in his provocation. All that was left to do was to retaliate with a knocking blow to the serpent's head:

'Oh!, I don't know... just consider this: women usually require male approval throughout most of their lives, if not permanently – first, from their grandfather, who tops their father still on account of precedence, unless the power of both is combined; second, just the father; third, the husband; fourth, and if none of the above are applicable, the male entrusted with the highest authority in their family or society. Now, why do you figure only men are entitled to be a part of the clergy?'.

Everyone stared at Theophilus – the robed guards, the populace, Cyril... even the surrounded Pagans; the Pope, however, kept his eyes focused on Olympius. In fact, he took a couple more steps forward, gently hit the floor with the crosier, making little noise, and started squinting his sight, upsettingly asking:

'What is your point...?'.

'It's quite simple... that which you hunt so passionately is what you unknowingly stand for – witchcraft. Your deity's only way of obtaining general approval is but to claim to be male...', Olympius responded, dramatically pausing for a few seconds before getting to the plot twist, 'even though she is not'.

Rattled beyond belief by this festering blasphemy, both the Parabolani and the Christian mob turned the agora into an uproar, unsheathing swords and threatening to throw stones at the High Priest; the square was drowning in upheaval – not even the rioters themselves could understand each other, but there was really no need... the clashing of blades and rocks was a powerful enough language that spoke no more than a few words, of which «intimidation», «conflict», «bloodthirst», «wounding», and «killing» were rough examples. Speaking of «blood», the boiling, pulsating stream running through the Patriarch's vessels in his head turned his whole visage rubicund. He faced the agora once more, saw the duality of reactions from his enraged followers and the mocking Pagans, and cried out to the full extent of his vocal range, emphasizing the first syllable of his one-word address:

'SI-LENCE!'.

The Pagans could understand why the Patriarch would tell them to hold their tongues; his flock, on the other hand, was confused – even Peter the Reader puzzledly ogled him with one eyebrow lifted, round like an arc, whereas the other was flattened against his eye. He simply failed to understand how a statement as daring as Olympius's had not triggered the Pope's order to attack. As vexed as he too felt, Ammonius restrained himself from warping his face, a reaction which did not at all pass unnoticed to Cyril, who, regardless of his tender age, was already perfectly capable of understanding how facial expressions and other body-emanating language made one's feelings rather transparent.

Having confirmed everyone in the square was again at ease, Theophilus turned to the High Priest, pointed the top of his crosier the Pagan old man's way, and calmly said:

'I'm willing to forgive the sickly atrocity you've just spoken and even forget about it if you take it back – now'.

'And why, pray, would I do that?', Olympius asked him in a defying tone.

'Have you any idea whose body it is my men are holding down there?', the Patriarch inquired, pointing to the sarcophagus with his left arm and hand fully extended.

The High Priest's best option, now that he had been finally confronted with the presence of Alexander the Great's remains in the agora, was to deny his knowledge of the truth:

'Why would I have any idea whose body that is? And what are you doing carrying a broken sarcophagus around? What, are you a tomb defiler? Of course you are! I knew you stood for witchcraft – necromancy, to be precise. What is your plan? To raise that poor devil back to life and contaminate everyone here with whichever ailment afflicted them? It wasn't leprosy, was it?'.

Because Olympius's tone significantly changed the moment he was asked if he knew who the remains purportedly belonged to, the Pope saw fit to insist on his questioning the High Priest, just to see how long it would take him before he admitted the truth:

'Save the diversionary mumbling, heathen – it's too late for that. You know who this is, now tell your people!'.

'Tell them what?', Olympius asked as his voice went higher, 'I don't know who you had your lackeys pick up from the hypogea beyond the wall'.

The Pagans in the square were indeed growing curious regarding that meaningful a presence of a dead person among them, but they simply could not take a guess at who it might be; the fact the sarcophagus looked so unusual did not at all contribute to their learning of Alexander's rape by the Christians, though the situation would change soon enough.

'It's a glass-made casket filled with crystallized honey! How many people have you heard about who were entombed in this particular manner? Are you not an academic? You know your History, so just tell them they've no choice but to bow to me, or I will see that their treason is paid dearly!', Theophilus exclaimed as a last warning addressed to the High Priest. Hesitating and gulping, Olympius continued to refuse the acknowledgement of a lost cause. Both factions present in the agora ogled him while reflecting all sorts of emotions, ranging from confusion to impatience. He was secretly buying his followers the necessary time to assemble behind the Christian front and engage in bloodshed, whose approach he noticed from the corner of his eye as he swept the crowd visibly disturbed from the top of the stairs leading to the Neoplatonic School. After taking a deep breath, the High Priest uttered these words, denying Alexander one last time:

'It could literally be anyone – this land didn't always belong to the Ptolemies, it wasn't always Hellenic; it once prospered on its own for millennia, long before your god was engendered by the imagination of weak-minded men'.

And with that, Theophilus recovered to his original position by the feet of Serapis's representation, still meeting Olympius's gaze while breathing sonorously, after which the Bishop told the High Priest:

'Very much unlike Peter, you will not be made a saint after denying the true identity of this body thrice, the one rock, the only cornerstone who legitimized your presence here in the first place, no matter how hard you repent'.

Only the Christians seemed to understand what Theophilus had meant by a triple denial, judging from their mocking laughter, which eventually spread across the agora again like wildfire (their mood seemed to change like a burning candlewick in the wind, somehow). As for the Pagans, most of them were simply clueless as far as the whole argument was concerned, though the reference to a legitimizing cornerstone had unveiled a bit more information; still, it was hard to maintain a proactive cognitive process under the pressure of an impending blade, no matter where it was pointed at.

'So be it', Theophilus said, facing forward and opening his arms wide yet again, elevating his voice to add, 'ECCE HOMO! Behold the remains of Alexander the Great, founder of Alexandria, currently held by the Church, ruler of this city under the yoke of Theodosius Augustus by choice of the Holy Trinity! Bend now or watch your beloved relic burn! Bring forth a lamp and cover the heathen with oil, so that he may be purged from "Hephaestion's thighs" to dust!'.

The Patriarch's reference to Alexander's companion of a lifetime was obviously not an innocent one, as rumors about the Macedonian leader's sexuality persisted still long after his death. In Christianity, anything that was even remotely related to sodomy was viewed as plain abhorrent. As for the Hellenic culture, bisexuality was more of a common practice particularly in Athens; other city-states, however, did not necessarily view it as such, though it was philosophically considered that interactions of a sexual nature between men were as equally part of the living experience as was a relationship between a man and a woman, instead of the result of being cast astray from the rules and other sorts of social convention. Still, in three-hundred-ninety-one-Alexandria, under the laws promulgated by Theodosius the Great, passive homosexuality constituted a crime punishable by burning; as for the active parties, the sword was the primary death penalty. Although he had been dead for nearly seven hundred and fifteen years, Alexander's remains could still be completely destroyed, whether it was true he had maintained an intimate relationship with Hephaestion or not.

A mist of revolt and shock invaded the spirits of the surrounded Pagans, for they did not believe for a moment the founder of the city had been involved with a man who was but the closest Alexander had ever had to a brother, given his only full sibling was his sister Cleopatra, daughter of both Phillip II of Macedonia and Olympias; the remainder of his siblings (three sisters and two brothers) were the children of his father and his several concubines. Alexander often compared Hephaestion and himself to Patroclus and Achilles, respectively, for which reason both contemporary and later historians believed the two men had been lovers in fact, even though no straightforward mention is made to the nature of the relationship kept between the main character of Homer's 'Iliad' and his companion, mistakenly killed by Hector, heir to the Trojan throne. The shocking part of the Pagans' reaction to the events unfolding in the agora was the fact the remains of the legendary leader who had once set out to conquer the world, building a much larger empire than any other single man so far, were about to disappear forever, blown by the wind in a posthumous execution run by a man whose life accomplishments were a joke when compared to Alexander's.

The people still tried to run for the sarcophagus now lowered to the ground and dampened with lamp oil, but the Parabolani made sure their blades would not let them take another step forward. Atop the stairs leading up to the Neoplatonic School, Olympius was feeling powerless, seeking to prevent himself from looking beyond the square, so as not to expose the few men he had managed to gather. It was when the sarcophagus was about to be set ablaze that the youth who had discreetly left the scene raised his sword and reflected the light of the setting Sun, signaling the High Priest that everyone was in position. Taking a deep breath as a burning torch was brought to the vicinity of the remains, threatening to ignite the oil at any moment, Olympius harnessed all the strength he had left in his lungs and cried out loud while pointing his right arm in an aggressive fashion:

'CHARGE!'.

Momentarily distracted by the High Priest's yelling, the populace, the Parabolani, and Theophilus himself looked at him with the element of surprise stamped across their faces, while those standing in the outer rim of the agora were being slaughtered one by one, gasping their very last breath as they heard the Pagans behind them screaming, "ATTACK!", simultaneously having their back and torso pierced by blades whose edges were now steaming with their fresh blood.

Now that the first blow had been suffered, resulting in inevitable casualties, just like Theophilus had predicted on his way to the square, the Christians in the inner perimeters were able to react and counterattack; those equipped with stones began throwing them at the Pagan army, preferably aiming at their heads to kill them straight away or at least knock them down to crush their skulls soon afterward and splatter their brains all over the ground. Others either hit other body parts, breaking them and rendering them useless, or simply missed, not to mention those who could not even release the payload before having their hands or arms severed in full, both sides screaming in either pain or aggression.

The Parabolani, on the other hand, quickly

made use of their already drawn swords and mortally wounded the captive Pagans before moving back to the source of the impromptu bloodshed. Said villainy and utter lack of compassion only increased the Pagan rioters' will to finish Theophilus' soldiers off, speaking of whom, both him and Cyril abandoned the scene escorted by a small number of people who were told to pick the sarcophagus with Alexander's remains back up and carry it to Saint Mark's Cathedral, where it would be kept safe; the corpse's sudden disappearance would certainly hint at its destruction and permanent loss, scarring Hellenism for millennia to come. And so, the Patriarch and his nephew fled back to their stronghold, leaving their lackeys to deal with the Pagan uprising.

In a rather tragic scenario, the dominant color spattered across the agora's canvas was blood-red, gushing like a fountain from severed bodies and their respective limbs, twitching as if they were still attached to the nervous system, although, beyond a certain a point in time, it became next to impossible to figure out which trunks all those chopped heads, arms, and legs had originally belonged to.

As for both Peter the Reader and Ammonius the Parabolanus (the latter, especially), they could not be living any bigger joy than this – an abundant bloodbath to quench their feral bloodthirst. The concept of civil war somehow brought along with it somewhat of a sense of both guilt and incongruence, as one would figure fighting one's fellow countrymen was no more than a useless (if not petty) spilling of good blood; a holy war, however, meant that, regardless of whether or not people were entitled to Roman citizenship in this particular imperial diocese, there was no such thing as "fellow countrymen", for there could be no tolerance as far as claiming the veracity of different faiths other than Christianity was concerned, thus making these people enemies of the State's official religion and, subsequently, the State itself. Again, if Evagrius was not willing to enforce the law with his own soldiers, then God's warriors had no choice but to cleanse the city themselves.

We even dare say Ammonius was not ashamed of the path that had led him to the present anymore... he had always known the Lord had spared him from paying for sins he had never committed to begin with; his crossing of the desert, not unlike the Son's, was a way of letting him know his suffering on earth would one day be compensated with the joy of making sure the world was at peace and rid of chaos before departing his body to join the Creator – an event he had proudly taken part in, butchering every single heathen in his way with nothing to fear.

We know the environment in Alexandria was all the more turning into a volcano waiting to burst and do irreparable damage, but this was just beyond imaginable. A once prosperous and culturally diverse city, gifted with a Great Library no other power could match and turn into the guardian and preserver of the world's knowledge, Alexandria was now closer to being razed to the ground than ever before, and the sad part is Nature had nothing to do with it, except that of Man.

Chapter XIII
Fall Back

The Sun was already ending its journey across the celestial dome when the battle between Pagans and Christians eventually erupted and burst into flames in the agora. Nightfall was bound to engulf the city sooner or later, naturally making it difficult to keep a fight up; although moonlight could have provided some visibility, the Moon itself could not be spotted anywhere in the sky, as it had just begun a new cycle, accompanying, therefore, the Sun into its horizon hideout. Not just that, the death toll was already high enough on both sides, though the Pagan faction was clearly the one feeling overwhelmed, for it seemed that, while their numbers kept being cut, the Christians' kept increasing.

'Where are they all coming from?!', a Pagan soldier rhetorically asked out loud, swinging his sword against the attacking mob.

'I don't know, but there's a much larger swarm of these fanatics hiding in the city than I could ever imagine!', another replied.

Meanwhile, Olympius had already climbed down the stairs of the Neoplatonic School, taking every detour he could find to stay behind his improvised warriors. On his way, however, he could see dozens of people closing in on the agora, intending to either support the battling sheep or seek sheer revenge on behalf of any relatives or close friends who might have fallen.

The High Priest was clueless as to what to do next; the soldiers were trying their best to hold the line and prevent it from being breached, but said purpose was beginning to prove herculean. For a moment, Olympius considered surrendering, when a rather unexpected event unfolded – the oil that had been poured on Alexander's sarcophagus was still spilled on the ground, stepped on by both Pagans and Christians; not too far away, there lay the lit torch which would have otherwise burned the Macedonian general's remains. Jumping back and forth both aggressively and defensively while trying to avoid tripping on the severed bodies beginning to pile, the rioters ended up kicking the torch close enough to the stream of oil, thus igniting an accidental funerary pyre which spread not only to the fallen, but also the living, making no distinction on grounds of creed. The sudden light irradiating in the middle of the square, together with a completely different sort of screaming matching that of excruciating pain, caught everyone by surprise. Running around against each other trying to put their burning clothes out as their flesh was singed and their body hair lit up like multiple candle-wicks, both confusion and the foul stench of the human sacrifice in progress became dominant, especially after the pile of bodies was converted into what it seemed like a bonfire, eventually claiming other victims.

To the like of wild animals, the enclosing backup of Christians was easily startled for a while, a chance the High Priest did not allow to go to waste, confident the protective hand of Serapis, looking down to the scene of desolation embodied in his magnanimous statue, was behind this lucky turn of events, despite the taking of Pagan lives as well, tangled in the middle of the inferno just like ember.

Crying out as loud as he could, Olympius ordered the warriors to fall back and run for the Serapeum; those who failed to do so within a certain time limit would have no choice but to fend for themselves, as the gates would be slammed shut, not to be open until some sort of agreement could be worked out between both parties. The only question was figuring out who could possibly mediate the negotiations, one we should probably ask at a better time, for it was imperative that, at this precise moment, everyone fled, apart from those volunteering to delay the incoming Christians for as long as they could.

Taking a route back to the Serapeum was now riskier than ever, considering the Epsilon Quarter was probably swarming with enraged enemies, but there was really not much of a choice, for which reason they split up into several groups and ran as fast as they could. One of the groups took charge of protecting Olympius, whose age forced him to pace quickly, rather than sprint.

Most streets seemed deserted, though, having been built within a perpendicular layout, every corner was the object of suspicion. Regarding the residential buildings bordering the sandy gangways, they too appeared to be empty, for no light source could be found inside, making it harder to discern any obstacles that might lie ahead. As the squads made their way, one of them eventually became the scapegoat of the retreat when Christian citizens, hiding in the darkness of their homes, quietly approached the windowsills and began throwing stones at the group, immediately killing a handful with direct blows to the head, while others were severely injured, rendered unable to move on after having either their knees, legs or both struck, falling facedown on the ground, painfully scraping their flesh as their broken bones and other injuries took care of letting their blood gush freely inside the body, ultimately resulting in their demise. Whereas some were perverted enough to wait for the Pagans to die on their own from these severe wounds, others were much too impatient to withstand the screaming and would just rather finish them off by dropping a good-sized piece of rubble on the head or the neck, instantly snapping it. Having been warned by the soldiers the Christians had missed to beware the windows, half of each squad remained vigilant looking up, while the other kept facing forward, bearing their common destination in sight. Just a few more steps and they would soon be protected by the high walls around the Serapeum while maintaining a good enough distance from any attempts at being hit by more rocks or other harmful ammunition projected toward the entrails of the temple grounds, of which arrows are but an example.

Naturally, after the carnage endured in the agora mostly from the Parabolani, together with the surprise attacks engendered by the people, very few soldiers made it to the walls encircling the Serapeum, arriving either alone and unharmed, alone and wounded, accompanied and untouched (apart from maybe a couple of scratches), or accompanied and carrying with them just a small number of men who could barely stand, let alone walk. Behind the squad protecting Olympius, there was still another throwing blades at the citizens hiding in the buildings, some of which could not help but fall from their windows, either already dead or still drawing breath, though life would immediately leave them after being further pierced once they hit the ground, blowing their head with a great deal of force (thus splattering their brains all over), or simply snapping their spine. In turn, behind the squad in question were the soldiers who had held the line before breaking it up to run for their lives while they could. Some of them were already so very exhausted they could not go on, ending up either slashed or overrun by the stampede of Christian rioters, to the horror of those looking back from a safe distance.

It took one final push and, along with the people who had not left the Serapeum ever since the High Priest had given the order to prepare for battle, the soldiers were now protected under sanctuary, joined shortly after by Olympius and his guards. Looking at the reduced number of warriors in front of him (few of which were unharmed), the High Priest, bearing a desolated look on his face, eventually asked them:

'What...? Is there no one else...?! Is this all that's left...?'.

As much as they wanted to, none of them could provide him with a plausible answer. He then looked outside and, unable to see anyone else running away from the incoming mob, Olympius had no choice but to give the order:

'Close the gate and hold it steadfast. We've done all we could... now we're in Serapis' hands'.

Following this remark, several youths pushed the magnanimous wooden gate, shutting and barring it from the evil lurking on the other side, who repeatedly called them out as "cowards".

Back in the agora, from the entrance to the Neoplatonic School emerged Hypatia, followed by Theon and a few disciples. The Lady could not help but genuinely cry while throwing her arms around her father's neck (who, in turn, protectively took hold of her), as the great pyre of dead bodies burned toward the night sky and the stench traveled across the streets. Far away, to the South, torches could be seen moving quickly toward the Serapeum. The damning fires of hell were on their way to making short work of one of the main landmarks of Ptolemaic Egypt. The worst part, however, was neither Hypatia nor anyone else in the Neoplatonic School could do anything to prevent the impending catastrophe, inertly watching the running shadows of men projected on the building walls to the like of the manacled slaves in Plato's cave; though unaware of the intelligible world, they could at least bask in their blissful ignorance, something which, as far as these academics were concerned, was utterly impossible to reproduce in the present situation, hopelessly wishing they could break free at any point from the invisible shackles Theophilus had placed over their souls' wrists and necks and revert the calamity that had befallen their beloved Alexandria.

Chapter XIV
The Last Stand

Over the following days, both Alexandria's harmony and peaceful environment, which had already been fading away for several years, eventually reached its full depletion. The entire city was under siege by its own inhabitants, paradoxically behaving like invaders cornering and trapping their counterparts in the only place left the latter could describe as being their "safe haven", for, like we said before, more than civil, this was a holy war, greatly benefitting the Christian allegiance. Hypothetically, should the followers of Our Lord be the ones trapped at a certain point in future history, it is likely they might not enjoy a simple, theoretical vocabulary distortion, ultimately resulting in the ugliest, practical consequences.

Now, given the fact provisions in the Serapeum's storages were not meant to be distributed by a few hundreds of people all at once without regular resupplying, every single resource had to be duly rationed before the Pagans ran out much too soon and either starved, thirsted (as there was no running water), or both without coming to an understanding with the Christians camping on the outside, thus making sure no one could escape without a confrontation. There was also the question of how to dispose of their bodily excrements, for the sanitation system did not run through the temple complex. In order to avoid spending drinking water washing up the few buckets available, it was best to just sterilize them with urine as much as possible, forcing the healthy practice of personal hygiene the Greeks had been used to for centuries to stoop exponentially low; once such containers were filled, it was only a matter of mimicking the regular habit of throwing it all out the window, though, in this case, it had to be over the wall. You may have probably guessed this was one way to both provoke and push the Christian campers away from the temple's immediate vicinity, considering quite a lot of them had already been caught by surprise after unpleasant episodes of unusual «rain»; their reaction was to either retreat, wash up and come back later, or retaliate by making use of a bow and arrow, precisely the sort of volley counterattack that had already made a small number of unnecessary victims (resulting in their subsequent burning for public health reasons), which led Olympius to instruct everyone not to toy with the very people it was imperative to make peace with, something that constituted yet another problem – how could agreeing to a truce become feasible, when all diplomacy had severely gone awry up until then? The surrounding forces outside were certainly not going to stay put while the High Priest or any other negotiator majestically walked out the front gate; also, it did not seem like Theophilus would want to go to the Serapeum himself or send his treasured nephew on his behalf, and the undeniable proof was his favorite henchmen, Peter the Reader and Ammonius, were in charge of the camps both West and East of the temple grounds, making it, perhaps, the Patriarch's own small-scale version of the entire Roman Empire, just one step away from conquering the fort where a handful of stubborn people insisted on hiding out in; the difference was, instead of commanding the troops by himself like a general, he simply put a couple of pawns on the field to do the job.

To the Pagans' misfortune, what they did not know was that, in order to impress Theodosius regarding his enforcement of conversion of the Egyptian Diocese's capital city, Theophilus had already taken care of writing and sending an eloquently worded letter in Latin to the Augustus in Constantinople, aided by none other than Cyril, who had just finished Grammar school and could certainly benefit from a favorable imperial opinion of him in the future, when required.

In turn, Orestes, having stayed behind with his colleagues, Theon, and Hypatia in the Neoplatonic School on that fateful night an ugly turn of events had taken place, took it to himself to at least try to have the Emperor spare the lives of his people, even if the Serapeum, a Pagan temple which should have already been closed according to the Theodosian Decrees (not to mention pillaged and plundered), was not, probably ending up being razed.

Unwilling to abuse the correspondence service by traveling either via the cursus publicus system's fast section (the cursus velox) or slow section (the cursus clabularis) without a license from high officials, even though his petition was comprised of extreme importance and urgency, Orestes gathered it was likely best to take advantage of the summer weather and ask that his missive be sent in the care of one of his servants by sea on the first ship available to depart the Alexandrian Great Harbor toward Constantinople through the Mediterranean, the Aegean, and the Propontis (via the Hellespont). Had the youth chosen to pay for a carriage driven by a pair of oxen (forced to stop along the road in several overnight mansiones), the trapped Pagans would most likely be already dead before the letter even got to Constantinople, making it a total of approximately one thousand two hundred and sixty leugae, completed (on average) in about one month and a half. Waiting for a response (and supposing Theodosius replied immediately after receiving the letter) would take yet another month and a half, which is to say nearly three months would go to waste before this entire endeavor reached its completion stage (all sorts of delays excluded, such as the animals dying from heat and exhaustion or the partial destruction of the carriage on the road, for example) – the whole summer, no less, during which food would become much too hard to preserve and water would certainly not last without a well nearby connected to the Fluvius Novus, which was precisely the case. Being under siege was a big enough a problem as it is, let alone the fact this particular city was surrounded by the scolding desert, sending its infernal temperatures from every direction, apart from the North, which brought with it a wee bit of cooling from the sea currents. And so, in order to make haste, Orestes inked a message (with remarkable penmanship) on a piece of papyrus (as opposed to Theophilus and Cyril's preference for parchment), eloquently addressing Theodosius and his magnanimous qualities as Augustus of the East, pleading innocence on behalf of his Pagan counterparts, supporting both their actions and this begging for mercy on account of having been provoked as Greco-Roman citizens by the same people who had dug out Alexander's tomb and sarcophagus, which, as if it that was not disrespectful enough to the memory of the founder of the city, could have ended completely destroyed beyond recoverability. Perhaps it is too great a risk to claim that, behind these unquestionably honorable intentions, Orestes cared also for his own future, which, as it was customary for young aristocratic men bearing an educational background thriving in excellence, would undoubtedly sit somewhere within the world of Politics, thus laying down a well-maintained path toward some sort of government position that would make his family proud; the fact he was being tutored by Hypatia the Philosopher (despite her Pagan upbringing) was all but in his extraordinary favor, considering both her name and teaching qualities had been heard of all across the Empire.

In turn, and predicting any Pagan communications could be secretly sent to Theodosius behind his back, Theophilus took care of admitting to the finding of Alexander the Great's body, though he made no mention concerning an attempt at either burning or in any other way erasing the remains from History, claiming, rather, the Pagans had been the ones breaking into the tomb in the first place (even though the entrance to it was located in the Christian catacombs), knowing perfectly well it had lastly been sealed by Caracalla, a predecessor of Theodosius, thus constituting the burial chambers as State heritage in need of preservation, a duty the Patriarch boasted to have taken upon himself, keeping it safe in Saint Mark's Cathedral, where he could personally see to its conservation, also reassuring the Emperor his nephew, Cyril of Alexandria, would competently perform the same task once he departed this world and his successor took his seat. Now, although the Emperor did not have a direct say in the election of new patriarchs throughout the Empire, garnering his support would certainly turn out to be a road toward success, for which reason expressing his views as the current Patriarch at this time seemed quite legitimate and opportune to Theophilus.

For the time being, and unable to figure out whether the Emperor had in fact been contacted by the opposite party, neither Orestes nor Theophilus could help but continue to wait for a response to the current predicament as stated by themselves. Only after confronting both accounts would Theodosius be able to decide to the best of his judgment.

Chapter XV
Imperial Resolution

Much unlike the distance, speed, and time one would expect to travel on a journey between Alexandria and Constantinople by land, the corresponding sea connection proved a great deal faster, less complicated and undoubtedly not as risky as the former. Sailing a one-way course of approximately eight hundred and thirty leugae at an average speed of five knots only took about seven days at sea, reducing the three-month roundtrip journey by land to just a little under a couple of weeks onboard, keeping both goods and travelers safe throughout the entire endeavor; naturally, and to the like of either a horse or ox-pulled wagon, the speed rate at which ships sailed did not exclusively rely on human action, given that factors such as currents and the wind played a role of the utmost importance. Still, and considering it was mandatory for Theodosius the Great to compare the accounts of the two clashing factions of Alexandria in hopes it could all be resolved without resorting to unnecessary violence the city had been cursed with for quite a few good decades, waiting between two to three weeks for the return of an imperial decree was absolutely worthwhile – both civil cohesion and human lives were at stake, even if some regarded others as social parasites, a rather sad (if not catastrophically genocidal) way of looking down on fellow human beings. Yet another worrying issue regarding this matter is the fact there were three sides to this so-called holy war, not two; so far, the Jewish people has been kept out of the equation – it is the part they might still play in the near future that reveals itself to be problematic, though, as of this moment, there is no telling what is yet in store for them.

Despite the hot, arid weather taking Alexandrians by assault, the Christian citizens did not seem like wanting to step away from the Serapeum, keeping but a safe distance from its walls on account of the aforementioned questions of personal hygiene the Pagans had had to adapt themselves to under siege. However, and so as to avoid any further provocations and subsequent confrontations, the prisoners of their own temple thought it would be wise to just burn their excrements for as long as they could keep a fire going, though the stench never really disappeared, worsened by the scalding sunlight. Outside, the Christians obviously shared the same needs, but they could easily change their guard and take shifts while going home to relieve themselves, wash up and bring more food and water supplies – exactly the downside of remaining vigilant in a finite space barring the exiled within from the natural resources they needed to stay alive and, most of all, conscious, for neither worn-out brains nor bodies were enough to hold one on one's feet.

Because of the ongoing situation of political instability taking the city by storm, Theon, in the quality of Director, eventually decided it was best to suspend pro tempore all classes taught at the Musaeum, something the institution's academics agreed with, choosing to stay home and keep out of any extra trouble. As far as his daughter is concerned, convincing her proved rather herculean, for Hypatia's strong spiritedness kept telling her there was nothing to feel guilty about; her conscience was clear regarding her political spectrum and ambitions – there were simply none. In fact, her being a philosopher did not mean she merely took interest in a theoretical way of describing the world Humankind lived in and where everything else emanated from. On the contrary, she was a great deal more of an astronomer and a mathematician whose purpose was preserving and perpetuating knowledge, that much has been proven, which is why she could not find any reason whatsoever not to carry on with her instructional duties. Regardless of her affection and respect for Theon, this was a resolution she was willing to defy and debate until her father ran out of arguments to refute her cause. In the end, and only after an immeasurable amount of persuasion from her own disciples did she give the idea up; it naturally did not make any sense keeping the Neoplatonic School open if no one intended to show, but it had nothing to do with the disciples (either Pagan or Christian) not wanting to be seen near her, far from it. The real reason behind their backing down was related to a genuine concern they all shared for the Lady; being educated young men allowed them to see beyond the pointless quarreling people like Theophilus enjoyed instigating – the issue lay in the hands of those who aimed at nothing but their own greed for power. Fearing Hypatia could get seriously injured for wandering the streets on the way to the Neoplatonic School and back, her disciples were more than willing to pause their studies and prioritize the Lady's safety, asking her to remain home with Theon. Orestes, who did not want anyone to learn of his backdoor moves, was the one disciple insisting a great deal more that Hypatia accept this general decision; if rumors began spreading about how important Hypatia was to those young men, she would surely become an inevitable target in need of being taken down. Theon was growing old and tired; no one could predict when his soul would leave his earthly vessel to rejoin the One. His only heiress was his daughter and, having made it clear she had no intention of wedding anyone, choosing to remain engaged to Philosophy for as long as she lived, the line would necessarily die with her. Still, whether it was sheer stubbornness or not, the Lady offered a counterproposal and suggested resuming her lessons at home, somewhat of an approach to tutoring, instead of attending school per se; she had both the necessary instruments and the room for her disciples to join her and her father. And so, because she had met them halfway, they all concurred with the new setting, including Theon, who was more than happy to welcome the youths to his abode and participate in whichever topics Hypatia chose to lecture about. The peristylium balcony, the exact place where years before the Lady had gone during bedtime to look at the stars, could work as the perfect venue to engage in some astronomical observations at nightfall.

In a way, one might think Hypatia was being somewhat insensitive regarding the ordeal taking place at the Serapeum, but we dare say that is not the case – at all; on the contrary, this was her way of coping with a too sad a moment to stay still and do nothing. She was continuing the Grecian legacy, something that, in the end, Olympius hoped she could maintain, should the worst befall the Pagan cultural heritage; right now, it did not seem anything could have been worse than an angry mob encircling the last standing building of the Great Library.

* * *

A few more days of impatience went by before news finally reached the Great Harbor of Alexandria. Ever since he had sent one of his servants with his missive addressed to Theodosius in Constantinople, Orestes would try to discreetly walk by, in search for the slave he had entrusted the important mission to, but the youth could never find him. Sometime later (maybe three to four days, he could not be precise about it), the aristocratic young man began to notice someone else was constantly present at the harbor around the same time of day, also looking for updates concerning a certain arrival. Of course, because he had to keep his distance, Orestes never gathered who or what the ominous-looking man was waiting for and whence, but the aggressive visage he often displayed, together with his black garments (featuring a hood covering his head), were enough to arouse suspicion in Orestes's heart. The man was unquestionably a Parabolanus, a fact which ended up confirming Orestes' thoughts – the Patriarch had definitely been on the move, just like him. He only hoped he had not sent the letter too late, prompting Theodosius to only read Theophilus's account of the latest events and decide in his favor, giving the Christian zealots the right to punish the "revolting" Pagans.

As the Sun kept revolving around the Earth, all the more resources at the Serapeum kept depleting, bringing death closer to the exiled (some of them even looked undead already).

Olympius had run out of ideas long before. Had he dared show his head from the top of the wall, it would probably not take too long to have it pierced by an arrow or a spear, depending on the perpetrator's strength and marksmanship. All communications were simply broken down; the only thing left to do to keep everyone's morale up and somehow relay reports on the situation to the outside was to turn to Serapis (he who had the whole of Alexandria in sight) and pray for deliverance.

It was back at the harbor, at an unexpected time of day, when neither Orestes nor the hooded Parabolanus were looking for any arrival in particular, that a small ship bearing a vertical insignia on its stem (a vexillum, commonly known as the labarum of Theodosius, based on that of Constantine the Great, the first emperor to use it as a personal mark, with the first two Greek letters of the word «Christ» combined into a Christogram) was coming in to unload a small squad guarding someone who appeared to be an imperial official. His orders were to head to the Prefect's palace immediately upon arrival, so as to let the governor know about the decision and procedures to adopt regarding the "Serapeum issue".

Little did Evagrius realize that, along with these directives, a formal admonishment was attached to the Emperor's decree; to put it quite simply, it was a strongly-worded letter asking the Prefect the reason why he, as the Roman Empire's highest official and representative in the Diocese of Egypt, had not sent a formal report of his own (which was no more than his duty), forcing the Emperor into making a decision concerning a serious crisis of civil instability based on two entirely opposite accounts, contradicting each other on almost every single aspect, except for the events both Pagans and Christians were agreed upon, though the way they claimed they had been triggered differed substantially. Ultimately, and because Evagrius had (though indirectly) «forced» Theodosius to make haste as far as this matter was concerned, so did the Emperor forcibly summon the

Prefect to Constantinople, relieving him of his command as soon as a new governor for the Diocese was chosen, something Theodosius was unable to do until he was assured by his envoy that order had been restored in Alexandria by the now Acting (de jure) Roman official, and not a Patriarch or a High Priest, regardless of whose side the Emperor took.

Evagrius, of course, after having broken the imperial seal and read both the decree and his own punishment, gulped quite audibly, but not necessarily because he was being terminated – in fact, he was relieved about it. He had never accepted the position so lightly to begin with, as he was aware, based on the accounts of his predecessors (mostly Eusebius), the peaceful center of knowledge of the Western World had become everything but quiet, which made the task herculean just thinking about it. However, and because he was likely to never accomplish another achievement of the sort again, Evagrius eventually accepted, fearing, nevertheless, he would suffer the same fate as the former Prefect of Judaea, the very man the Roman State, now fully converted to Christianity, had no issue condemning to the fires of hell for siding with the Jews in both the torture and murder of Our Lord, who "was crucified under Pontius Pilate". The only difference was, to the best of the contemporary historians' knowledge, Pilate had never been subjected to the hearing Tiberius, then Augustus of the newly-formed Roman Empire, was to preside in order to take satisfaction from the governor, as he was already dead by the time he arrived in Rome, replaced by the sordid Caligula; Pilate's death (about six years after the Crucifixion of "Jesus of Nazareth, King of the Jews" and three after the Revolt of the Samaritans) is, therefore, a mystery, though evidence of his actual cause of death has been tampered with for nearly four centuries, now, ranging from suicide all the way to martyrdom. Whichever fate awaited him, Evagrius was certainly unwilling to face his deliberate death, rather wishing he would depart this world when his time came and God had no other plans for him.

Seeking to pace his anxiety, the Prefect finished reading both documents, nodded toward the imperial envoy in silence and left the palace on his horse, both accompanied by the messenger and escorted by their respective personal guards, riding out through the streets as they headed for the Serapeum.

The closer the two men got to the Pagan temple, the worst the stench became, nauseating them like never before in their entire lives. The incineration of human bodies, feces, the heat urine was exposed to, along with dozens of people on the outside who simply did not care for bathing or going back home, just relieving themselves wherever they pleased, made the air foul and poisonous. No matter how hard both them and their military personnel tried covering their noses with their neckerchiefs (either the focalia that prevented their armor from hurting their neck or the sudaria used to wipe their sweat), the odor was much too intrusive for the brain to ignore; the only option was to inhale through their mouths, even though they considered it to be a free pass for some infectious disease that would eventually drive them to their deathbeds.

Despite their incoming presence, no one really paid attention to them, either because the Parabolani and other members of the Christian mob were distracted or because they felt like deliberately ignoring the Prefect, refusing to acknowledge his authority over Theophilus's, continuing to block, therefore, the path leading up to the main gate.

For a while, Evagrius looked like he was not planning on ordering the campers to move aside, rather preferring to assess the situation from afar, much to the imperial envoy's incredulity; it really seemed to him the governor had a severe lack of backbone, for which reason he decided to make himself heard, bringing Roman authority back to a land of petty hoodlums:

'Hear ye, hear ye! Make way for the Prefect of the Roman Diocese of Egypt, legal representative of the Emperor, now!', he authoritatively cried.

The command, while still ignored by most Christians, who merely looked at each other, then back at the soldiers, then at the ground yet again, had been heard by a vigilant atop the walls of the Serapeum:

'The Prefect! The Prefect's here! Go inside and call for the High Priest! Get everyone out here, quickly!', the man told a few youths, who immediately climbed the stairs of the temple and began warning the elderly, including Olympius himself.

Meanwhile, and just before resorting to a slightly more intimidating means, the imperial envoy took a firm hold of his horse's reins and cried yet again as he made the beast stand on his posterior legs, making it look like he was prepared to stomp any resistance, if necessary:

'Move aside, scum! Make way for the Prefect, I said, or I'll have your heads right here and now stuck on a pole for the vultures to pick!'.

Peter the Lector, who had been watching ever since the military committee arrived not a while ago, walked over to the messenger and asked, simultaneously making fun of him in his face:

'Who are you supposed to be, exactly? No, wait, don't tell me... you are... the spine Evagrius never had, aren't you? You've finally decided to show up! That is remarkable!'.

Bearing a stern look on his face without ever blinking not even once, the envoy, used to the kind of discipline and respect for authority made constant over at Constantinople and the battlefield in general, immediately went for his sword and unsheathed it at a rather impressive speed, placing the edge of the blade next to the reader's neck, spelling out almost every word he uttered as he lowered his upper torso to make himself clear. In turn and feeling provoked, the zealots prepared to stand and defy the Roman committee, something that eventually impressed the emissary (whose guards unsheathed their blades as well), but not in a favorable way:

'I gather you're the one who's deluded enough to think you're in charge... well, let me tell you this: no one claims authority on Roman soil apart from the Augusti and the representatives Their Graces choose to enforce the Law. Now, should you or your "little army" even dare stand against us or any other Roman soldier, I will have you beheaded, gutted, speared, shot, and burned – not necessarily in that order. Do I make myself clear?', he asked Peter.

Enraged and trying his utmost to restrain himself from doing something stupid, the lector slowly turned his head to the crowd and parroted the Roman's words out loud as the latter's blade slid softly on his neck:

'Stand down and make way for the Prefect! Make way, now! No sudden moves...!'.

Carefully observing the mob's movements without flinching, the imperial envoy was at last satisfied to see the civilians comply, turning to Peter one last time as soon as everyone moved and cleared the path to the gate to tell him:

'Good… very good. It seems like the people actually do respect you, and that's fine, it really is… but as long as there are Roman officials nearby, they are the real authorities, not you, not anyone else. You're here to raze this Pagan temple to the ground? Well, had you chosen to strike me, the Prefect, or any one of our men down, the entire city would burn up in flames, not just one temple – plus, you'd be in the middle of the inferno. Think about it next time you feel like challenging the Roman Army'.

And having said that, the Roman recovered and pulled his sword away from the lector's throat, but not without leaving a mark that soon began to bleed, which almost made Peter bite himself from the stinging and consequently drove his hand to the flesh wound; feeling his blood leaking and gushing strongly to coagulate the cut as soon as possible, he took a look at the palm of his hand and saw the red fluid of life tainting it. He could only but look at the envoy with fire in his eyes as he also gnarled. The Roman grabbed a cloth, wiped his sword and put it back in the scabbard, simultaneously looking at the small damage he had done, saying:

'Don't worry about it – it's just a scratch. Think of it as a token of my appreciation for your civilized behavior', he mockingly concluded.

As a precaution, the guards had their swords and spears at the ready, just in case Peter or anyone else attempted on their lives after this short, humbling episode.

Far ahead, standing on top of the front wall, the exiled Pagans observed the scene rather amused as the committee began to approach without rush; one of them even said:

'Will you look at that… Roman soldiers finally standing up for themselves and putting this scum in their rightful place. I just hope they'll keep it up from now on!'.

The High Priest, however, felt far from excited, ending the youth's hopes right on the spot:

'Don't be so hasty, lad. The Emperor is Christian, the Empire is officially Christian… therefore, the Law is on their side. Not only that, the bishop had a chance to let Theodosius know what happened the way he wanted the Emperor to know. We, in turn, had no say in this. Our death warrant is now literally closing in on us as we speak', he sadly argued, unaware Orestes could have just made the difference. Still, as far as the young man was concerned, Olympius had made a good (yet discouraging) point – even if the Pagans had had a chance to tell Theodosius their side of the story, it was likely he would not have even considered reading it; after all, Theophilus was not called the «Patriarch of Alexandria» simply because of a formality… the Prefect was the Emperor's representative, whereas the Pope was God's, and given Theodosius was the Augustus by the will of God, there was really not much that could be done to refute the ugly truth. The imperial envoy's attitude toward Peter the Reader might have been entertaining, but under the present circumstances, namely chaos and the Prefect's lack of self-respect (or sheer cowardice, to some), the emissary probably felt it was appropriate to mark his territory; the Emperor was waiting for the man to report to him, so, in the end, what was the chance someone would tell on him? And if they did, whose account would tip the scale regarding being favored – the emissary's or someone completely unknown to Theodosius? Looking back, one could probably ask oneself the same question about Orestes's version of the facts; after all, aristocracy was a numerous class, whereas the Emperor was but one person, which means he did not know all of the aristocrats in the entire Roman Empire, turning Orestes into no more than a young man with a common Greek name who could either be an aristocrat or a common plebeian, for all Theodosius knew.

It is that precise mystery regarding the young disciple's attempt of success Evagrius was prepared to publicly disclose after unrolling the scroll of parchment and discreetly thanking the emissary for his performance. Looking to sound confident, the Prefect harnessed all the vocal strength he had available and proclaimed, as both Theophilus and Cyril arrived at the scene on a chariot, tipped off by a devoted Christian who had run to Saint Mark's Cathedral at the sight of Evagrius:

'Hear ye, hear ye! Gather round so that you may hear, one and all, the decree of our Emperor: "I, Flavius Theodosius Augustus, Emperor of the East, hereby declare, after having been made aware of the events that have recently unfolded in Alexandria, capital city of the Diocese of Egypt of the Roman Empire, by both Pagan and Christian parties, that the insurgents exiled in their temple are to be spared and, therefore, released unharmed from their captivity at once. However, and as a token of appreciation for my being merciful to the rebels, they are to abandon the Serapeum and the Great Library, for Theophilus, Patriarch of Alexandria, now personally entrusted by me with the necessary authority, shall dispose, in the name of the Father, the Son, and the Holy Spirit, of the entire complex as he pleases". That is the Emperor's verdict. Now that you've heard it, concede and obey. My men will lead you out through the back', Evagrius concluded, momentarily halting the conflict.

Theodosius's two-part decree, simultaneously subdivided into an indult and a sentence, was crucial for both the holding of accountability and the definition of a new era, which is to say that, while Orestes had successfully proven to the Emperor (or convinced him of, to say the least) his fellow Pagans' innocence, on the other hand, disturbing the remains and, therefore, memory of the legendary founder of the city, whose tomb was property of the Roman State, Christian in its faith, had been enough to grant Theophilus, the man supposedly abiding by the law as Patriarch, the freedom to enforce, precisely, the Theodosian decree declaring the mandatory sealing (if not total destruction) of Pagan temples – the final blow the heathens were to endure before the Pope could proclaim absolute victory of the Holy Trinity (through him) over the demonic tide flooding Alexandria with evil and sin.

Now, throughout the first part, everybody's expectations were extraordinarily high, peaking toward an outburst of cheering from the Pagans the moment Evagrius read the Emperor's pardon, which, in turn, immeasurably rattled the Christians, forbidden from pushing their purge any further. Once the second part was parroted, beginning with that mischievous conjunctive adverb, then they all quieted down again; the cheering switched sides and was the first to leave the Serapeum, taking over the mob and the Parabolani, who craved their entering the heathen sanctuary as quickly as possible, effectively erasing Paganism from the city's history.

Taking advantage of his reinforced authority, the Prefect of Alexandria dispatched his troops accordingly to make sure the "insurgents", as the Emperor had labeled them, came to no harm, setting a safety perimeter at the back of the complex.

As the exiled began making their way out, climbing down the walls and stepping away from the main gate, Olympius, the very leader of the counterattack that had led them all there, appeared to have frozen in place; he simply refused to climb back down, ogling from above a triumphant Theophilus, who, in turn, looked back at him, accompanied by Cyril on horseback in his vicious smirking. Noticing the High Priest was not moving, one of the youths went back and asked him:

'Sir? Aren't you coming?'.

'No...', he said, 'our bodies may have been spared, but not our souls. Having the Serapeum demolished at the hands of these animals is as maleficent as destroying Serapis himself, and... without him here to protect us, sooner or later we will all have perished, regardless of how long our earthly vessels may yet endure the vicissitudes of the world. Go', Olympius told the boy, looking him in the eye as he put his hand on his shoulder, adding, 'go and save yourself while there's still time... mine is already up', he concluded.

The young man's gaze was focused back on the High Priest's; a couple of tears gushed from the corner of his eyes, streaming over his cheeks. He nodded once to signal his understanding, took a couple of steps back, then turned around and followed the others inside the complex as they prepared to leave. When Olympius looked back down to the entrance, both Theophilus and Cyril had already strutted away, remaining afar as the Patriarch allowed his nephew to enthusiastically give the order:

'Brethren, listen to me now! You've heard the Prefect – our Emperor gives us permission to dispose of this sacrilegious place as we may well please! Thus spake Theodosius Augustus, whose words, whispered unto his ear by Our Lord, are divine law on earth, so let us not deprive Him any longer of our tribute to Him! His will be done – bring it down!'.

The Christian campers, now standing on their feet, reached for the sky wielding their blades as the Sun gave them a good shining, screaming victory in ecstasy. Waiting for more men to bring back thick pieces of lumber from the catacombs nearby, the group that remained began throwing themselves against the gate, trying to pierce through the strong wood with their swords, thus facilitating the others' task of throwing a good-sized log through it.

Watching from above, Olympius found himself in the deepest anguish as the ornamented gate was being slashed splinter by splinter with the purpose of weakening its integral structure right at its core, eventually breaking its tension. Shortly after, the High Priest could see a battering-ram making its way through the crowd from the catacombs just a hundred pedes away – it was almost time.

The old man finally decided to climb down and wait for his death in the middle of the courtyard; he could almost feel the log coming at him with extraordinary momentum. The cheering on the outside, apparently split into two halves, led Olympius to believe the besiegers had stepped aside to allow the those carrying the ram to run freely and break down the gate, along with the fact no one was striking the large, wooden door anymore. He gulped and closed his eyes, his fingers intertwined, trembling. After what it seemed like an eternity, the gate suffered its first blow, making the High Priest jump in fear. He did not know anymore whether it was best to keep his eyes shut or just face the music. A second blow came without warning, forcing him to flinch and blink strongly due to the loudness of the impact. The gate was beginning to yield, its hinges pulled out of both sides of the wall. The timber block was practically the only obstacle left to break and overcome; the Serapeum had not exactly been conceived to withstand a siege, so the fortifications it possessed were really nothing special, let alone of a military nature. After a while, encouraged by the men positioned at either flank, the bearers of the battering-ram struck the gate yet again, their screaming made louder at each running step they took forward. Part of the hinges were knocked out of the wall for good, the timber block cracked. It would probably take one more ram to pry the gate open. Olympius turned around, looked back at the statue of Serapis and prayed hard for the god's forgiveness, for he, the High Priest, had failed to defend the deity's home, where Ptolemaic Egypt had eventually sprouted nearly seven centuries before. Again, without warning, the battering-ram splintered through the gate and the timber block, cracking it in two. Because of the momentum applied by the running zealots, the latter only came to a stop when they hit the temple stairs, piercing through Olympius's flesh like the fangs of a lion, slashing him in two. His blood was spattered all over the courtyard, his innards projected with massive force, visibly steaming due to his body temperature. The last look on his face what that of horror, horrifying, in turn, anyone who looked back at him, his eyes slowly invaded by darkness within. The ultimate guardian of the temple was down.

Having relayed his orders to the lector, Pope

Theophilus rode with Cyril via Aspendia Avenue back to Saint Mark's Cathedral, located near the agora, where Hypatia had come out to watch from afar. Despite the distance, the scene was perfectly visible, and her good eyesight also helped. There she stood, the last of the Hellenes after her father, right in the center, between the Lighthouse and the Serapeum, also the last two remaining structures of a city which had known prosperity ever since its foundation, now crumbling apart at each day that went by. Theophilus was making sure it stayed that way, ordering Peter to take care of bringing all idols down, once he was done with the entire structure of the temple, leaving no stone unturned.

The Lady looked serene, but... on the inside, only she knows the damage she was presently taking, her mind, her spirit, her all corroded entirely toward irreparability, unable to utter any words to express the ongoing tragedy, not just the city's, but her heart's. Her chin fell on her chest – she was stepping on burnt blood and ashes, all human. Suddenly, her legs gave in, as they could not support the weight of the upper half of her body anymore. There she sat and stayed, covered in the dusty remains of what had once been people. Anyone recording that moment for posterity could have easily said that Hypatia was the phoenix responsible for the respawning of the Grecian heritage, reborn from the ashes of her own people, unprepared to go down – no, not that easily, not as long as her body drew breath.

Chapter XVI
The Fragmentation Consolidation

Over the course of nearly twenty-five years after the complete destruction of the Serapeum under Theophilus' orders, the city of Alexandria never again recovered from its political crisis. Every last remnant of Greco-Roman Paganism was wiped out along with its Egyptian crossovers, apart from the Neoplatonic School, the only building of the nature left untouched by the Patriarch, and all because of the strong influence a young man who was approximately Hypatia's age had exerted over the old Pope. This youth was none other than Synesius, born into a wealthy family who lived in the vicinity of Cyrene, located about three hundred and fifty leugae West of the capital of the Diocese of Egypt, also in the North African seaboard.

Around the age of twenty, Synesius departed his hometown accompanied by his brother, heading for Alexandria in order to study under Hypatia, who he befriended and cared for deeply, having made her his confidant for the rest of his life. For years they exchanged letters on Neoplatonist Philosophy and other subjects, perhaps the most important of which was Astronomy, as he sought instructions from the Lady on how to construct an astrolabe – an instrument conceived for both measurements of the celestial dome (which was itself reproduced on the face of the device) and star-assisted navigation. Now, while Hypatia was not its original inventor (but rather Apollonius of Perga), it is true the daughter of Theon highly contributed to the device's perfection.

Throughout most of his forty-year lifespan, Synesius had always identified himself as Pagan, though he eventually yielded to Christianity during the final stage of his life (beginning in four hundred ten), consecrated Bishop of Ptolemais by Theophilus himself at Alexandria, soon after his popular appointment. It took him a great deal of internal conflict and debate before taking up the position, showing resistance mostly on the grounds of doctrinal ideology. Staying married to his wife of seven years was imperative if he was to accept his new duties as a man of the Church, something he was eventually allowed. His tenure as bishop, however, was most likely the worst part of his life, for the loss of his entire family (his wife and three sons) quickly depleted his own health to the extent of being bedridden, whence he bade Hypatia goodbye through means of a letter, passing away in four hundred thirteen.

It became quite clear his utmost successes, apart from wedding the woman he loved and building a family in Alexandria (whither he returned shortly before permanently moving back to Cyrene), were the obtaining of tax remissions from Aurelian, the Prefect of Constantinople, where he had been sent to with that exact purpose after being appointed imperial envoy by the citizens of his hometown. While in the capital of the Eastern Roman Empire, Synesius dedicated himself to Poetry, composing an allegory whose main characters were based on the Prefect, doer of good, and one of the Augustus' ministers, Gainas, a Gothic leader who, to the like of his peers, heavily manipulated Arcadius (and, therefore, practiced evil), the eldest son of Theodosius the Great, the last to rule as sole Emperor before the Roman State definitely split into two in three hundred ninety-five, the year of his death. Synesius was also offered a grant and exempted of obligations as a civil curio, a leading citizen (of Cyrene, in this case), quickly losing his wealth, though Aurelian compensated him once he returned to power. He also proved himself a competent military strategist by repelling frequent attacks from Cyrene's neighboring tribes.

And so, in short, it was because of his appreciation by high officials in general from both the government and the Church that Synesius had always been able to keep Hypatia safe, preserving her outstanding reputation as both a pedagogue and a supreme moral authority in Alexandria.

However, and because there was not much more to do concerning Paganism in the city, the Patriarch's bloodthirst had to be quenched some other way, mostly via the elimination of opposition within the Church itself, regardless of him having supported his rivals for years. Theophilus's turncoat attitude toward the followers of Origen (a Christian scholar from the second and third centuries) came to life after his pastoral address of three hundred ninety-nine proved a complete disaster with Alexandria's Christian majority, mostly made up of monks who believed the exact opposite of what Origen had stood up for regarding his theological views – an incorporeal Father; the monks, on the other hand, believed God to be anthropomorphic, which is to say bearer of human features.

Indeed, Origen characterized the Father in quite a platonic fashion, branding him the creator of all things (the one true essence), though his power had limitations, a factor which prevented him from revealing himself to the world, thus requiring mediation from humans, who could easily attain both creative and rational thought via the Logos (through which the Lord had revealed himself to Humankind), eventually leading them to their communion with the Father, together with their continued resemblance to Jesus Christ, nevertheless holding on to their own individuality and free will.

As far as salvation and the concept of Holy Trinity were concerned, Origen played a role of great importance in the understanding of said matters, though his somewhat extreme points of view eventually earned him his excommunication as a heretic long after his death, for the generally accepted (if not enforced, on account of the reformation of the Nicene Creed, produced during the First Council of Constantinople, in the year three hundred eighty-one) correlation between the Father, the Son, and the Holy Spirit was completely different in the eyes of Origen – he rejected the hypostasis (or underlying reality) in which the Father and the Son were consubstantial; as far as he saw it, that was the true heresy of the subject, which he dodged by claiming a Subordinationist approach regarding the Trinity: the Father, as Godhead, was both superior and invisible to the Son, just as the latter was to the Holy Spirit, inclusively suggesting a relation between the three based on precedence, though he did realize the necessity of the Holy Spirit's inflation when speaking of God. In fact, and despite this connection now regarded as heretical between the entities of the Trinity, all three were necessary to achieve salvation.

This was, quite bluntly put, the basis of Theophilus's pastoral missive in three hundred ninety-nine, the same that ended up enraging the monks living in Alexandria, who threatened to riot against the Patriarch. His only way out, thus preventing a catastrophic conflict, was to persecute all Origenism out of not only the capital city, but also the Diocese of Egypt in its entirety. In order to obtain the necessary legal authority to undertake this enterprise, Theophilus summoned a council the following year, in four hundred, in which he called upon Pope Anastasius I of Rome (whose term lasted just a little over two years) to officially acknowledge both the writings of and Origen himself as heretical. The Patriarch of Alexandria was now free to persecute those preaching the teachings of the ancient scholar, the Nitrian Monks (whom Ammonius had been a member of, if you will recall – perhaps delivered from their clenches by God, as he had always thought, having foreseen these events as an omniscient Lord), expelling their leaders, The Four Tall Brothers, from the city and their followers from the monasteries located across the desert, in four hundred and three. Any monk who showed resistance was killed, placing the total number of purges close to ten thousand, thus putting an end to one of the events the First Origenist Crisis was primarily comprised of.

Once they fled Alexandria the same year, The Four Tall Brothers sought sanctuary from John Chrysostom, Archbishop of Constantinople – yet another target whose downfall Theophilus deeply craved, disregarding the means to his end, an event which was bound to soon take place.

Still during the year four hundred and three, the Bishop of Alexandria, accompanied by both Cyril, now aged twenty-seven and a master of Theology (having completed his studies the previous year), and twenty-nine suffragan bishops subordinate to Theophilus, traveled to Constantinople to retaliate John Chrysostom's persecution accusations on behalf of the surviving Nitrian Monks, which had led to the summoning of Theophilus by Arcadius to Constantinople one year before in order to be disciplined in a synod presided by none other than the newly-appointed Archbishop of the capital city of the East. However, because of the weakmindedness of the Emperor, his consort, Aelia Eudoxia, easily persuaded the Augustus into leaving the Patriarch of Alexandria alone, having him oppose Chrysostom instead (mainly because of his public lecturing on extravagance regarding feminine attire, accusations she took personally), which, in turn, led to the turning of tables, as Theophilus presided over the Synod of the Oak, whose purpose was the very deposal of Chrysostom.

The Patriarch of Alexandria made sure his accusations against the Archbishop of Constantinople, even though unfounded, were based on Origenist sympathies, given the fact he had offered The Four Tall Brothers shelter. However, when Chrysostom realized Theophilus, who had been ordered to travel alone, had brought with him a massive envoy, not to mention he had bribed a few more of his enemies with riches and all sorts of gifts during his stay at an imperial palace, where he had held multiple conferences, the Archbishop refused to recognize the authority of neither of those men – especially the prosecutor, Severian, Bishop of Gabala, whom Chrysostom had previously banished from Constantinople.

Only after the third calling was the Archbishop deposed under the Emperor's consent. Willing to avoid unnecessary violence, Chrysostom eventually surrendered himself and prepared to depart into exile, but the populace was not planning on easing the procedure, inclusively threatening to set the imperial home ablaze. Not just that, Aelia Eudoxia, with child at the time, suffered a miscarriage. Reading this entire conjecture as a sign of God's wrath, the Empress Consort pleaded with her husband to have the Archbishop reinstated.

Amid the sudden change of events, Chrysostom hesitated to return, but the people convinced him to stay by welcoming him back with great joy. With the tables turning once more, Theophilus and his party were the ones who had to run away for their lives, immediately returning to Alexandria.

The Archbishop's tenure, however, did not last long, for a silver statue of Aelia Eudoxia was erected close to his cathedral, leading him to label said demonstration a product of Paganism. This time, the fear of God had not been enough to prevent the Empress from finally having him kicked out of the city, sending him to his exile in Cucusus, about four hundred and thirty leugae to the Southeast. During his three-year stay there, he pleaded with ecclesiastic authorities (namely Pope Innocent I of Rome, Venerius, Bishop of Mediolanum, and Chromatius, Bishop of Aquileia) to intercede on his behalf, though the enterprise bore no fruit. In fact, other letters he sent directly to Constantinople, where his influence was still strong, were the reason why he was sentenced to further exile in Pitiunt, North-Northeast of Cucusus, comprising a total distance by land of about five hundred and twenty leugae. It was on his way there, at Comana Pontica, after moving but less than a third of the entire journey, that John Chrysostom succumbed, his last words allegedly being, "Glory be to God for all things".

In the year of Our Lord four hundred twelve, Theophilus, the twenty-third Patriarch of Alexandria, died unexpectedly after nearly three decades of papacy. Despite his old age, none of his closest followers (not even his obvious successor, Cyril) could have guessed God would have set his transition from the earthly realm to the heavens ever so smoothly, without any warning at all, which is probably why, even though his nephew was bound to succeed him as Patriarch, personally trained by him most of his life, the old man had not yet publicly announced his decision, as his health seemed to be just fine.

Now, while some may think a reign of terror had finally come to an end (a rather tardy one, come to that), allowing an opportunity for serious change in the city founded by Alexander, the truth of the matter is that same legacy would only be further perpetuated under the twenty-fourth Patriarch, Cyril of Alexandria, who had had to wait but three days after his uncle's death before being appointed as Theophilus's rightful, legitimate successor. Through the course of this three-day period, however, a small clash took place between him and a local archdeacon, Timotheus, who was himself a contender to the position, having garnered a great deal of support, especially from the local government, headed by none other than Orestes, the same young man who had pleaded to Theodosius the

Great for the lives of his fellow Pagans, the disciple of Hypatia, friends with Synesius, who, in turn, had no sympathy whatsoever for Cyril, branding him inexperienced, if not much too violent in the following months before his death, therefore requesting via one of the many letters he wrote Hypatia that the Lady, as a Neoplatonist philosopher, interceded on behalf of the citizens for the greater good of Alexandrian society, eventually convincing her to become a faithful political advisor to her former pupil, now exercising his duties as Prefect, the highest Roman official in all of the Diocese of Egypt.

Orestes' support of Timotheus unavoidably played a critical role in his relationship with Cyril for the next three years, as both men kept clashing to a devastating extent, made transparent across the whole of Alexandria. The moment he was appointed Pope, Theophilus's nephew, taking after his uncle's teachings and example, severely punished Timothy and his followers, engaging in other ruthless activities with complete disregard for the Prefect's authority, putting an end, for instance, to the Novationist doctrine adopted by Dionysius I, the fourteenth Patriarch of Alexandria, which comprised benevolence regarding the reacceptance of Christians back into the Church after having apostatized on account of their being previously persecuted in order to save their lives. Cyril was definitely not as tolerant as Novatian, the theologist responsible for the doctrine, had figured the Church should be, which resulted in his sealing off and plundering Alexandria's Novationist headquarters, inclusively stripping Theopemptus, appointed bishop of this particular branch of Christianity, of his power and wealth, leaving him miserable and rendering him both religiously and politically insignificant.

Expelling Novationists from Alexandria was but the first leg under his tenure of the holy war his uncle had begun twenty years before. There was still much to be done, especially regarding the Jewish population and the two remaining pieces of Paganism left in the city after Theophilus's first purge – Hypatia and the Neoplatonic School, of which she was now proudly in charge on the one hand, but distastefully on the other, as her heading the institution meant her primordial idol, Theon, her father, was dead, having passed away in four hundred and five, aged seventy. The last Director of the Musaeum had literally spent half of his life raising and advising Hypatia on how to maintain the Hellenic legacy alive and fend for herself in a patriarch's world, rejoining the One after his body exhaled for the very last time with relief, perfectly conscious he had fulfilled the promise made to his dying wife regarding their daughter, the result of their love, whom they had always been proud of.

Chapter XVII
An Attempt at Secularism

It was the beginning of the year four hundred fifteen, mid-winter; a coastal city, Alexandria's weather was strongly influenced by the cool temperatures brought in from the Mediterranean to the North, but also from the surrounding desert, whose temperatures could easily reach a freezing point, especially at night.

Orestes, having been appointed the lawful representative of the Augustus of the East (Theodosius the Younger) for the Diocese of Egypt, had it in his mind to start the new year via the enforcement of a few reforms regarding public order and safety in the city, frequently put at risk by Cyril's constant intrusions in civil affairs, if not fully disrupted by his inciting the Christian faction (now a majority) to riot as soon as they felt offended or even intimidated, regardless of there being someone behind the alleged plots against them.

It was precisely because of this rioting streak Orestes was planning on marking his territory once and for all, making sure Cyril understood that the former, in the quality of Praefectus Augustalis, outranked the latter, a cause that his predecessor, Evagrius, had lost during Theophilus's crusade against Paganism, making it impossible for the following prefects to regain political control of the city and reestablish governmental authority.

The plan was to change the rules applicable to certain demonstrations of the performing arts in the city's amphitheater (located behind Saint Mark's Cathedral, now larger than ever, overlooking the harbor in the old Pagan center, the Broucheion), whose seats were mostly reserved for the Jewish community – if you will recall, the Parabolani were forbidden from attending these events because of their violent nature. The spectacles mainly comprised mime shows and dancing, which always seemed to constitute the necessary pretext for cyclical outbursts of conflict, perhaps a surreptitious way of moving the Church of Alexandria's purge of both political and religious opponents, one small group at a time. And so, having grown tired of dispatching his men to quell this outraging and uncivilized behavior, Orestes decreed that no religious groups would ever again take full control of public venues, introducing a «first come, first served» policy. Still, and because there was a risk of either faction attempting to fill the venues in question with their own folk, thus barring the entrance to their opposition and, yet again, incite a riot, there would always be a limited amount of both Christians and Jews allowed to enter the premises with the purpose of equally distributing the available seats.

The edict on its own, once it was released and put up on the amphitheater's wall, could be regarded as a reason for the populace to clash right on the spot, as it had drawn the attention of a great number of individuals from both sides, already complaining about the new regulations, which, bluntly put, stripped the Jews of a few rights while, simultaneously, stopped the Christians from engaging on and provoking them.

From the inside of Saint Mark's Cathedral, Cyril's attention had been drawn to the loud reaction by that same group of people gathering in front of the amphitheater, whose number increased at each passing moment – a rather intriguing event as far as the Patriarch was concerned; the presence of Roman soldiers contributed all the more to his curiosity. However, quenching this thirst for knowledge on his own would certainly turn out to be counterproductive, as his going over to read the piece of parchment pasted on the wall would be obviously regarded as an attempt at breaking order; also, given the fact he was the Patriarch, Cyril had no need to leave the Cathedral unless it was absolutely necessary, as he had lackeys at his disposal, just like his uncle before him. Now, neither Ammonius nor Peter the Reader performed this kind of petty duties anymore, given the former had been promoted to general of the Patriarch's personal militia, the brotherhood who had sheltered and nurtured him back to his health and strength, whereas the latter had been relocated to the catacombs, put in charge of overseeing the structural integrity of the tunnel network Theophilus had begun years earlier, through which holy war had been taken by surprise to Pagan homes in the middle of the night, destroyed and rebuilt as Christian quarters, eliminating all sorts of heathen residue from the streets. Also, and still in regard to this, considering Alexander's body had been found back in three hundred ninety-one and transferred from the Rhakotis to Saint Mark's Cathedral, the sarcophagus was now duly repaired and sealed under the magnanimous building, immediately adjacent to Mark's tomb, also a founder of Alexandria in his own way – the first to instill the values of Christianity in the city; holding both tombs underneath the Holy See's floors was an indisputable claim of power by the Church in Africa. As to the reason why Cyril had directed Peter to his underground predicament, it mostly had to do with the look on the lector's face the Patriarch had never forgotten about, an expression of ridicule addressed at his uncle, Theophilus, when threatening to dispose of Alexander's remains right in the center of the agora, should Olympius fail to back off on his blasphemies. The former patriarch's passiveness and patience he kept showing the tumultuous crowd, preventing them from moving on to a bloodthirsty approach straight away, had but inflamed the lector's heart, who could not discern at all the old man's intentions. Questioning his uncle's authority was something Cyril had never been prepared to accept, let alone from a minion like Peter, whose sight he could not withstand for too long, thus choosing to send him underground, not only avoiding his face completely, but also restraining him from the excessive authority Theophilus had entrusted him with. As far as Peter was concerned, of course, and granted his mind tricks and flattery toward Cyril had never borne fruit, disappointment and anger were the two main emotions radiating his soul, a great deal more twisted now than ever, constantly trying to figure out what was it he could do to impress the Patriarch, having come up with nothing so far.

In short, since Cyril had deliberately disabled

one of his uncle's favorite henchmen while entrusting the other with more important duties, he always kept someone else far more appropriate for these tasks, and that was Hierax, a Grammar tutor who admired Cyril more than anyone, always drinking the Patriarch's sermons at the Cathedral to the like of wine brewed from angels' sweat. The man would literally do anything to get the Head of the Church of Alexandria's attention and appreciation, regardless of the importance or quality of his feats. Deciding to show some false compassion for his follower, blindly supporting him no matter what, Cyril had him called in, asking his messenger to add he had a task of the utmost importance for him.

It did not take long for Hierax to arrive at the Cathedral; not only did he live nearby, his excitement had also fueled his speed. Led to Cyril's chambers in the back of the building by a Parabolanus, Hierax was told all he had to do was knock on the door and wait for the Patriarch to let him in. Once the Parabolanus was gone, Hierax made sure he was at his best, dusting the sand on his garments with his hands, rearranging them so they would look tidy and clean. He then took a deep breath and softly knocked on the door.

'Enter', Cyril uttered from the inside, his voice muffled by the thickness of the wooden door.

Promptly did Hierax oblige, leaving but a

small space between the door and its frame, just enough for him to slide through without exposing too much of the room to the outside, even though no one was really looking – it was likely no more than an idiosyncrasy of his subconscious. Having passed, he closed the door behind him and saw Cyril looking out the window, still focused on what he did not know was an edict from the Prefect. The Patriarch had both his right arm and hand already extended for Hierax to hold and bow to it as a sign of his acknowledgement of the Pope's clerical superiority. Instead of doing just so, however, the Christian enthusiast added a few features of his own, which comprised kneeling and kissing Cyril's hand, after which he saluted the clergyman and asked him:

'What is thy bidding, Holy Father?'.

Caught by surprise the moment Hierax's lips touched his hand, the Patriarch lost his focus and his attention was drawn to what the man next to him had just done:

'Oh! No, no, you don't have to- that's quite all right, thank you. Stand up, if you will', Cyril said, pulling his hand away from the man with disgust, though trying not to discourage him by outrightly wiping his hand in front of Hierax.

'May I say what an honor and privilege it is to be directly summoned by you, Holy Father. Whatever you ask of me shall be done, no questions on my end', the man said.

Happy to hear such dedicated words, Cyril looked out the window once more and asked him:

'My dear Hierax, do you happen to know what all that turmoil might be about, by any chance?'.

The follower asked for the Pope's permission and walked closer to the window, realizing a great deal of people kept gathering in front of the entrance to the city's amphitheater, heavily guarded by Orestes' soldiers, whose sheer presence bore the purpose of intimidating anyone willing to start a brawl.

'No, sir, I wouldn't know anything about that, but… everyone does seem to be arguing about the parchment on the wall', Hierax replied, making use of his keen eyes.

'Indeed', Cyril confirmed, 'it does look like the whole fuss is somewhat related to that. Judging from what I've gathered so far, it would seem as if the document was produced by the Prefect's office, which would justify those guards being there, would you not agree?'.

'Right you are, sir, absolutely right, yes', Hierax said, using his words as a means of applauding the Patriarch's shrewdness.

'I'm glad you agree. Now, what I need you to do is go out there and find out what it's about. Don't talk to anyone, whoever they are. You do realize it would be inappropriate for me to walk the distance myself, right? These are dangerous times we live in', Cyril said, looking at him from the corner of his eyes, his head facing forward.

'Yes, sir, undoubtedly! It's too great a risk for you to wander about the streets, whether it's the middle of day or night. I'm more than happy to oblige and straighten out the meaning of all this commotion for you. Is there anything else you'd like me to take care of, sir?'.

'No, my dear Hierax', Cyril responded, 'your devotion to me is a devotion to God, and that's simply more than I could've asked from any other sheep in my flock', he concluded, placing his right hand on his follower's left shoulder.

'Thy blessing, Holy Father', Hierax asked of the Patriarch, taking his hand and kissing it again, though merely bowing, this time.

'Dominus vobiscum', the Patriarch uttered.

'Et cum spiritu tuo'.

Hierax walked backward to the door while bowing and, having found the knob, he stepped out, closing the door again in front of him, rising only when Cyril could not see him anymore, which was the moment he made haste to fulfill his shepherd's bidding. From inside the room, after observing how his enthusiast had taken his leave, the Pope looked out the window once more and openly wiped his hand, thinking aloud:

'How very interesting... this was easier than I'd thought. Well, Uncle' he said, communing with Theophilus's memory, 'I guess I may have found my own Peter. Let's just hope this one lasts as long as yours, but without ever asking too many questions. In fact, the less he thinks, the better'.

Due to the amphitheater's proximity to Saint Mark's Cathedral, it only took Hierax no more than a few moments to show among the crowd, who did nothing but shout accusations back and forth.

'You Jewish filth are all alike! The moment you grab something, you never let go! The more you've got, the more you want, and the more of you we get rid of, the more of you show up – by the double! You're like weeds sprouting all about!', one of the Christians said; in turn, a Hebrew retorted:

'Who in God's name are you to judge?! If it hadn't been for us, you'd have no reason to exist at all! Jesus was a Jew! He – was – a – Jew! He was no king, but he was certainly Jewish. Where would you be without us?'.

The Christian side of the mob was beginning to go up in fumes because of the opposite faction's nerve – so much so that yet another member could not help but ask:

'What, so now Our Lord is your property? Now you recognize Him as one of you?! Then why would you be as hypocritical as to force Pilate into sentencing Him to His death?! He told you he'd die for your sins, he destroyed the Temple and rebuilt it in three days, just like He said He would, and still you don't believe He's the Son of God! You people reek of falsehood! It's no wonder Our Father's abandoned you – you broke the Covenant! You murdered Our Lord in His human form! His blood is on your hands, He, who rescued you from this accursed, forsaken land! But it wasn't good enough, was it…? You had to come back and reclaim it, because that's exactly what you're sentenced to doing until He tries you on our very last day on this world. No territory will ever flourish for you again, no matter where you go, and mark my words – no one will ever let you stay anywhere, for the peoples of all lands will unite and cast you out to reclaim the same deliverance Our Lord died for to give to us… deliverance from the likes of you, the salt of the earth!'.

A sudden urge to demonstrate keriah and spit near their rivals' feet came over the multitude of Hebrews close enough to listen to the accusations. In turn, their choice to straightforwardly manifest their outrage was met with anger from the Christians, who kept stepping closer to their enemies. Foreseeing a clash, the Roman Kentarch who was at the scene ordered his subordinates to stand in line between both factions, pushing them away from each other as much as they could, as they all prepared to fatally throw stones – something they seemed to have in common, even though they failed to realize their God was one and the same.

If Hierax waited much longer before reading the parchment on the wall, he would almost assuredly lose his chance for good, as the soldiers would have to clear the area and escort each side to their respective quarters, which is why, taking advantage of the hood his robes were featured with, he tried to hide his face as much as he could, also rejoicing on the distraction of both the mob and soldiers. Cyril's patsy eventually realized it was indeed an edict promulgated by Orestes, establishing the seating rules everyone was already arguing about. Having been a short read, he almost immediately began clapping his hands, drawing the attention of the Kentarch, who noticed him just standing there in the passageway the soldiers had left unoccupied, addressing him with these words:

'Hey! What are you doing?! How did you get past my men? Get behind the line, now!'.

The Christians up front immediately recognized him based on his flinching posture, typical of a dirty rat used to running for its life, though he was being quite bold as far as this moment is concerned; one of them even shouted his name:

'Hierax! What are you clapping for? Get away from there! These dogs will stone you to death if they grab a hold of you!'.

The Hebrews shared that thought, though they had a twist of their own:

'Yes, begone, pig! Your sty is oinking back for you!'.

The fight, of course, escalated quickly. In need of backup, the Kentarch ordered a couple of his men to leave quickly and return with both the Prefect and more soldiers in order to contain the imminent riot. Hierax, on the other hand, tried to do some damage control, seeking to protect himself, though he made it look like he just wanted both sides of the quarrel to ease down, making use of his Rhetoric skills:

'Friends, please, please! There's no need for confrontation! Let us all douse the fire in our hearts, huh...? Peace be with you and shalom as well!', he said, including everyone in the conversation. Confused, the crowd stopped pushing the soldiers for a moment, quieting down and relieving the Romans for a while, who reassembled the lines; even the Kentarch was surprised that a man of no importance had done such an impressive feat, but there was much more to it.

'What are you supposed to be? A turncoat? "Peace" and "shalom"...? What's the meaning of this? We know you're Cyril's little lamb! And answer his question, what was the applause for, anyway?', a Hebrew asked him, inadvertently making the Christians look at Hierax as well, waiting for a response to the question they had asked first.

'W-Well, erm... I just don't think it's wise to fight about something as insignificant as this, I-I mean... the Prefect's decreed that the theater's capacity be equally distributed, so... why not just do that? Everyone gets a chance to watch the spectacles and... we're all happy...! Isn't that deserving of a good round of applause...? I do. Who's with me?', he said, raising his hand in the air, waiting for someone to mime his gesture, but no one did.

Meanwhile, the Kentarch's envoys were returning to the scene with Orestes leading the way, followed by more men to help. The moment Cyril saw the Prefect stepping in, he stepped away from the front of the window, though keeping his watch while secluded in the darkness of the room. As Orestes came closer, the Kentarch ran toward him, informing him of the ongoing events. However, because everyone seemed to have calmed down, he ordered everyone to wait before announcing his presence, having recognized Hierax as well. Should the man encourage another brawl between both factions, instead of breaking them up, then Orestes could make use of the situation for his own benefit.

'They've had the theater to themselves for too long. Nobody else ever gets a chance to enter. We say it's our turn to strip these swine of their privileges and claim the building! In fact, we should claim everything they've got! Each day they spend alive is one more day of complacency on our behalf they don't deserve! We should ask the Holy Father to let us annihilate them from our country, so prosperity may blossom once more!', a Christian shouted, garnering full support from the crowd standing behind him, who kept yelling, "hear, hear!".

Hotheaded, Hierax thought he would be the perfect man for the job, deciding on the spur of the moment to volunteer:

'That's a brilliant idea! I was just with him, so I can go ahead and ask him!'.

The moment those words left his lips, he instantly regretted them, driving the palm of his hands to his mouth, as if he were trying to seal it, perhaps preventing it from articulating any vocables at all, but it was too late; the Hebrews were already holding stones, so it was merely a question of throwing them at the other side, who, in turn, started doing the same. The soldiers in-between had no choice but to run backward and hold both fronts back-to-back, adopting a testudo formation to protect their heads, most of all.

This was Orestes's cue to intervene, ordering his accompanying soldiers to help their counterparts by unsheathing their swords and poking the rioters with their spears as well. The aeneator joining the Prefect's party blew the buccina the hardest he could, nearly deafening everyone, which forced the people to cover their ears and drop the stones in their hands. The Kentarch then made himself heard and announced Orestes:

'Hear ye, hear ye, one and all! Make way for the Prefect!'.

Moving toward the center of the crowd, protected from both sides by the soldiers already on the spot and the others he had brought with him, Orestes looked directly at Hierax and said:

'My Kentarch tells me there was trouble going on over here, but that's not exactly new. The twist to this plot seems to have come the moment you arrived. What game is it you're playing here, Hierax?'.

'P-P-Prefect', the man stammered, 'there's... there's no game being played, I-I was just walking by, the parchment on the wall happened to have caught my attention, and I read it to... to satisfy my curiosity. And nothing more'.

'See, now why don't I believe you? This is just another one of Cyril's tricks, isn't it? Is this what he wanted? For me to step out of my palace and restore order, whereas he sits back and relaxes while he sends his flunkeys to do his dirty work for him? Well, my friend...', Orestes told him, putting his hands on Hierax's shoulders, 'you and your beloved Patriarch are in for a treat, a surprise neither of you will ever forget, and let this be a message to all of you here and now!', he concluded, turning his back on the Grammaticus as he spoke to everyone, the Hebrews included. Approaching him, the Kentarch asked:

'What are your orders, Prefect?'.

Ogling the back of Saint Mark's Cathedral, perfectly aware Cyril was somewhere inside watching, Orestes enounced loud and clear, pointing to Hierax without even looking at him:

'Take him inside and put him on stage. As for the rest of you', he said, addressing the crowd, 'you'll be the first to abide by my new law. Take a seat. Stand, if you must. The spectacle you're about to watch is a reenactment of the best part of a Greek tragedy – hubris! Now, move! Battalion – escort them all in!'.

The soldiers promptly obeyed and began pushing everyone inside the amphitheater by making use of their shields, also poking the rioters in the back every time they showed resistance. Orestes then turned to the Kentarch and said:

'Bind his wrists, hang him from there and flog him all over until everyone has seen enough to not even think about disrupting public order or questioning my authority ever again, but don't kill him, do you understand?'.

'Yes, Prefect. I'll take care of it at once', the Kentarch replied, going inside the building to oversee the preparations for a public display of torture devised to show Cyril and his followers whose side the Law was really on.

Despite ordering the punishment, Orestes did not stay behind to watch it. He returned to his palace accompanied by his personal guard, but not without piercing the Patriarch's eyesight with his own (now that he had revealed himself), flaming vividly – as was Cyril's.

Chapter XVIII
Thirty Pieces of Silver

Over the next few weeks, the city of Alexandria eventually cooled down regarding both the religious and ethnic tensions, despite the most recent events. After being flogged for everyone to mandatorily see during an immeasurable amount of time, the Kentarch in charge of the punishment released Hierax, merely cutting him loose from his bonds. The stage was tainted with his blood, and a great deal of people attending could not help but regurgitate; the sight of bare flesh and the screaming from the defendant, whose vocal strength diminished at each lash of the whip, were much too difficult to withstand. No matter how much they pleaded with the Roman guards, neither Christians nor Jews were allowed to leave; all exits were sealed.

The point Orestes was trying to make with Hierax's public torture, apart from the one concerning a political paradigm, was also an educational one, which is to say that the audience was supposed to learn from what they saw, the classical premise of Grecian Theater. The most important difference between rehearsed, hypothetical situations staged for competition in the Great Dionysia of Athens and this particular episode was, perhaps, the gruesomeness of what happens in real life when someone challenges the power they owe allegiance to. It is one thing to bet on verisimilitude, but a completely different one to engage in actual suffering from having to face the consequences of one's actions.

Cyril did not necessarily care for Hierax – so much so he refused to even look at him and hand him over to the Parabolani, who could have taken care of the Grammaticus at the Cathedral. However, the Pope simply told him to begone, slamming the door shut on his face. Unable to walk anywhere else, left unaided (under Orestes' orders, no one could help him even if they wanted to, as the penalty would be severe), he lay by the stairs, subjected to the most assorted infections, and died in a matter of hours. Still, because he was a Christian, the Patriarch had earned a good enough reason to speak outrightly during the funeral, when delivering his sermon:

'As thou art all well aware, a heinous crime has been recently committed against one of our brothers – it was no more than a couple of days ago. Orestes, the Prefect of Alexandria, ruthlessly ordered that Hierax, herein laid to rest, be tortured in public, which ultimately resulted in his untimely death. A man of God, whose eternal peace and protection he now rejoices in, our brother was outrightly convicted to the harshest sentence – without the possibility of fending for himself in a court of law, being tried by a group of his peers, or even facing the counts he was never charged with to boot! I say unto thee, brothers, the Patriarch of Alexandria will not stand by as he watches his flock being slaughtered – no, I thoroughly reject it! Let it be known the slightest provocation against any of us shall be met with wrath beyond imaginable! We are the true Children of God, who smote heathens like the Prefect himself into the eternal firepits of hell! Not only is he a Pagan pretending to be one of our own, he's also a Pagan in league with the murderers of Our Lord? Acting on behalf of their interests? When does the blasphemy come to an end?! Mark my words, brothers – this will never again be tolerated! The right hand of God will crush them all into oblivion!'.

The Christians attending the service erupted in

both applause and excitement, agreeing, as always, to means of force when it came to overcoming any obstacle they might be presented with. In the back, however, not all men were as thrilled as the rest; they had no reason whatsoever to be cheering – at all, for, having adopted the same covert methods Cyril was fond of as a self-defense strategy, three Jewish envoys, disguised in Christian robes, had heard more than enough. It was imperative that, instead of waiting for a surprise attack by a crazed mob, drunk with power they should have never obtained, the Hebrew community depleted their strength and morale. How they would do it, however, was something yet to be spoken of and discussed with the rabbis back at the Jewish quarters.

* * *

When order finally seemed to have taken over the city, much to Orestes's contentment, the apparent cease-fire came to an end and war was resumed. There was no prewarning or any other sort of diplomatically-natured methodology employed, on the contrary – a carefully planned covert operation was now set in motion in the shape of a ruse (or a deception, if you will).

The month was February and, while still enduring the chill of winter, the populace of Alexandria lit bigger fires than throughout the rest of the year, when the desert would blow its scorching heat, somewhat cooled down from the shoreline. Still, and because not every home was a villa featured with hypocausts, where fires were set to heat room floors and walls via internal plumbing, the usage of candles and lamps always increased during this season in particular, not just for comforting purposes, but also to allow people to watch where they were going. Of course, the more inflammable substances used, the greater the risk of an accidental fire – or even arson.

The Church of Alexander, the nineteenth Patriarch of Alexandria and a contemporary of Constantine the Great, was only one of the many houses of God to have been built over the remnants of Pagan temples following the campaign for their destruction by Cyril's uncle and predecessor.

During the course of a starry night featuring a spectacle of lights coming from the surrounding insulae, where common citizens lived in their respective apartments, the general environment was one of peace and relative quiet. There were Parabolani patrolling the streets, even though it was up to the government to ensure everyone's safety, but ever since the capturing of Hierax by Orestes, the Patriarch, though having backed off, had decided to remain vigilant, so he would not be caught by surprise yet again. However, and because there did not seem to be anything to be concerned about at that particular time, the militia was not so susceptible to being easily triggered, which turned out to be perfect for an assault that promised to weaken Cyril's forces. Completely relaxed, a squad of Parabolani was nearly scared to death at the sound of screaming voices whose location was quite impossible to determine, as they seemed to be coming from all over:

'FIRE! THERE'S A FIRE!', one of them said, apparently from the North.

'THE CHURCH IS ABLAZE! SAVE THE HOUSE OF GOD, QUICKLY!', another one shouted from the opposite direction.

'BRING WATER! WE NEED TO DOUSE THAT FIRE BEFORE IT'S TOO LATE!', a third yelled from the East.

Confusion and chaos had just found the perfect conditions to settle, even promising to linger for a long period of time. Running against each other, the brothers eventually panicked, unable to react in an orderly fashion, asking one another the most assorted questions:

'Where is all that screaming coming from?!'.

'Where's the fire?! Does anyone know what church is burning?!'.

'O Lord, what do we do, what do we do?!'.

One of them recovered from the upheaval and quickly told the others:

'Just head for the well, get some buckets and

fill them up! Now!'.

'But… but where do we go then?! It could be any church! Does anyone see smoke in the sky?!'.

Looking to help clarify which building they needed to save, one of the Hebrews who had disguised himself weeks before during Hierax's funeral service came out in the open yet again undercover, drawing the attention of the disoriented men:

'Brothers! Over here, come quickly! It's the Church of Alexander that's burning down! Hurry up, there's no time to waste! Follow me!'.

Immediately responding to the dispatch, the Parabolani started running who they thought was one of their brothers' way, praying to God they could get there before the church endured serious damage. Arriving at the scene after just a few moments, the sacred building named after one of the Patriarchs of the city seemed to be still intact. Also, no puffs of dark smoke could be seen reaching for the night sky, which increased the brotherhood's morale, making them confident they could extinguish the fire before it spread any further.

Spotting a well nearby, the covert Hebrew told them all to start filling up the buckets:

'Grab one of those and head inside! The altar is being consumed and it won't take long before it reaches the roof! Go, go, go!'.

One by one, the members of the brotherhood

entered the church and started looking for brightly colored flames to throw the contents of their buckets at; the problem was darkness was taking over and no source of light could be spotted anywhere. The men kept looking around, spilling water on the stone-cold floor, which eventually made them trip over each other. The moment the last Parabolanus went in the building, having crossed the iron gate that kept the altar safe, the Jewish man, who had kept himself at the well for some time while filling buckets for the others, ran ahead and shut the gate, putting a chain and padlock through it, tightly securing the prisoners. Unaware of what was happening, one of the brothers asked out loud:

'Where's the fire?! Can anyone see any flames?!'.

'No', another replied, 'it's impossible to discern anything in here!'.

'All right, just settle down!', someone else cried, but no one was actually planning on staying quiet, for which reason the same man yelled over everyone, 'ALL OF YOU, SHUT IT!'.

The noise soon died down, allowing him to go on:

'There's something wrong about all this. It's freezing cold in here, there's no ember in sight... I think we've been just made fools of. Who was the man who brought us here? Did anyone get a chance to see his face?'.

'No, Brother', someone said, 'it was dark, he had his hood on... he just told us where the fire was, and we came running as fast as we could. I think he was the one pouring water into our buckets... by the way, where is he?'.

'Precisely', the first brother replied, 'where are you? Are you in here? Where's that accursed fire you were yelling about? Hello...?'.

On the story above, a noise was heard, coming from the galleries looking down on the altar. It had sounded like a stone hitting the floor, possibly dropped by someone. As soon as they heard it, the brother who had just finished talking signaled everyone with his finger on his lips to keep quiet, softly shushing them, even though his gesture could not be perceived.

'We're not alone in here...', he whispered, 'someone try to reach the gate and see if we can get out, but silently!'.

The message was passed on from one mouth to another until it reached the other end, where a brother drove his hands to the iron bars, shaking them gently at first; since they did not move, he tried again just a little harder, raising his hands a bit more, looking for something that could have trapped the gate in place. It was then he felt several pieces of thick iron connected to each other tied so tightly they barely moved. The man was beginning to feel his heart trying to burst out of his chest, a condition which only worsened as soon as he felt the padlock securely fastened – he had just realized they were not going anywhere, saying almost inaudibly:

'We're locked... it's a trap'.

The men closer to the altar could not hear him and asked him a bit louder:

'What was that...? What did he say?'.

Panicking for good, the Parabolanus faced his brothers, despite not being able to see them, and screamed in horror:

'IT'S A TRAP!'.

His words immediately triggered yet another moment of chaos, but certainly not as frightening as before, when being told about the imaginary fire. From above, hands holding a multitude of stones came out of their long sleeves, and the little amount of moonlight that entered the church from the roof was reflected on silver rings the expectant Jews were wearing on their fingers, one per man, in order to make it clear for each other they were on the same side. The man operating under the Christian disguise, having already worn his ring, gave the command:

'FOR YAHWEH!'.

The trapped Parabolani screamed together in horror as they looked up and saw what appeared to be wraiths bearing silver, though they would never have been able to confirm such a vision, for they were struck down with good-sized pieces of rubble flying from all over toward them, similar to a hailstorm, only made of rock, not frozen water. Some of them died instantly from the force with which one or more stones were aimed at their heads. Others had their bones broken and some others, because the space was too small, were simply stomped on by their own brothers, crushed or smothered to death. Because the fences did not go all the way up to the ceiling, there was a bit of room left for an attempt at escaping, but the spear-headed railings were as deadly as the endless rocks projected against them, so much so that some of them slipped while climbing and either got stabbed or were severely wounded, cutting their veins open and bleeding out.

Those who were still alive and unharmed did not feel like going without a fight, and so, feeling around the floor with their hands while looking for used stones, the moment they caught some, they quickly threw them back at the perpetrators of the deception they had been led into like stuck pigs, angrily injuring them, even killing a few (perhaps four or five). As soon as the Hebrews realized a retaliation was taking place, they invested their last drop of strength in putting the escapees down, though they could not be certain they had killed them. Fearing things might get any worse, a total of thirty men were expected to exit the church as the Parabolani were left dead, if not to die overnight. However, having suffered at least four casualties, the number obviously did not match, but none of them had realized it until they returned home and gathered the following morning, meaning evidence of their ambush had been left somewhere in the church; the screaming had naturally drawn the attention of both citizens and other members of the brotherhood, for which reason the Hebrews had had to make haste, but... incrimination was now something impossible to avoid, no matter what they said or did.

* * *

The next morning, around sunrise, Cyril was warned of the events that had occurred overnight. Usually bearing a serene expression on his face, no matter how dark his mood, this time he could not help himself, transpiring violent anger through the language of his entire body. The Patriarch did not even waste much time getting properly dressed to go out on the street, having simply worn a phelonion while leaving behind his polystavrion-patterned camelaucum. Escorted by watchful Parabolani, including Ammonius, the Pope quickly arrived at the Church of Alexander, well-lit with the aid of candles and the imminent sunlight. What had been a total mystery just a few hours earlier was now a horrific truth stained with blood, both dripping and spattered everywhere on account of the impact sustained. The militia of Christ, who answered directly to Cyril, had been brutally slaughtered. Some of the struck-down men had even become unrecognizable, their visage disfigured from constant beating and crushing, whereas others had their face intact, though not their limbs, twisted out of their sockets from either trying to escape or being hit, seeking to support their weight some other way, ultimately failing. Then, of course, there were others hanging from the grating's spearheads, keeping their pierced bodies in place through their mauled flesh. Because they had only been dead for a few hours, the smell of putrefaction was not yet contaminating the air. Dozens of stones were all over the floor, having cracked, chipped, and broken it (along with the altar and other relics). The Patriarch, who had been chewing on the inside of his cheeks while sweeping the scene of desolation with his eyes for some time during which the brotherhood remained silent, seeking to contain their tears and anguish, was now prepared to utter a few words, despite the blow his eloquence had just endured:

'Is... is there anyone alive?'.

'No, Your Grace, they're all dead...', one of the men already there told him, adding, 'but not all of them are our brothers'.

Drawing his attention, Cyril looked at him and asked:

'What do you know? Speak'.

The Parabolanus signaled the men up in the gallery, who, in turn, threw down one of the Jews caught in the middle of the retaliation from their captives like a sandbag – they usually had no regard for their opposition, let alone at that moment.

'He's wearing a silver ring, sir, just like the other four. We think this is how they told each other apart while… while…', but he could not finish the sentence, yielding to sobbing.

Cyril walked closer to the body and knelt, picking the Hebrew's hand up in order to meticulously inspect the ring. Having seen enough, he dropped the dead man's hand (his ring echoing when it hit the floor), rose to an upright posture once more and told the militia with a broken voice:

'Collect all bodies. It's our job to provide our brethren a proper burial. Gather the corpses of the criminals as well without messing them up too much. Put a cross together for each of them and make use of the spare nails. The Jews have had their chance to gift us with a public display aimed at us with the sponsorship of the Prefect; it's only polite to reciprocate'.

Having given the order, Cyril left with the men who had accompanied him, except for Ammonius, who said:

'You heard the Holy Father; we're putting an end to this. My only regret is having waited this long'.

Chapter XIX
Yom Hadin

Before the last days of February were out, Cyril, the Patriarch of Alexandria, had taken it to himself to tie up a few loose ends which were severely disturbing his peace of mind. After ordering his men the cleanup of the Church of Alexander, the successor of Theophilus presided over a funeral of dozens of Parabolani, his equivalent to Orestes's personal guard, interred all at once in the sepulchers located in the Gamma Quarter. Directly above was the Delta Quarter, the last remaining space in Alexandria where the Christians had not yet made themselves at home.

Although the Patriarch had been trying to seize great power and influence over the authority of the

Prefect for the last three years, seeking to belittle Orestes in all matters of government, including those utterly unrelated to the ecclesiastical sphere, it would not be too hasty of us to state there was also a desire for peace, as the general populace, no matter how respectful of their Patriarch, was beginning to show signs of exhaustion over their feeling unsafe just by leaving their homes and going out on the street, as they knew not when the next clash between rival factions would ensue, and none of this uncertainty made them comfortable, which is why negotiating a truce with the Prefect was not at all ruled out from Cyril's strategy to bring Orestes closer to him. Still, forgiveness was not something the Pope was willing to hand out that easily, for which reason he sought to bring the culprits of the butchery that had taken place at the Church of Alexandria to justice, regardless of requiring that the Prefect determine the appropriate disciplinary measures, which brings us to yet another political move that should be taken into account: when Hierax turned out to be essential for the rioting between Christians and Hebrews, Orestes immediately took care of showing everyone what could happen, should any more attempts at violence flood the streets of Alexandria ever again. However, when it came to disciplining the Jews responsible for the carnage the Parabolani had suffered, the Prefect chose to remain within the walls of his palace, without publicly condemning the crime. Of course, such an attitude did not at all mean Orestes condoned the attack, as the Jews had clearly stooped much too low, to the like of Cyril himself, though they genuinely believed the Prefect would definitely side with and support them, but, even though he did not, his abstaining said otherwise. Deep down, Orestes was happy to know the Patriarch's militia had taken a critical blow, which could, perhaps, put him in his rightful place, but the Prefect's ongoing experience dealing with Cyril should have counted for something, for it was obvious the Pope would sooner or later retaliate. Orestes would never be able to appease both sides, and the problem regarding this sort of situation was the rivalry could come to halt at any time and yield to unanimity as far as deposing the Prefect was concerned, and that is what troubled him the most.

One night, as March came closer, several Parabolani silently entered the Jewish quarter. A few started digging a total of five holes in the ground, whereas the rest kept watch. The purpose of these orifices was to support five different wooden structures – crosses, each of them holding one of the five Hebrews killed in the attack at the Church of Alexander by nailing their hands and feet to the timber. The configuration of the holes, should it have been possible to see it from above, was supposed to create a cross-shaped layout, beginning in the middle of Meson Pedion (which led to the Canopian Gate), resembling the lower tip of the cross. The center point was located in the crossing to the Northwest. From there, the left and right tips were placed in the crossing to the Southwest and the middle of the street leading to the sepulchers, respectively. Finally, the upper tip could be found at the crossing that led to the Macedonian Camp. The symbolic intention contained therein was to both Christianize the Jewish quarter and figuratively crucify the murderers of Christ while five of them, despite being dead, were actually on the cross.

The Sun was preparing to rise in a few moments, for which reason the brotherhood worked fast to raise the crosses and plant them in the ground, adding a few rocks to prevent them from turning over and falling. They did, however, have something else prepared up their sleeves – in order to draw the attention of the sleeping Jewish community, also symbolizing the fires of hell burning through their territory, the Parabolani gathered multiple bales of hay from a stable nearby and placed them at the base of each cross. Those keeping watch had oil lamps with them; grabbing five, they simultaneously threw them at the crosses (one lamp per cross), immediately setting both hay and timber alight.

Given the fact the victims were being executed

posthumously, there were no screams of agonizing pain spreading across the quarter, but the fires, distributed by that many locations, eventually drew the attention of the residents, who recognized the men about to be consumed by the flames. The only garments they had been dressed in were pieces of cloth covering their private area, though the silver rings were still on their fingers.

It did not take long before the Hebrews coming to the windows started screaming on behalf of the singed, dead men, triggering them to leave their homes and head for the cross in their respective location. However, as soon as they set foot outside, they were captured by the overwhelming numbers of Parabolani, whose orders were to round the Jews in one place, plunder their homes, destroy them, and kick them and their families out through the Canopian Gate, forcing them to abandon the city with nothing but the clothes they wore and head for the desert once more, just like their ancestors had done in the Book of Exodus, led away from the Egyptian land and Pharaoh's sacred cat claws by Moses.

Of course, despite Cyril's orders, some of the Parabolani were under the impression (or so they had convinced themselves) the Patriarch had not necessarily emphasized the part of his instructions that said the Hebrews were to come to no harm during the roundup, for which reason blood was obviously shed. In order to make the evidence of the sinful part of their crime disappear, the bloodthirsty members of the brotherhood took advantage of the five fires burning vividly and threw the bodies in them; the smoke ascending toward dawning daylight was not dark enough to conceal the five sacred wounds of Christ that had now befallen over the Savior's assassins.

Although the militia was supposed to expel just the attackers present at the Church of Alexander and their families while leaving their homes uninhabitable and collecting their riches, such criteria were disregarded far more than just once, ultimately resulting in countless deportations that, come the morning, made the Jewish quarter look like ancient ruins. Theophilus and Cyril's campaign against opposing forces of the one true faith was nearly at an end – Christianity had come to Alexandria to stay and rule alone completely; yes, it had taken much too long, but divine justice, though tardy at times, always finds a way, which could not have made the Patriarch any happier about himself.

Chapter XX
Between a Rock and a Public Place

'I WANT HIM IN FRONT OF ME, HERE AND NOW! NO EXCUSES, NO SUBTERFUGES, NO PRETEXTS! HAVE HIM SURRENDER AND BRING HIM TO ME – AT ONCE!', Orestes angrily cried the following morning from his office in the Prefectural Palace, located in the former Broucheion, in the Alpha Quarter, with a view to the Great Harbor.

'Yes, sir. Right away, Prefect!', his Kentarch replied, on his way to seize Cyril with all the men he had under his command.

Keeping Orestes company in his office was his political advisor, Hypatia, who, willing to show her respect for Synesius' dying wishes (which she could not dispute, as she would only be contradicting her own principles), had accepted to guide her former disciple in the complex conundrum of governing a city permanently at war.

Although Cyril kept moving his forces across the whole of Alexandria, either forcibly converting its inhabitants to his views on Christianity while claiming the territory as the Church's property, or expelling those who refused to apostatize their original faith (if not killing them), the Neoplatonic School was still standing. Apart from a few symbols and monuments (such as the obelisks, for instance), the institution headed by Hypatia was the only Pagan structure the Patriarch felt reluctant to touch, perhaps following the footsteps of his uncle and predecessor, who had agreed with the late Bishop of Ptolemais to let the Lady be, considering she had never imposed any particular belief on her students, as she had always said they were free to adopt any creed they so desired, which is precisely what had held her popularity and influence in place throughout a teaching career spanning just a little over twenty-five years (the city itself had not been at peace for much longer).

Hypatia's views on contemporary Alexandrian politics were, therefore, an object of respect and credulity from the people in general, for neither Christians nor Jews (despite the latter never having been present in a single lecture of hers) regarded the Philosopher as an obstacle to public order merely based on the way she had been raised by her father, still to this day dearly remembered by everyone who had been lucky enough to meet him. As per Theon's own wishes, Hypatia had attained an enviable status in Alexandria, and not only inside the city's aristocratic class, but also among most of the population; only the Parabolani or the people directly related to them refused to recognize the Lady as a valuable asset, which she was not only because of her father's dedication to her, who had taught her everything he knew (leaving her his legacy for her to continue and improve on), but most assuredly due to her own principles as a woman of the highest moral standards as well.

The fact Orestes always turned to Hypatia for her support in a time of need (which, given the state of things, was pretty much every day) was regarded as perfectly acceptable as far as the citizens were concerned. They knew the Prefect had always had a strong connection with the pedagogue, especially because he had, indeed, studied under her, for which reason there was absolutely nothing odd about this friendship. Under the eyes of the institution led by the Patriarch, however, the picture was only bound to be deliberately twisted and distorted. While it is true Synesius had successfully influenced Theophilus, the same story was not applicable to the latter's nephew and successor. Cyril had always been aware of Synesius's opinion of him; in fact, Hypatia's former disciple had never tried to hide it, preaching it publicly. He was a man of the Church as much the current Patriarch of Alexandria, so what did he have to lose? Synesius's misery had been a product of natural catastrophes, not the wrath of God (although Cyril eventually ended up thinking the exact opposite, judging the loss of the Bishop's entire family and his own death as divine payback for never fully renouncing his Paganism).

'He's cornered me', Orestes suddenly unwound while leaning against the balcony's balustrade, 'the bloodthirsty bastard's cornered me! I punish one of his own for inciting sedition, but say nothing regarding his deserved blow at Alexander's, so he retaliates against the people supporting my government the most as a fair response. What happens then? He kicks out the majority and serves his own justice over my authority! He eagers for my seat... a complete merger of both political and ecclesiastical powers, fully centered in him, the ultimate authority, second only to the Emperor... I just know it, as much as I'm aware he'll never give up until he gets what he wants'.

Hearing nothing from the inside, Orestes turned around to face Hypatia, who was apparently distracted, having adopted her usual pensive posture, which comprised leaning on her lap while looking into the void. The Prefect could not help but feel ignored, raising his hands mid-air as he asked her:

'Does my ordeal somehow bore you, Hypatia?'.

Mentioning her name eventually caught her attention, making her wake up from a sort of trance that seemed to be taking over her. She averted her sight to Orestes, sat upright and genuinely asked:

'Pardon me? Were you saying something just now?'.

Disappointed, Orestes walked toward his seat and let himself fall into it, crossing his arms as he ironically replied:

'Yes, but I gather it's nothing too important, it's… simply the future of the city that's at stake', he said, shrugging his shoulders, 'and my head along with it. This whole situation has "Pilate" written all over it. In the end, it's my fault and mine alone… I washed my hands over the matter, allowed the Hebrews to serve their own justice as well. I didn't want anyone accusing me of taking sides, but… I just walked right into that, didn't I?'.

As soon as he stopped talking, Orestes leaned forward and buried his face in the palm of his hands. Hypatia ogled him with sincere concern, gulped slightly and said:

'Orestes, I… I honestly don't know what to tell you'.

'You don't…? Well', he gasped, 'that's it, then – my tenure as Prefect is over. I might as well let Cyril sit in this chair, while I'm at it… if you're at a loss for words, Alexandria is at a loss for something greater. I suppose tyranny must be on its way, by now', he said, laughing nervously.

'Orestes', Hypatia began, pausing shortly to change her address to the appropriate style, 'Prefect, you know that a great responsibility is inseparable from a great power. Right here, right now, you're that great power, the highest Emperor-appointed official. You're his representative and you have as much authority as he does in Constantinople – that is every prefect's job, no matter where they're sent to within the Empire, and you know it. However, there is something important you must also realize, which will at some point turn out to be key in your relationship with Cyril – two grown men who continue to put their own pride in front of the city and the population's best interests will never manage to come to terms… that is not what Politics is about, I taught you this years ago! Your job is to fend for the greater good of Alexandria, but you're allowing yourself to be consumed by this endless quarrel between you and the Patriarch. The more you need to show who's in charge, the less respected you'll be. Instill fear, threaten Cyril and his paranoid fanatics with blood and the war will only be perpetuated; give him an animalistic response, and so he shall respond to you in return. If you choose to leave now, what do you think will happen to your reputation? You'll be branded a coward, perhaps even charged with desertion, if the Emperor fails to accept your resignation. Where will you go? More importantly, how will you live the rest of your life? Running between places until your legs give up on you and you're found on the side of the road, rendered unrecognizable after being preyed upon?'.

Orestes, who had been closely paying attention to Hypatia's speech, felt like interrupting her to tell her how he felt:

'For someone who didn't know what to say, Lady… your eloquence is quite overwhelming, and not in the best of ways…!'.

'Would you rather have me pat you in the back and tell you everything is going to be all right, no matter what you do? I apologize if my choice for words is too harsh for your ears but running on account of your giving everything up will not only provide Cyril the authority to meddle with secular affairs, it'll also confirm that he's won. It might not be a fight to the death stricto sensu, but he'll likely take over at the blink of an eye and all your efforts to maintain order in the city will be forgotten'.

'Very well', Orestes said after a short moment of silence looking Hypatia in the eye, asking, 'what would you have me do?'.

The Lady took a deep breath, looked down to the floor for a while, then stood up and slowly walked toward the Prefect as she said:

'The decision is yours alone to make, but my advice for you to resolve this matter permanently is to, first of all, think of the people's welfare, not your own. You're the head of government, you're responsible for all Alexandrians, whether you like them or not. Second, don't retaliate Cyril's attacks proportionately; punishing his men will both make him take pleasure in further defying you and show the populace you're no different. The people look up to you, Orestes... you have their support. Keep them by your side, and they will always be your most powerful ally, much stronger than the Emperor himself. When Theophilus tried to rid Constantinople of Chrysostom, the people turned on the royal house. Had Arcadius failed to bring him back as soon as the Archbishop was preparing to leave, he could've been eliminated that same day, just like Cyril and his uncle, who constituted a purpose common to all – keeping their beloved clergyman in the city by any means necessary, but because the two of them craved the opposite, they had to run for it. Side with the people, don't be another tyrant... you know sooner or later they fall, but it's the blood that's spilt in the meantime that elevates the cost of an enterprise as pointless as waiting on a miracle'.

Orestes was still overwhelmed by the Lady's discourse, but not in a bad way, not anymore. They were looking each other in the eye, standing quite close to one another, when the Kentarch returned and opened the door without knocking, gasping for air as he said:

'Prefect, the Patriarch says he agrees to speak to you, but refuses to come here. We tried bringing him by force but couldn't even get close to him. We were heavily outnumbered by his own guard and had no choice but to retreat quietly…'.

Orestes quickly stepped away from Hypatia the moment the Kentarch finished his report and approached him while lifting his eyebrow:

'He set his dogs on you…? He had the nerve to threaten my soldiers?! This just keeps getting better… then tell me, my good Kentarch, where would His Eminence like to meet?', he asked, referring to Cyril in a disgusted manner.

'In the agora, sir. Somewhere spacious, public… without any guards involved from either side – just the people'.

'Do you think we can trust him?'.

'He threatens to drop the dialogue, should any soldiers be spotted, sir'.

Orestes looked back at Hypatia with his hands on either side of his waist, seeking to obtain her opinion, but all she did was stare back at him bearing a serene posture. Ultimately, it was all up to him.

'So be it', the Prefect told the Kentarch, asking his guest, 'will you be all right on your own, Lady? I don't mean to be long'.

'I'll be fine. Just go', Hypatia replied in a peaceful tone, walking toward the balcony.

Orestes nodded toward her and patted the Kentarch's shoulder, meaning to give him a few instructions once he closed the door, leaving the Lady inside:

'I require two things from you – first, have a few guards posted in the middle of the crowd without wearing their uniform; just give them regular clothes where they can conceal a small blade. Second, make sure the Lady is safe in there and is waiting for my return; I don't want her wandering around the streets on her own, are we clear?'.

'Absolutely, Prefect!'.

'Good man'.

* * *

Already stationed at the center of the agora, the Patriarch of Alexandria awaited the Prefect of Alexandria's arrival, holding a large book behind his back. Approximately twenty-five years later, no one could tell a horrific butchery had taken place in that very same spot. All signs of blood and ash were now gone, sprinkled, nevertheless, with fresh drops spilt every now and then from the ongoing rioting, sadly keeping shady memories alive.

People had begun to gather around Cyril, but never as close enough as to prompt a surprise attack from his security detail; even though no Parabolani were in sight, the populace was just much too scarred and calloused to go ahead and take any chances without carefully pondering the consequences of their actions. The Pope's stern expression on its own kept most individuals away. As moments went by, all the more people came to the public square, waiting for something to happen. Now, even though no one had any idea what was going on, some of the members of the general populace were reluctant as far as staying was concerned. Whenever Cyril came out on the street, it was customary for violence to surprisingly erupt, as had Vesuvius over three hundred years before, taking both Pompeii and Herculaneum by storm; an immense graveyard had been carved in stone by the hands of Nature herself.

Believing nothing was actually going to take place, those who had waited for a while started to go away, only to be held back by other citizens, pointing out the coming of Orestes to the agora. It could not have been a coincidence that both the Prefect and the Patriarch were meeting each other precisely at a location where the majority of citizens walked by every day. The whispering that had been playing in the background ever since Cyril's arrival was now mute; countless hearts started beating strongly in people's chests – silence was king.

As soon as Orestes walked toward Cyril, keeping a good distance, nevertheless, the latter was the first to speak as host of the encounter:

'Your Excellency', the Patriarch said, both saluting and bowing to the Prefect.

Orestes knew perfectly well Cyril loved playing mind games; in fact, he had never met anyone as cynical and two-faced as his ecclesiastic counterpart, but, and bearing in mind Hypatia's advice, he decided to play along, also taking a bow as he saluted him, but not as low as the Patriarch, soon recovering:

'Your Eminence. As far as I can tell, we were supposed to meet in private at the Prefectural Palace. Would His Grace be so kind as to explain the reason behind his changing of venue?'.

The audience continuously averted their eyes from one man to the other without moving any other body parts; it was as if they all had turned to stone.

'Of course, I'd be very much obliged to provide Your Excellency with a plausible explanation. You see', Cyril commenced, walking toward Orestes still concealing the book, 'both the Prefect and the Patriarch are leaders of this city in their own way.

The first, appointed by the Emperor, who, in turn, is appointed by the Father, is responsible for all political affairs, which is to say the secular half of government, whereas the latter, appointed by his peers, who, in turn, are consecrated under God's blessing, most naturally, takes charge of the pastoral tasks necessary to ensure that, come Judgment Day, every single person here is delivered from evil and sin, thus allowing them to pass the gates guarded by Peter into eternal peace and glory under the Creator's careful watch. Would you not agree, Prefect?', he asked, pausing his walk.

Standing right where he was, Orestes slightly shrugged his shoulders and said:

'Yes... yes, I suppose so. What of it?'.

Resuming his slowly stepping forward, Cyril finally came to a stop, just about five pedes away from Orestes, who refused to flinch – not even for a moment, and held the book between them both, asking:

'Do you recognize the book I'm now holding in front of me, Prefect?'.

'I do – those are the Holy Scriptures; any Christian would recognize them at length', Orestes replied.

'My point exactly', Cyril uttered, 'and this is the reason why I asked you to come to the agora, to show you the one bond all these people are brought together by, including you and I – the word of God'.

'I'm sorry, but I don't quite follow', Orestes told the Patriarch, somewhat exasperating from impatience.

'The Lord speaks to us all through me, my son. I am the Father, the Son, and the Holy Spirit combined in this earthly vessel of mine made of flesh and bone. The Word of God finds its way into articulation through the mouths of select men. No one's authority is valid without the Trinity's consent, and by the transitive property of congruence, the Lord selected the Emperor, who in turn selected you, a sheep of my flock. Take the Good Book as my personal gift to you, prove you're a Christian in fact, and acknowledge your fate is in the hands of the Lord. Take it', Cyril said out loud, raising the Holy Scriptures above both their heads.

Orestes, who had not moved until then of his own accord, was now stuck and overrun with shock. It had all been an ambush, a twisted ceremony witnessed by the people of Alexandria so as to confirm the Patriarch's authority over the Prefect's. He had not seen that coming, not at all. Even though Hypatia did not cross his mind at that particular moment, we believe it is safe to say she knew not what the proper response to something like this was, let alone Orestes, despite his being a politician. During the course of a deafening silence, the Prefect's visage grew more and more rubicund with anger. Experiencing his emotions breaking through his very skin, Orestes knew, nevertheless, that accepting Cyril's gift would mean showering him with absolute power. Either doing that or running away would forever stain his reputation, branding him a coward even after he died.

With flames vividly piercing his eyes, the Prefect was rendered speechless. No one can tell how long that moment of silence lasted. Breathing heavily as his rage increased, Orestes turned his back on the Patriarch and walked away to the North, headed for the Prefectural Palace. In turn and almost immediately, Cyril turned his back as well and walked East, to Saint Mark's Cathedral.

Viciously ogled by a member of the crowd, Orestes's attention was drawn by the same person screaming to his face while the crowd made way for him to pass:

'PAGAN!'.

It was Ammonius, the General of the Parabolani, Cyril's favorite. Offended by the provocation, the Prefect responded:

'I am NOT a Pagan! I was baptized by Atticus, Bishop of Constantinople! I am as Christian as you are!'.

Moved by impulse, Ammonius grabbed a stone from his pouch and threw it at Orestes, hitting the Prefect in his forehead. The blow was so strong that he immediately started gushing blood all over, his fall cushioned by the populace. Orestes' undercover guards ran for the Prefect straight away, trying to shield him the best they could from more stones that came from every direction, hitting not just them, but the Gentiles as well. Cyril had taken the same precautions by hiding his men among the crowd; perhaps they were not so different after all, but it was not until much later that the thought crossed the Prefect's mind, currently in danger. Severely outnumbered, the guards fled for their lives, leaving Orestes to die. Thankfully, because of the people's reaction to yet another surprise attack they were much too tired to allow, the undercover Parabolani were chased away, whereas Ammonius was seized as he tried to finish the job, letting at least one guard fulfill his duty by taking hold of the Prefect and rushing him back to the Prefectural Palace nearby, aided by the citizens themselves, now turning against Cyril's reign of terror. They simply had had enough; their only hope now was that Orestes could be saved in time.

Chapter XXI
Dies Irae, Dies Illa

After enduring a violent attempt on his life, Orestes was able to quickly recover, remaining conscious at all times throughout the cleaning and suturing procedures his doctor performed on him while he lay down, successfully stopping the bleeding and preventing infection.

Outside the Prefectural Palace, the Kentarch in charge of the Prefect's soldiers stood guard at the top of the stairs while his subordinates were placed at the entrance as if they were somehow glued to each other, having adopted an oblong square formation in order to flank and stop anyone from trying to get past unnoticed. It was merely a safety procedure, given that the people standing in front of the palace were the same who had helped bring Orestes back, joined shortly after by an enormous crowd who had begun praying to God for their Prefect's well-being. In his chambers, he could hear the populace chanting in unison, though he was not necessarily sure of what was going on, for which reason he asked no one in particular:

'What... what's that? What's that singing...?'.

The doctor took the liberty of responding based on the most probable cause, almost done sewing Orestes's cut:

'I believe that might just be the people, sir. It seems like your being in danger has brought them together, a feat no one who's ever taken upon this office hadn't accomplished in a long, long time'.

Despite being aware of his surroundings, his mind unaffected, the liqueur he had forcibly drunk to numb his nerves down was obviously taking its toll, which led him to closing his eyes as he revived the conversation between him and Hypatia only a few moments before, especially the part concerning siding with the people for the greater good. Enouncing his thoughts out loud, the doctor and the rest of his staff heard him say these words in a broken voice:

'She was right all along...'.

The doctor put what he was doing on hold for a moment, looked the Prefect in his closed eyes and asked:

'What's that, sir?'.

Orestes opened his eyes again, blinking repeatedly in order to restore his visual acuity, and said:

'Erm… nothing, it's… nothing… just thinking aloud. Do-do any of you know where Hypatia is?'.

One of the soldiers standing by the doors to the chambers replied:

'The Lady Hypatia insisted on returning to her home, Prefect. The Kentarch told her he had direct orders from you not to leave her by herself, but she kept replying she wanted to go back, so the Kentarch had no choice but to let her walk away, though he pleaded with her that she accept being escorted. I was one of the soldiers accompanying her home, sir. She's safe'.

'Well done, soldier, very well done, indeed…', the Prefect told him.

'There's one more thing of the utmost importance I must tell you about, sir – we've captured the perpetrator. There were more hiding in the crowd, but the people chased them away. The one who assaulted you, however, is currently under our custody'.

'What's… what's his name? Who is he?', Orestes asked.

'A man known as Ammonius, sir. From what we were able to gather, he's one of the Patriarch's main henchmen. In fact, we believe he might be the head of the Parabolani'.

The Prefect could see the details of the man's face in his mind; he remembered that, immediately after having been provoked, he had seen a thick, black beard and fiery eyes concealed under his hood. For some reason, Orestes seemed to recall having spotted that same, cloaked visage at a time, but he was not sure when or where, until it finally came to him, still uncertain, though quite positive it could not be a mere coincidence – the man wandering about the Great Harbor back when the Serapeum was under siege, it had to be him. Just as the future Prefect had been waiting for his servant to return from Constantinople via the Mediterranean, so had that man. Whether it was his former Pagan self taking over him or not, he knew that man, Ammonius, could not go unpunished; letting him rot inside a cell was too painless a death for him to suffer as payback for his crime. Having made his decision, Orestes sat on his bed, much to the doctor's surprise, who told him:

'Prefect, you need to rest! You could've died; I wouldn't advise you to stand and walk around all of a sudden'.

'Right you are, my good doctor, but, like you said, I could've died, even though I'm here, safe and sound, thanks to your handiwork. Soldier, take me to Ammonius – I want to have a word with him'.

'Yes, sir', the military man responded, opening

the door for Alexandria's commander-in-chief.

Both the soldier and the Prefect went down several flights of stairs until they reached the holding area, where a few cells had been installed. The guard pointed the one Ammonius was in and was then asked to wait by the doors, a command he promptly obeyed after handing over the keys.

Orestes walked toward the front of the cell. Standing in the back, with chains restraining his neck, wrists, and ankles, was the skittish prisoner. The darkness of the cell made him look far more aggressive than when daylight illuminated his expression. It was almost as if a demon lived inside him. He had his eyes closed; blood covered quite a few parts of his robes. The Prefect, though trying his best to seem awfully sure of himself, could not help but feel somewhat scared. Still, he put his hands behind his back and jested with the captive, asking in a high volume:

'Comfortable?'.

Ammonius did not flinch for a second. Instead, he retorted with his eyes still shut:

'I heard you coming in. Don't bother toying with me, foot soldier; it won't do you any good'.

He had not realized it was the Prefect who was talking to him, something Orestes took advantage of:

'Your throw didn't do you any good, either. Here I am, good as new'.

The Parabolanus quickly opened his eyes and, much to his surprise (which he could not hide, not even in the dark), he saw the Prefect's face shining from the lamp hanging to the side.

'It can't be…', he said, 'I hit you… I hit you, I hit you, I HIT YOU!', he repeated and cried, spewing bloody saliva from his mouth as he yelled; his expression had drastically changed.

Orestes, bearing a smirk on his face, jiggled the keys, took hold of the oil lamp, opened the lock and entered, slowly approaching the prisoner.

'Believe me now?', he asked, pointing to his forehead.

Ammonius followed his finger and saw it – the suture binding Orestes's flesh where he had been hit. He bore the same expression Saint Thomas had been reported to transpire in the Gospel of John the moment Jesus Christ revealed himself to his apostles after the Resurrection, something which ended up earning him his «Doubting Thomas» nickname.

Enraged beyond belief, the Parabolanus tried breaking free from the shackles, but they were secured tight, allowing him but to go back against the wall. Assuming, however, the Prefect was in range, he suddenly ran toward him, only to be strangled by the chain around his neck, thus chafing his flesh and making him bleed even more, which, in turn, forced him to retreat and fall on his knees as he screamed in pain. A stream of tears began running down his face, washing away the dirt. He looked at Orestes from below and asked him:

'Please... please, have mercy...! You're a merciful man...! I know you are! Please, show me your mercy, I beg of you!'.

Lowering the lamp to have a better look at the Parabolanus's face without, however, kneeling or bending his back (with the purpose of maintaining his posture of authority), Orestes uttered with disgust:

'You should've thought of that before letting Cyril in your mind, twisting and warping it for his own pleasure. Do you think he praises you...? Don't be fooled. In the end, you mean nothing to him. You're no more than a minion – expendable like everyone else'.

'NO! No, you're lying! The Holy Father loves me as much as every lamb in his flock! Heaven is in store for me, I know it is! Just let me go! Please, don't kill me!', Ammonius kept shouting and crying, seeking to reason with the Prefect.

Orestes stood still for a moment, suddenly kneeling and grabbing the former Nitrian monk's chin, yelling at him in his face:

'Kill you?! KILL YOU...?! Do you take me for an animal, scum?! A barbarian to the likes of you and your friends, headed by Cyril, the Bloodthirsty Monster?! Well, let me tell you this – even if I were as vicious as you, I wouldn't kill you, and do you know why? Because you – are – just – not – worth – my – TIME! I am Orestes, Prefect of Alexandria, appointed by Flavius Theodosius Junior Augustus, Supreme Leader of the East. I am the legal authority of this city, the Emperor's representative, and an attempt on the Prefect's life is an attempt on the Emperor's life just as much. Theodosius the Great spared the lives of my companions when you trapped them in the Serapeum, and for that, I'll forever be thankful to him and his descendants for as long as I live. He was merciful because I presented him good cause', he told Ammonius, who looked at him with surprise; Orestes then kept going, 'indeed, I saved my people, I did everything I could to rescue them because I believed my faith as vehemently as you, but never – NEVER as far as to kill for it, and that, my pathetic little friend, is where we differ, so no, I shan't kill you, but I'm not returning you back to Cyril untouched. There's yet a lesson to be learned before you achieve deliverance. GUARD!', he called, letting go of Ammonius and standing back up.

As the soldier made his way into the holding area, the Parabolanus made sure he told Orestes one more thing:

'PAGAN! IDOLATER! MAY YOU FOR-EVER BURN IN THE FIRES OF HELL!', he cried, spitting the Prefect on his feet.

The soldier showed soon after and reported for duty while Orestes wiped himself on Ammonius' robes, forcing him against the floor.

'Yes, sir?'.

'I'm done with the prisoner. Lead him to the theater, use the backdoor when you leave, and once you're there, strip him of his clothes, strap him, beat him and leave him. I'm sure Cyril won't take too long to collect him before he dies. As far as I can tell, he is, after all, of great importance to the Patriarch'.

'Right away, Prefect', the guard said, receiving the keys from Orestes on his way out of the cell.

Seeking to stand on his feet but failing, Ammonius yelled at Orestes for the last time:

'DIES IRAE!'.

The Prefect stopped, turned around and eerily replied:

'Kyrie eleison'.

He left. As for Ammonius, released from the wall by the guard, he saw his past coming back to haunt him. His time had come, as promised by the desert horned viper he had come across with during his stay at the oasis, whose reality he could not question anymore. Led by the guard through the back of the Prefectural Palace, more soldiers joined the party and quietly headed for the theater.

Orestes, on the other hand, showed up on his office's balcony, saluting the people praying for him in front of his home, who, to their greatest contentment, cheered him the moment they saw him. The Prefect, reminded once more of Hypatia's words, thanked the citizens for their dedication and let them know that, had it not been for their heroic move, he would not be standing there.

Several hours later, at nightfall, Cyril, who had seen Ammonius being taken to the theater, dispatched a few Parabolani to retrieve him, hoping he would still be alive, but, because the Roman soldiers had stayed at the venue for quite some time, enjoying their own spectacle, it was already too late – the General of the Parabolani, the Patriarch's favorite, was dead.

At the See, his body was cleaned and dressed properly for the funeral mass during which the Pope announced he had proclaimed Ammonius a martyr, renaming him Saint Thaumasius the Wonderful, with the purpose of having him interred under the Cathedral, which he did.

A few days later, however, unable to douse the anger of the Christian populace, the same people who had witnessed Ammonius' criminal actions against the Prefect, Cyril was forced to exhume the body and have it transferred to the sepulchers like the common man he was, and not one who had died for denying God. The title the Patriarch had conferred upon him was, most naturally, discarded – the citizens simply found it offensive to venerate a man who, to the best of their knowledge and apart from the conflict of three hundred ninety-one, had attempted against another's life. His past, however, would be the primary count to be read out during his trial, after which he could only be sent to, in his own words, "the fires of hell".

Chapter XXII
Pharos, a Doused Candlewick in the Dark

One of the worst curses Mankind must endure to avoid total annihilation in an impending future, whether on account of natural disasters or human miscalculations (unless they are deliberate and, therefore, planned), is the ever-present learning process of trial and error. This means that, in order for some people to be able to live up to a ripe, old age and perish of natural causes, others must withstand (against their own will, as is most common) the sordidness of being put to the test, like subjects of an experiment (hence the «trial» part) whose purpose is, from a constructive point of view, to improve certain features of either day-to-day life or periods in time during which special circumstances take place; should the viewpoint turn out to be of an evil nature, however, simply for the sake of satisfying one's sick pleasures, then it is quite likely the subjects may be selected, regardless of their being aware of their fate or not, to just die at the hands of their equals, even though the latter might believe they are somehow superior for one reason or another.

Of course, not everything a certain group of people is put through is specifically conceived or thought of as an experiment – quite the contrary, for the knowledge we already possess as humans capable of processing and retaining information constitutes a fundamental basis for us to undertake innovative enterprises, thus broadening both our horizons and abilities as a species who do not know how to yield to limitations. It's the fact we insist on making our lives better and acquiring as much sapience as possible that gives our existence some purpose, but not all of it. Still, it is precisely when we believe we understand all risks involved in these ventures, for either good or bad, that we are caught by surprise, forced to face the consequences of the «errors» made during the «trial» stage.

So, in the end, and in order to avoid both our annihilation as a species and the painful learning process that comes with our very survival, what is there left to do? The answer lies with us, for if we can feel proud of ourselves for the ability to retain and process constantly incoming information, then it is up to us as well to stop certain events in the history of Humankind from repeatedly happening to the like of a vicious cycle. That is why we must never discard History, whether it is ours or somebody else's, because, as the scrupulous men and women we are supposed to be, dominant on earth, regardless of our being affected by specific situations or not, it is our duty to put a halt to the very implosion of both our civilization and the world we were given for a home. Allowing the objectification of human beings whose story is bound to fall into repetition sometime today, tomorrow, in a few days, weeks, years, or even centuries, somewhere close to us or thousands of leugae away, makes us accessory to that exact crime, for we are never exempt from such great responsibility.

* * *

After having successfully reacquired the support of the citizens of Alexandria thanks to Hypatia's advice, Orestes had at last left his mark in the city as the Prefect who had been able to corner the Patriarch into respecting the will of the people by withdrawing from his attempt at controlling government affairs, stripping a criminal with a peculiar passion for brawling from his undeserved sainthood, and encroaching the general population into yielding to his personal desires, which was a clear abuse of power.

The capital of the Diocese of Egypt had not been this much quiet as it was today. A truce was both finally and ironically in order, as the principal warmongers seeking domain over the urban center had been employing violent measures to ensure order, though, quite naturally, to no avail. Plato had debated the issue long before Christianity even dreamt of possessing such great influence over the very Empire that had once sought to obliterate it – tyranny is always bound to collapse, sooner or later; it is the meantime that is hard to endure, especially when one refuses to give into conformity and hopes to be alive the day freedom comes to the like of divine deliverance, no matter which Creator is responsible for it.

The Parabolani were, to put it quite bluntly, crippled; their General had died at the hands of the Prefect and Cyril did not feel like risking any other attacks, regardless of having or not the element of surprise by his side. The Patriarch had come to terms with reality – when the people unite like a flock of sheep and think like humans, precisely, willing to challenge their self-proclaimed shepherd, there is absolutely nothing to be done about it. Without power and influence, there is no one weak-minded enough to be toyed with and, in turn, instill fear in others by means of force – or is there?

It turns out that, fortunately for Cyril and the Parabolani now in hiding, there actually was one man left after all, an individual whose self-righteousness was inexistent and had no issues whatsoever about getting rid of anyone or anything in his way, turning people on the same side against each other if necessary. Whether it was the result of a cosmic conspiracy, no one knows, but the fact Peter the Reader was still alive, having chosen to stay away from the most recent conflicts while literally working underground, in the catacombs, seemed to prove Cyril had been right all along as far as excluding him was concerned, for the lector was free to walk about without arousing the population's suspicions or being arrested by Orestes's guard, now in charge of patrolling the streets of Alexandria just like they were supposed to.

Although Peter, much like the Patriarch and the late Ammonius, enjoyed brutality (for which reason he had at first created a bond with the former monk), he was anything but a fool, let alone easily influenced; on the contrary, that was another of his specialties – convincing others what they were doing was right and aimed at their own salvation, even though they were mere instruments for him to get what he wanted and, right now, he wanted to rebuild the Parabolani and have them labor under his yoke while, nevertheless, serving

Cyril.

A plan was taking shape in his mind. He knew the Prefect had not suddenly become wise enough to isolate the Patriarch and disband his militia all by himself; Orestes had an important aid and ally he could rely on, which was no secret. Everyone knew his former Pagan tutoress, Hypatia, Head of the Neoplatonic School and daughter of Theon, the last Director of the Musaeum, provided her counsel in matters of local government, just as Peter was certain she took advantage of the Prefect's admiration for her to numb down his mind and have him do as she pleased. As an idolater of false deities, Hypatia was obviously well-versed in the arts of witchcraft; not just that, she was secretly conspiring against the Church by preventing Orestes from converting completely to Christianity, still hanging on to his Paganistic roots. Her being alive was the one reason Cyril could not get back on his feet, which is why something had to be done about it.

* * *

On the evening of March, the eighth of the year of Our Lord four hundred fifteen (under the Julian calendar), as the cool air of winter became more agreeable with the spring equinox's final approach to the Northern African seaboard, Hypatia was returning home from her usual walk around town before retiring, accompanied only by a slave, who was in charge of commandeering the horse and the chariot. Against Orestes' wishes, no matter how strongly he pleaded his case, the Lady had made it clear to the Prefect she had no desire of being treated like someone special or better than the city's general population, given her role as her former disciple's political advisor was not official, but merely symbolic, for which reason she had categorically denied being escorted about by soldiers of the Prefectural Palace whose presence could likely be required somewhere else on the grounds of significant events, far more important than looking out for her safety, which she had completely discarded as something to worry about, for public order had at last been restored, there having been no Parabolani in sight for several weeks since Cyril's defeat. Although he was the highest official of Alexandria, Orestes could not force Hypatia into doing what he wanted, nor did he mean to – all he was trying to do was to protect her, despite her skepticism. However, and even though her statesmanship was both admirable and commendable, the Lady's concern for the citizens' greater good as a collective eventually turned out to set her fate in stone, a cross most altruistic people are doomed to bear.

Having made use of the underground network

he had been responsible for expanding over the last three years, Peter the Reader managed to convince about a dozen men to do his bidding by accompanying him through the tunnels he knew better than anyone, with the purpose of resurfacing close to the street coming from the Public Gardens, an area Hypatia's route was comprised of.

One by one, the men led by the lector emerged and waited for the Lady's chariot to pass while headed for the agora. Sometime later, around nightfall (still dropping in somewhat early), a couple of the vigilantes turned to Peter and warned him she was on her way, standing next to the driver. Confirming there was no mistake, the lector gave the order and the men, assembling in line with their leader at the center, constituted a barrier the horse was unwilling to break through. Hypatia told the slave to stop the chariot, turned to them and delicately asked:

'May I help you?'.

They were all looking at her menacingly, but Peter was, without a doubt, the scariest of all. After standing still with his hands behind his back for a moment while looking her in the eye, he cut the Lady's prompt short, walked toward her and grabbed her arm, saying:

'Quiet, witch! Come with us – now!'.

The few people still walking down the street had failed to show resistance despite what they saw, not to mention that, out of fear for their own lives, they could not call out for any guards. The slave still tried to react, saying:

'Hey! Where do you think you're taking the Lady Hypatia? Let go of her!'.

His mistress, however, signaled him to stay quiet, adding:

'It's all right. Just take the chariot and head back home. I won't be long', but in her heart she knew it not to be true.

'But Mistress…!', the slave insisted, drawing the attention of the men.

'Please, just do as I say', Hypatia replied.

The slave reluctantly nodded as he looked at her and drove away the moment the obstacle was cleared, looking back from afar, his sight distorted on account of the tears.

The men's intention was to take the Lady somewhere secluded where she could also be purified and cleansed of her sins for being both a heathen and a sorceress, and so Peter dragged her with the assistance of a few others into the old Emporium Caesareum, which was now a church (currently under refurbishment, as seen from the masonry materials nearby). Once inside, Peter threw Hypatia on the freezing stone floor for his men to tear through her garments and leave her in a state of nature. Having hit the surface hard, the Lady was already bleeding from her mouth, her gentle lips cut open. Because of the violence with which the zealots had undressed her, their acutely shaped nails also tore through her delicate skin, left bruised and scratched; her hair was loosened and consequently pulled, making the Lady gasp in pain. Aware of what was coming her way, Hypatia sought to sit down, covering her intimacy with her tainted arms and hands, turning to Peter with tears in her eyes, cascading down her visage:

'Is this how I shall depart this world...? Having a martyr made out of me...? Silenced for cherishing the truth above all things...?'.

The lector looked down on her, then back at his entourage, ordering a few of them to go outside and bring back terracotta-made roofing shingles. As he and the rest of the men remaining with him waited around her, in a circumference whose center point was Hypatia herself, more fragile and broken than she had ever been made, Peter knelt, grabbed the Lady's hair, pulled her head close to his face and condescendingly said:

'Heathens aren't entitled to martyrdom, you foul wench. Your refusal to apostatize and accept the one faith only means the demons inside you must be purged, don't you see...? That is the only truth you had to accept, and yet, you just had to do as you pleased, directly disobeying male authority, selling yourself out to the Prefect in exchange for your life... giving him the backbone he never had… it's no wonder you've survived this long, but let me tell you this – should anyone even think of adoring or turning you into an idol, I will make sure the Patriarch knows about it, I will personally take care of it, and Orestes won't be able to do anything about it, because the only reason he had to stay in office will be no more by this time tomorrow'.

As the lector concluded his speech, the men he had sent outside returned with several intact shingles in their hands. He then let go of Hypatia and threw her back against the floor; seeking to maintain the concealment of her body from the eyes of the men encircling her, the Lady lost her balance and hit her head. Whether it was a strong enough blow to kill her instantly, no one knows, though it is likely she may have just passed out – having her scream would have attracted too much attention, consequently resulting in the foundering of the plan, for which reason pushing her with enough force may have probably been deliberate.

Peter then distributed the roofing tiles among his minions, told them to break the shingles on the floor into sharp pieces of terracotta, and the deed the lector had been craving took place at last – Hypatia of Alexandria was brutally, viciously, violently murdered by a dozen of Christian zealots who scraped and tore her flesh from her bones, literally turning the church into a slaughterhouse. A pool of blood, every last drop of it, spread across the floor where the lynching continued. To the killers' collective surprise, Hypatia, having been rendered unrecognizable, was still able to scream from excruciating pain for a moment as her life hung by a thread, but was quickly silenced by smothering and piercing of the neck.

Even though the Lady was far beyond salvation, turned into a carcass preyed upon by wildlife, rather than a dead human body, the scraping continued, eventually moving on to dismemberment and decapitation. Willing to make the last living representative of Paganism in Alexandria disappear forever as to never again be remembered, Peter ordered everyone to gather the smaller pieces of flesh and put them in a pabillus, a kind of wheelbarrow. As for the bigger pieces, such as the head and the mutilated limbs and trunk, those were to be dragged along the ground. Grabbing the torn garments as well, Peter took hold of a lit torch, stepped outside the Caesareum and watched out for guards, but there was no one to be seen, and so they all left.

Headed for the Cinaron, located at the tip of the central pier of the Great Harbor, it was like a burial procession was happening at that moment. A trail of blood eventually took shape across the desert sand, reduced along the way. Having reached the Northernmost point of the pier, the pabillus was voided, the small pieces of flesh and bone topped by the rest of the carcass. After covering it all with the Lady's torn garments, Peter threw his torch on the pile and set both the rag and the remains on fire, abandoning them like waste without ever looking back, followed by the other zealots.

Hypatia of Alexandria was physically no more, her ashes blown by the wind toward the Mediterranean, the smoke from her charred flesh making its way up to the celestial dome where, together with her father, Theon, and the mother she had never met after giving up her life for her daughter, the Lady became a star in the night sky herself, her nous rejoining the Demiurge, the Creator from whom all things emanate, maintaining the identity she had always lived by in the phenomenal world.

Revolted about and sickened by the news the following morning, Orestes, pulling his hair with pain and in despair, immediately gave up his position as Prefect of Alexandria without notice and left the city, never to return. Without any opposition left to take down, Cyril, the Patriarch of Alexandria, acquired full control of both the capital city and the whole of the Diocese of Egypt, reinstating the Parabolani brotherhood as responsible for Alexandria's official safety and law enforcement, headed by none other than his new favorite, Peter the Reader.

As for the general population, disgusted by the inhuman disposal of Hypatia, they still tried blaming the murder on Cyril, but no evidence of his link to the crime was ever found, and their short-lived freedom and relief came to an end.

The Neoplatonic School, once a place of Philosophy and Science that brought members of all peoples from just about anywhere together under the charismatic and majestic character of a true leader, was demolished and replaced with a new church.

* * *

Hypatia of Alexandria would be remembered later on in Socrates Scholasticus's account of Christianity's rule across the Roman Empire, from the beginning of the fourth century (with Constantine the Great as Augustus) to the end of the first half of the fifth century, still during Theodosius the Younger's tenure as Emperor of the East, soon to become the Byzantine Empire.

Despite all efforts to erase Hypatia's influence over Alexandria throughout the nearly forty-five years of her life, her legacy lives on to this day. A martyr, not on the grounds of faith, but rather Knowledge, Philosophy, and Truth, Hypatia continues to inspire millions of people all over the world, both men and women, to defy those who proclaim themselves an authority never to be questioned, pursue an education and continuously acquire sapience, actively participate in civilization-related affairs, claim for an egalitarian society in which men and women share the same rights and are treated accordingly and alike, and, above all, win our freedom as thinking human beings allowed to speak our minds, never to be subjected to either the silence, violence, or darkness of tyranny, whichever its nature or intent.

Biography

Tiago Lameiras was born in Lisbon, Portugal, in 1990. He holds a Bachelor's Degree with Honors in Theater – Acting, from the Higher School of Theater and Film of Lisbon. He is presently completing his doctoral thesis in Communications, Culture, and Arts – Cultural Studies Specialization, at the School of Arts and Humanities of the University of the Algarve, Faro, Portugal.

His titles are comprised of: *Portvcale – A Epopeia Portuguesa da Contemporaneidade* (2010), *Viagem ao Centro de Ti – Romance Trovado* (2012), *A Mão de Diónisos* (2013), *Actor Being: A Role in Mankind, Utopian Ambition: Constitution of the 2100 Atlantian Republic* (2016), *Sonata, Epistulæ* (2017), and *Persephone's Fall* (2018).